Unsolved Mysteries
of History

Unsolved Mysteries of History

An Eye-Opening Investigation into the Most Baffling Events of All Time

PAUL ARON

John Wiley & Sons, Inc.

New York • Chichester • Weinheim • Brisbane • Singapore • Toronto

ISBN 0-471-35190-3

Printed in the United States of America

10 9 8 7 6 5 4 3 2 1

Contents

Preface   xi

Acknowledgments   xiii

1   Were the Neandertals Our Ancestors?   1
Some see them as brutish and dim-witted, others as our closest relatives. Scientists continue to debate whether modern humans evolved from Neandertals, interbred with them, or wiped them out.

2   Who Built Stonehenge?   10
Credit has gone to Greeks, to Romans, and to Druids, among others. But Stonehenge was built more than a millennium before any of these people reached England. The key to solving the mystery may come from a new look at an old legend about Merlin, the wizard of King Arthur's court.

3   Why Did the Pharaohs Build the Pyramids?   18
Most Egyptologists were convinced that they were tombs. The problem was that as explorers and archaeologists entered one pyramid after another, nobody could find any bodies.

4   Who Was Theseus?   26
Theseus's greatest deed, according to Greek mythology, was the slaying of the minotaur—a monstrous half man, half bull. Archaeological discoveries in Crete and the deciphering of the ancient Minoans' writing have convinced many that the story was not nearly as fantastic as it once seemed.

5   Was There Really a Trojan War?   *34*
*When a German millionaire with a passion for Homer
uncovered what he claimed was the legendary city of Troy,
historians had to reconsider whether there might also have
been a queen named Helen, a hero named Achilles, and
perhaps even a giant horse full of soldiers.*

6   Did Jesus Die on the Cross?   *43*
*To explain Jesus' empty tomb, historians have proposed a
variety of theories, among them: that Jesus faked his own
death so that he could "rise" again; that his body was
eaten by dogs; and that the story was devised by one set
of his followers to discredit other Christian sects.*

7   What Were the Nazca Lines?   *52*
*The most notorious explanation for the lines on the
Peruvian desert was that they were runways for UFOs.
This was recognized as nonsense. But how else could
scientists explain markings that can only be made out
from the air, yet were drawn thousands of years before
men could fly?*

8   Who Was King Arthur?   *59*
*Until recently historians assumed we could never know
where or when or even whether he really lived. Then
archaeologists uncovered the remains of what may once
have been Camelot.*

9   Why Did Mayan Civilization Collapse?   *67*
*Their sprawling palaces and dizzying pyramids were
engulfed by the Central American jungle long before the
Spaniards arrived. Only by deciphering their complex
hieroglyphics could linguists reveal what brought an
end to the Mayan world.*

10   Who Built the Statues on Easter Island?   *75*
*To try to prove that Easter Island had been settled by
American Indians, a Norwegian scientist determined to
travel from Peru to Polynesia—a distance of forty-three
hundred miles—by raft.*

11 What Was Joan of Arc's "Sign"? 83

The sign Joan showed the crown prince convinced him to entrust his fate—and that of France—to this seventeen-year-old, a peasant with no military experience, and a girl to boot. This same sign convinced the British to burn her at the stake.

12 Who Invented Printing? 92

Everyone knows it was Johann Gutenberg. But then why did his partner, Johannes Fust, sue him—and win? And why is it Fust's name that appears on the first printed books?

13 Did Richard III Kill the Princes in the Tower? 100

Was Richard the monstrous villain portrayed by Shakespeare? Did he murder his nephews, the rightful heirs to the throne? To find out, twentieth-century scientists exhumed the princes' skeletons.

14 Did Columbus Intend to Discover America? 108

Most historians believe he was searching for a new route to the Far East. An increasing number are convinced that from the start, he was out to discover a New World.

15 Did Martin Guerre Return? 117

One of the most celebrated trials of the sixteenth century was that of Guerre, who returned to his tiny village after mysteriously disappearing for eight years. Then another man showed up, also claiming to be the long-lost Guerre.

16 Did Mary, Queen of Scots, Murder Her Husband? 126

Three months after the murder of the king, the queen married the prime suspect. Was she an adulterer and a murderer? Or a pawn in a deadly game of politics?

17 Who Wrote Shakespeare's Plays? 134

His plays reveal a knowledge of law, classics, and court life that many say no son of a small-town glovemaker could have possessed. Were Shakespeare's plays written by Francis Bacon? Christopher Marlowe? Queen Elizabeth? Or that man from Stratford?

18 Was Captain Kidd a Pirate?   143
*He was convicted by a British court, but many have
questioned whether he had a fair trial. They've pointed out
that Kidd's voyages were sponsored by none other than
England's King William, and that critical evidence for his
defense conveniently disappeared . . . only to surface two
hundred years after he was hanged.*

19 Was Mozart Poisoned?   151
*Was he done in by Antonio Salieri, a lesser musician jealous
of Mozart's genius? Or could it have been the Freemasons,
whose secret rituals Mozart had cryptically revealed in
The Magic Flute?*

20 Why Did Freud Abandon His Seduction Theory?   159
*The entire Oedipus complex seemed to be crumbling after
the director of the Freud archives argued that Freud was
a fraud. The director was fired, but others continued to
question whether Freud had told the truth about the origins
of psychoanalysis.*

21 Could the *Titanic* Have Been Saved?   168
*Just miles from the sinking ocean liner sat another ship,
whose officers watched the Titanic's distress signals burst
in the sky—and then did nothing. Could the Californian
have reached the Titanic in time? And why didn't it?*

22 Did Any of the Romanovs Survive?   177
*DNA tests proved that bones found in a Siberian swamp
belonged to Nicholas and Alexandra, and three daughters
of the last czar and czarina—all killed by Bolsheviks during
the Russian Revolution. But the bones of their son and a
fourth daughter have not been found.*

23 Did Hitler Murder His Niece?   186
*After Geli Raubal was found dead in Hitler's apartment,
shot with his pistol, rumors surfaced that she was not just
his niece but his lover. The investigation into her death has
led historians into the very dark recesses of Hitler's mind.*

24 Why Did Hess Fly to Scotland?   195

*When the deputy führer parachuted into Scotland right in
the middle of the Battle of Britain, both Hitler and Churchill
contended it was the act of a lone madman. But many
believed there was more to the story.*

25 Was Gorbachev Part of the August Coup?   203

*To Westerners, the aborted right-wing coup of 1991 featured
Gorbachev as the innocent victim of devious hard-liners, and
Yeltsin as the savior of democracy. Russians have been much
more skeptical about the part played by both of the story's
heroes.*

Index   213

Preface

In Josephine Tey's classic mystery story *The Daughter of Time*, Scotland Yard's Alan Grant is laid up in the hospital after falling through a trapdoor. Frustrated and bored, he takes it upon himself to solve a five-hundred-year-old case: the murder of "the princes in the tower."

The prime suspect in the case—indeed, the prime example of evil incarnate, to judge from Shakespeare's play and, before that, Thomas More's history—was King Richard III. This was a man accused of murdering two kings, of marrying (and then poisoning) the widow of one of his victims, and of drowning his own brother in a vat of wine. So the murder of his two young nephews, each of whom stood between Richard and the throne, seemed completely in character.

Grant, however, has his doubts. Stuck in bed, he keeps staring at a portrait of Richard, one in which the king appears far too kindly to have done anything so heinous. He assigns his visitors to investigate, and he discovers, to his shock and indignation, that More was a very unreliable source; for Sir Thomas, though quite literally a saint after his 1935 canonization, grew up in the household of Cardinal John Morton, a bitter enemy of Richard's. In other words, More had it in for Richard.

The true villains, Grant concludes, were More, who framed Richard, and the historians who followed, who were too lazy to notice.

What's the moral? That fictional detectives are better investigators than professional historians?

Hardly.

As Grant begrudgingly concedes, most of his "discoveries" about Richard had been discovered years and in some cases centuries earlier, by members of the same historical profession that he holds in such disdain. It was historians who analyzed More's sources and motives, who uncovered an account of the princes' deaths written *before* More's, who pressured Westminster Abbey to open the tomb in which the remains of the princes were supposedly interred.

No Scotland Yard detective could have asked for a more tenacious investigation.

What Tey's story does illustrate is that the best mystery writing has lots in common with the best history writing. In both, things are not always as they at first seem; in both, the quest for a solution is jammed with surprises and challenges and thrills.

So here's the premise of this book: Historians make great detectives. And history makes for great detective stories.

As for the princes, the tomb in the abbey was opened in 1933, and the skeletons were examined by Westminster's archivist and by the president of Great Britain's Anatomical Society. What the forensic evidence revealed was . . .

One rule about great mystery stories: Don't give away the ending.

Acknowledgments

For allowing me to work part-time so that I could write this book, thanks to my editors at *The Virginia Gazette,* W. C. O'Donovan and Rusty Carter. For filling in for me during that stretch, thanks to my then colleagues Tracy Blevins, Brian Rafferty, Bill Tolbert, and Amy Williams.

For their useful ideas, thanks to Stephen Aron, Robert Thompson, W. C. O'Donovan, Monica Potkay, and my agent, John Thornton.

For his careful reading of the manuscript and his efforts to ensure clarity throughout, thanks to my editor, Chris Jackson. For their help through the publication process, thanks to Wiley's John Simko and Diana Madrigal.

Above all, for her incisive analyses of the book and its author, thanks to my wife, Paula Blank.

Chapter 1

Were the Neandertals Our Ancestors?

On an August day in 1856, in the Neandertal Valley in northwestern Germany, a workman in a limestone quarry uncovered the bones of what he thought was a cave bear. He put them aside to show to Johann Fuhlrott, the local schoolteacher and an enthusiastic natural historian.

Fuhlrott immediately realized this was something much more significant than the bones of a bear. The head was about the size of a man's, but it was shaped differently, with a low forehead, bony ridges above the eyes, a large projecting nose, large front teeth, and a bulge protruding from the back. The body, to judge from the bones that were recovered, must also have resembled a man's, though he would have been shorter and stockier—and far more powerful—than any normal man. Making the bones even more significant, Fuhlrott realized, was that they'd been found amid geological deposits of great antiquity.

The schoolteacher contacted Hermann Schaaflhausen, a professor of anatomy at the nearby University of Bonn. He, too, recognized that the bones were extraordinary: "a natural conformation hitherto not known to exist," as he later described them. Indeed, what the workman had uncovered, Schaafflhausen believed, was a new—or rather a very, very old—type of human being, one that would come to be called a Neandertal. Perhaps, Schaaflhausen may even have suspected, the Neandertals were ancient ancestors of modern man.

If the professor and the schoolteacher expected the scientific establishment to celebrate their discovery, they were sorely disappointed. Charles Darwin's theory of evolution, as spelled out in *The Origin of Species,* was still three years from its publication, in 1859. To most scientists, the idea that humans evolved from any other species, let alone one represented by these bones, seemed entirely absurd. Rudolf Virchow, the leading pathologist of the day, examined the bones and declared that they belonged to a normal human being, albeit one suffering from some unusual disease. Other experts followed suit.

By the end of the nineteenth century, however, Darwinism prevailed in most scientific circles. Some scientists, such as Gabriel de Mortillet in France, took another look at the bones and argued that modern humans evolved from Neandertals. The discovery of more Neandertal remains—in France, Belgium, and Germany—buttressed their case. These fossils dated back to between 110,000 and 35,000 years ago, making it impossible to dismiss them as either diseased or modern.

But the majority of scientists, led by another Frenchman, Marcellin Boule, still adamantly rejected Neandertals as human ancestors. The skeletons may have been ancient, Boule conceded, but they were no kin of his. This bent-kneed, squat-necked, curve-spined Neandertal was more ape than human, Boule argued. If modern humans had anything at all to do with them, he suggested, it could only have been that our *real* human ancestors, whoever they were, might have wiped out this "degenerate species."

For most of the twentieth century, the scientific rift only widened. On the one side were Mortillet's followers, who viewed Neandertals as our direct, albeit primitive, ancestors. On the other side were those who, like Boule, saw the Neandertals as at best our distant cousins, an evolutionary dead end destined to be replaced by modern humans. Only in the past few years have scientists begun, very tentatively, to build a bridge across this bitter divide.

Are there any Neandertals in the family? From left, Piltdown Man, Neandertal Man, and Cro-Magnon (modern) Man. Courtesy Department of Library Services, American Museum of Natural History.

One reason why Boule's followers were able to dismiss the Neandertals, well into the twentieth century, was that they could put forward their own and much more reassuringly familiar candidate for human ancestor. This was the infamous Piltdown man, discovered in 1912. An amateur fossil hunter named Charles Dawson found the Piltdown bones at a common by that name in Sussex, England, and they were an immediate sensation. Unlike Neandertal's skull, Piltdown's was in most respects just like that of a modern human being. Only the apelike jaw seemed primitive, and even there the flat-topped teeth added a human touch. Here was an ancestor whom Boule would have been happy to call his own.

The problem was that Piltdown was a hoax. Someone, probably Dawson, had fused parts from a modern human skull with the jaw of an orangutan, then stained them to make them seem older. The teeth had been filed down to throw investigators off the track. It was not until 1953 that scientists thought to look at the teeth under a microscope, at which point the file marks were plainly visible.

Now the scientific momentum shifted in favor of Neandertals as human ancestors. Instead of emphasizing how different they were from us, scientists started focusing on the similarities. In 1957 two American anatomists, William Straus and A. J. E. Cave, took a new look at the very same fossil that had formed the basis of Boule's description of Neandertals as brutish and nonhuman. This was the La Chapelle-aux-Saints fossil, found in a cave in southern France in 1908.

The first thing Straus and Cave noticed was that the Chapelle-aux-Saints man suffered from arthritis. Boule noticed this, too, but he ignored the implications. To Straus and Cave, the arthritis explained the Neandertal's stooped posture, and the rest of the Neandertal man suddenly didn't seem so different from a modern human being. The two anatomists concluded that if Neandertal man "could be reincarnated and placed in a New York subway—provided that he were bathed, shaved, and dressed in modern clothing—it is doubtful whether he would attract any more attention than some of its other denizens."

The post-Piltown period saw a reevaluation of Neandertal behavior as well as looks. In the 1960s the American anthropologist C. Loring Brace led the way with new studies of Neandertal tools, technology, and living arrangements. From the pattern of ashes they left behind, for example, Brace deduced that the Neandertals were baking their food in shallow pits not so different from those of later humans. Others noted that many Neandertal remains appeared to have been buried intentionally—a practice that was undeniably human. Carefully arranged bones of animals at various Neandertal sites seemed also to indicate some sort of ritual slaughter, and the Neandertal bones at the Yugoslavian site of Krapina were broken up in a way that hinted at cannibalism. These were rituals that, however macabre, were definitely human.

The glorification of Neandertals reached its high point in 1971, with the publication of Ralph Solecki's work at an Iraqi cave known as Shanidar. Soil samples taken from a Neandertal burial there found an extraordinarily high level of wildflower pollen, far more than could have been blown in on the wind or carried on animals' feet. Solecki inferred that the Shanidar Neandertals had placed offerings of flowers on their burial sites, and he called his book *The First Flower People*. As additional evidence of their humanity, Solecki noted that the remains of one of the older people buried there indicated he had a withered right arm and was blind. These conditions would certainly have led to his early death—unless members of his family or tribe took care of him.

With Solecki's book, the Neandertals' transformation was complete. No longer the apelike brutes of Boule's imagination, they were now sort of protohippies, a people in many ways more humane than modern humans. This was also the high point for what became known as the "regional continuity" theory, according to which modern humans evolved from Neandertals in Europe and the Middle East, and from other, similarly archaic people in other regions. But the Neandertal image (and with it, the regional continuity theory) was about to suffer another reversal. The attack this time came not from archaeologists or anthropologists, but from molecular biologists.

⁂

The biologists knew little about fossils, even less about archaeology or anthropology. But they knew a lot about a small segment of genetic material known as mitochondrial DNA, or mtDNA for short. A team of Berkeley biologists—Rebecca Cann, Mark Stoneking, and Allan Wilson—calculated the rate at which human mtDNA mutated, and in 1987 came up with a new estimate of human origins: about two hundred thousand years ago.

This hypothetical mother of the human race was dubbed, appropriately, Eve.

Here was a new human ancestor, and unlike Piltdown, this was no hoax. If the biologists were correct, and Eve lived about two hundred thousand years ago, then modern humans were on the scene more than a hundred thousand years earlier than scientists had previously thought likely. That meant the first modern humans were around well before the disappearance of Neandertals—some of whom still lived, judging from fossils found on the Iberian Peninsula, as recently as twenty-eight thousand years ago.

Proponents of the idea that Neandertals were our ancestors were thrown into disarray; after all, if some Neandertals were more recent than modern humans, that made it much less likely that the former evolved into the latter. And if modern humans were around *before* Neandertals even appeared, as now seemed possible, then the evolution was an out-and-out impossibility.

New methods of dating ancient remains supplied more evidence that modern humans dated back as far as, if not farther than, Neandertals. Scientists estimated that Neandertals were at various sites in the Middle East about sixty thousand years ago, well within the range they'd previously estimated. But the new dates for modern humans were a real shocker: it turned out that they were in the area about ninety thousand years ago—much earlier than previously thought.

Meanwhile, archaeologists were also redating sites in sub-Saharan Africa, where they found evidence of modern humans from as long as a hundred thousand years ago, and by some calculations up to two hundred thousand years ago. This dovetailed with the findings of the biologists that Eve's home—her Eden—had been in Africa. Cann, Stoneking, and Wilson had found that the mtDNA of modern Africans showed significantly more diversity than that of other races. They interpreted this to mean that Africans had had more time to evolve; hence the original human beings must have been African.

So, according to what became known as the "out of Africa" theory, the human race first emerged in Africa, then spread to the Middle East, and finally reached Europe. In the latter two continents, humans encountered the more primitive Neandertals, and—as was the case with so many other species who came into contact with humans—the Neandertals ended up extinct. By the early 1990s the "out of Africa" scenario had replaced regional continuity as the dominant theory.

The latest blow to regional continuity came in 1997, again from molecular biologists. Matthias Krings and his colleagues at the University of Munich managed to extract a snippet of mtDNA from the arm bone of an actual Neandertal—in fact, from Fuhlrott's original Neandertal man. They then compared the Neandertal mtDNA with that of living humans and discovered that they differed in 27 of the 379 spots they examined. (In contrast, the African mtDNA samples, which showed greater diversity than that of any other modern humans, differed from each other in only 8 spots.) The genetic distance between Neandertals and modern humans, Krings concluded, made it very unlikely that Neandertals were our ancestors.

∽

The regional continuity proponents didn't take any of this lying down. They questioned the validity of the genetic and dating evidence, and in 1999 they struck back with a dramatic discovery of their own. About ninety miles north of Lisbon, Portuguese archaeologists uncovered the skeleton of a 24,500-year-old boy who appeared to be part human, part Neandertal. The boy's face was that of an anatomically modern human, but his body and legs were Neandertal. The dating, which placed the boy after the pure Neandertals were extinct, seemed to indicate that the child was the descendant of generations of Neandertal and modern human hybrids.

If Neandertals and modern humans had interbred, the regional-continuity proponents were quick to point out, they could hardly have been as unlike each other as the out-of-Africa advocates had argued.

The Portuguese discovery could have further polarized the field, leaving both sides defending seemingly irreconcilable evidence and theories. To some extent, that happened: long-time defenders of each lined up to hail the new find or to dismiss it. But their rhetoric seemed somewhat more muted than after past discoveries, perhaps because the focus of the debate was changing. Instead of arguing about whether Neandertals or other archaic humans evolved into modern humans, scientists were increasingly focusing on the issue of how Neandertals and moderns interacted.

Did they fight with each other? Did they learn from each other? Did they speak, or breed, or perhaps just ignore each other?

Perhaps archaeologists or microbiologists—or practitioners of some entirely different discipline—will someday be able to answer these questions. For now, the answers are very speculative, albeit intriguing. The German anthropologist Gunter Brauer, for example, has proposed a more moderate version of the out-of-Africa scenario. According to Brauer, modern humans did indeed emerge from Africa, then went on from there to the rest of the world. But though they were in many ways different from the Neandertals they encountered in the Middle East and Europe, they were not so different that they couldn't interbreed with them. So, Brauer proposed, modern humans could have some Neandertal ancestors, even if the Neandertal genes are only a minuscule part of our makeup.

On the other side of the aisle, some proponents of regional continuity, such as the Tennessee anthropologist Fred Smith, readily conceded that a key genetic change in human makeup occurred in Africa. But Smith argued that the European and Middle Eastern Neandertals, far from being overrun by the newcomers, took them in and incorporated their genetic advantages.

Neither Brauer's nor Smith's compromise was fully embraced, nor can it be said that there's anything near a consensus on the place of Neandertals in human prehistory. But a majority of scientists would now agree that, whatever the relationship between Neandertals and modern humans, the two overlapped in time and probably in place. So somewhere, most likely first in the Middle East and later in Europe, these two kinds of people—people far more different from each other than any of today's races, yet each possessing some recognizably human characteristics—first confronted each other.

No one knows for sure what happened next.

To investigate further

Richard Leakey and Roger Lewin, *Origins Reconsidered* (New York: Doubleday, 1992). Leakey, who is best known for his discoveries of fossils much older than those relevant to the above discussion, is nonetheless insightful and provocative on the Neandertal question. He started off believing in regional continuity, partly because he found appealing the apparent inevitability of the emergence of modern humans from all sorts of archaic peoples around the globe. But he gradually came to lean toward "out of Africa," with its even more appealing implication that all the races of today's world are one people.

Erik Trinkaus and Pat Shipman, *The Neandertals* (New York: Alfred A. Knopf, 1993). A comprehensive history of the Neandertal controversies. Trinkaus, an anthropologist, is one of the leading proponents of regional continuity, but his historiography is admirably unbiased. The book's only flaw is the authors' tendency to interject thumbnail sketches of the leading scientists, whose lives—at least as described here—were not, in general, as interesting as their discoveries or ideas.

Christopher Stringer and Clive Gamble, *In Search of the Neanderthals* (New York: Thames & Hudson, 1993). Stringer is the leading proponent of the "out-of-Africa" theory, but like Trinkaus, he's fair to both sides. British authors such as Stringer, by the way, have stuck with the traditional "Neanderthal" spelling; most others now spell it "tal."

James Shreeve, *The Neandertal Enigma* (New York: William Morrow, 1995). A popular science writer's clear and often elegant account of the ongoing debate.

Paul Mellars, *The Neanderthal Legacy* (Princeton, N.J.: Princeton University Press, 1996). A technical but useful overview of Neandertal behavior, especially how they may have organized their communities.

Matthias Krings, Anne Stone, Ralf Schmitz, Heike Krainitzi, Mark Stoneking, and Svante Paabo, "Neandertal DNA Sequences and the Origin of Modern Humans," *Cell* 90 (July 11, 1997). The mtDNA analysis of the 1856 Neandertal specimen.

Ryk Ward and Christopher Stringer, "A Molecular Handle on the Neanderthals," *Nature* 388 (July 17, 1997). A less technical summary of Krings's findings.

Cidalia Duarte, Joan Mauricio, Paul Pettitt, Pedro Souto, Erik Trinkaus, Hans van der Plicht, and João Zilhão, "The Early Upper Paleolithic Human Skeleton from the Abrigo do Lagar Velho (Portugal) and Modern Human Emergence in Iberia," *Proceedings of the National Academy of Sciences* 96 (June 1999). The discovery of a Neandertal-modern human hybrid.

Chapter 2

Who Built Stonehenge?

The pyramids of Egypt, the Parthenon of Greece, the Colosseum of Rome: all conjure up images of great civilizations, of pharaohs and philosophers, of emperors and epics.

Not so Stonehenge.

The massive stone remains on Salisbury Plain are surrounded, not by ancient cities, but by modern highways, heading eastward toward London. There are no hieroglyphics to decipher here, no Socratic dialogues to interpret. The Stone Age and Bronze Age people who built Stonehenge also built lesser stone monuments, and their remains are scattered around the countryside. But they left nothing else to explain how or why they managed as prodigious a feat of engineering as Stonehenge. The ancient inhabitants of Salisbury Plain appeared in other respects to have a culture that was barely above subsistence level, and until late in the twentieth century, historians had no qualms about calling these people "barbarians."

No wonder, then, that from medieval times on, those who studied this ancient circle of stones looked beyond Salisbury Plain to explain who built it. The twelfth-century Welsh cleric Geoffrey of Monmouth attributed Stonehenge to Merlin, the wizard of King Arthur's court. According to Geoffrey's *History of the Kings of Britain*, the monument was commissioned by Arthur's uncle, one Aurelius Ambrosius. Ambrosius was looking for a suitably monumental way to commemorate a great victory over the Anglo-Saxon invaders. Merlin suggested taking a circle of stones from a place called Killarus in Ireland, and then arranged to float the premade monument to Britain.

In the seventeenth century, King James I was so intrigued by Stonehenge that he assigned his court architect, Inigo Jones, to investigate. After studying the monument, Jones could only agree with Geoffrey of Monmouth that the region's Stone Age or Bronze Age residents could not possibly have built it. "If destitute of the Knowledge, even to clothe themselves," Jones reasoned, "much less any Knowledge had they to erect stately structures, or such remarkable Works as Stone-Heng."

Jones concluded that a "Structure so exquisite" could only be the work of the Romans, and that it was a temple to an obscure Roman god.

The succeeding years saw continuing efforts to credit Stonehenge to builders from somewhere—almost anywhere—besides Britain. The Danes, the Belgae, and the Anglo-Saxons all had their backers, as did the ancient Celtic priests known as Druids.

The problem with all these theories was the same. Though radiocarbon dating would not be invented until the twentieth century, the cruder dating methods of earlier archaeologists indicated that Stonehenge was probably built before 1500 B.C. The Druids, most scholars also realized, arrived no earlier than 500 B.C., the Romans after that. That meant Stonehenge was built more than a millennium before either reached England.

So, well into the twentieth century, the question remained: Who built Stonehenge?

∽

An archaeologist's accidental discovery in 1953 pointed to a solution. On July 10, as part of his survey of the site, Richard Atkinson was preparing to photograph some seventeenth-century graffiti on a stone next to what's known as the Great Trilithon. He waited until late afternoon, hoping for a sharper contrast of light and shade. As he looked through the camera, Atkinson noticed that below the seventeenth-century inscription were other carvings.

One was of a dagger pointing to the ground. Nearby were four axes, of a type found in England at about the time of Stonehenge's erection.

It was the lone dagger, not the axes, that most excited Atkinson. Nothing like it had been found in England, or anywhere in northern Europe, for that matter. The most comparable artifact came from the royal graves of the citadel of Mycenae, in Greece.

Here, finally, was the link to a more sophisticated civilization, one that could reasonably have been expected to build something like Stonehenge. Even better, the daggers found in Mycenae dated to approximately 1500 B.C., about the same time Stonehenge was built, according to most experts of the 1950s. Unlike the Romans or the Druids, the Mycenaean connection made chronological sense.

Atkinson worked up an elaborate theory that Stonehenge was designed by an architect visiting from the more civilized Mediterranean. Perhaps, he speculated, there was even a Mycenaean prince buried on Salisbury Plain. The archaeological world, relieved to finally have a solution to the Stonehenge problem, embraced the theory.

But just as quickly as the Mycenaean consensus formed, it was soon torn apart. The 1960s brought the advent of a new form of radiocarbon dating, and suddenly archaeologists were confronted by strong evidence that Stonehenge was much older than previously thought—and much older than the Mycenaean civilization. The new radiocarbon dates confirmed that the citadel at Mycenae was built between 1600 and 1500 B.C., but they pushed the origins of Stonehenge way back, well before any Mediterranean influences could possibly be felt.

By this latest reckoning, the banks and outer ditch of the Stonehenge circle were begun in approximately 2950 B.C. Some wooden structures were added within the circle between about 2900 and 2400 B.C., then replaced by the familiar stone structure sometime soon after that.

The new dates undercut not just the Mycenaean theory but also the entire "diffusionist" mind-set that led to it. Stonehenge was simply too old to have been built by any of the great European civilizations, and non-European civilizations were too far away. For the first time, most scholars had to accept that the people who built Stonehenge were people who lived near Stonehenge, and that they did so without outside help. These apparently primitive people had somehow built one of the world's most enduring monuments.

᠎᠎᠎

As if that wasn't impressive enough, the people who built Stonehenge had made their task stunningly more difficult by using stones that came from 150 miles away, in the Preseli Mountains of southwestern Wales.

The "bluestones" (which are actually more of a splotchy gray) were traced to their source by the geologist H. H. Thomas in 1932. The three rock types in the bluestones are unlike any rock found near Stonehenge, but Thomas found that the same three could be picked out of natural rock outcrops between the summits of Mounts Carnmenyn and Foel Trigarn in Wales.

How did the people of Salisbury Plain get these stones, some weighing five tons, from Wales to England?

Thomas's discovery led some to look anew at Geoffrey of Monmouth's tale about Merlin's magic. Perhaps, archaeologist Stuart Piggott suggested, there were some genuine oral traditions embedded in the folklore. After all, Geoffrey had written of Merlin getting the stones from the west (albeit from Ireland, not Wales). Geoffrey had also written of floating the stones to Stonehenge, perhaps a residual folk memory of ferrying them across the Irish Sea. And Geoffrey may have even provided a hint as to why the people who built Stonehenge would go to such lengths to bring the stones from afar, when there were plenty of other kinds of rocks right around Salisbury Plain: perhaps the builders of Stonehenge, like Geoffrey's Merlin, believed these rocks had magical properties.

Most historians thought Piggott's suggestions a bit far-fetched, especially in light of Geoffrey's generally garbled version of history. But that still left unanswered the question of how at least eighty-five and possibly more stones got from the Preseli Mountains to Salisbury Plain.

Some, most notably the geologist G. A. Kellaway, argued that the bluestones were carried by glaciers, not people. But most experts lined up against Kellaway, since they didn't believe that the most recent glaciation extended as far south as the Preselis or Salisbury Plain. Even if it did, it's highly unlikely that glaciers would have gathered up the bluestones from one small area in Wales and deposited them in another small area in England, as opposed to scattering them all about. The absence of any other bluestones south or east of the Bristol Channel (with the possible exception of one now in the Salisbury Museum but of disputed history) makes a strong case against the glacial theory.

So, unlikely as it may once have seemed, the most common explanation was that the people from the Salisbury Plain area had lashed some canoes together and carried the bluestones across the Irish Sea. The journey was further evidence that the people of Salisbury Plain possessed surprising and extraordinary technological expertise.

∽

With the diffusionists in disarray, the 1960s saw even more remarkable claims made on behalf of the people of Salisbury Plain. This time they came not from archaeologists or geologists, but from astronomers.

The sixties were not the first time astronomy had come into play. Back in the eighteenth century, William Stukely had noted that the principal line of Stonehenge was "where abouts the Sun rises, when the days are longest," and many others who studied the monument had found other ways in which it was oriented toward the sun, moon, or stars. Yet none of those studies created a stir anything like that made by the Boston University astronomer Gerald Hawkins. His brashly titled book *Stonehenge Decoded* was published in 1965 and became an international best-seller.

Hawkins found that the alignments among 165 key points in the monument strongly correlated with the rising and setting positions of the sun and the moon. Even more controversially, he argued that a circle of pits in Stonehenge known as the Aubrey Holes had been used to predict eclipses of the moon. Hawkins dubbed Stonehenge a "Neolithic computer."

Atkinson, still the premier authority on Stonehenge since his discovery of the "Mycenaean" carvings, struck back with the

The sky figured prominently in John Constable's 1835 painting of Stonehenge . . . and in various twentieth-century theories that it was once an astronomical observatory. Copyright The British Museum.

equally bluntly titled article "Moonshine on Stonehenge." Atkinson argued that there was a good chance the celestial alignments could have occurred by chance. As for the Aubrey Holes as an eclipse predictor, Atkinson pointed to evidence that the holes had been used as cremation pits and had been filled up very soon after they'd been dug.

To some extent, the debate that followed pitted astronomers against archaeologists, with the practitioners of each discipline frequently having a great deal of trouble understanding the other's technical arguments. Astronomers came up with a variety of other ways by which Stonehenge could have been used as an astronomical observatory, some of which were less easily dismissed than Hawkins's. But the astronomers had a tendency to emphasize how different points were aligned with the sun or the moon, while ignoring the fact that one of these supposedly aligned points might have been constructed hundreds or even a thousand years later than the other. Archaeologists were quick to poke holes in most of these theories.

By the end of the second millennium, though the debate continued, there were signs of a consensus. The wildest theories, like Hawkins's, were discredited, even among astronomers, but almost all archaeologists (including Atkinson) recognized that at least a few of the celestial alignments, particularly the solar ones, were more than a coincidence. Most likely, most agreed, the monument was never used as an observatory, at least in the modern sense, but the people of Stonehenge probably did observe the sun from there, perhaps as part of some prehistoric ritual.

Yet even this imprecise kind of astronomy indicated that the people of Salisbury Plain studied the sky, and had some sort of system for keeping track of their findings. Clearly the builders of Stonehenge, however primitive they were in some respects, were remarkably sophisticated in others. In that sense, the latest discoveries, while deepening our understanding of Stonehenge, also have deepened the mystery surrounding the people who built it.

To investigate further

Geoffrey of Monmouth, *The History of the Kings of Britain,* trans. Lewis Thorpe (London: The Folio Society, 1966). Just as it was when Geoffrey finished it in 1138, the *History* is still entertaining, intriguing . . . and ultimately unreliable.

Gerald Hawkins, *Stonehenge Decoded* (Garden City, N.Y.: Doubleday, 1965). In spite of his flaws, Hawkins had a flair for drama, and the book still makes for exciting reading.

Richard Atkinson, "Moonshine on Stonehenge," *Antiquity* 40, no. 159 (September 1966). The leading archaeologist's response to Hawkins.

Jacquetta Hawkes, "God in the Machine," *Antiquity* 41, no. 163 (September 1967). Hawkes is rightly famous for saying that "every age gets the Stonehenge it desires, or deserves." Her words could just as appropriately be applied to just about every mystery of history in this book.

Christopher Chippindale, *Stonehenge Complete* (Ithaca, N.Y.: Cornell University Press, 1983). Though "complete" can only be an overstatement when the subject is Stonehenge, the book is a very thorough historiography that includes just about "everything important, interesting, or odd that has been written or painted, discovered or felt, about the most extraordinary of all ancient buildings."

Rodney Castleden, *The Making of Stonehenge* (London: Routledge, 1993). A close look at each phase in the monument's rise and fall.

R. M. Cleal, K. Walker, and R. Montague, *Stonehenge in Its Landscape* (London: English Heritage, 1995). A fat technical report that brings together all of the results of all of the twentieth century's crucial excavations.

John North, *Stonehenge* (New York: The Free Press, 1996). The latest and most thorough presentation of the astronomical thesis. North's thesis, which impressed many but convinced fewer, is that Stonehenge embodied many significant alignments, but that previous astronomers have failed to recognize them since they looked at the sun from the center of the monument, when they should have been doing so from outside the circle.

David Souden, *Stonehenge* (London: Collins & Brown, 1997). Commissioned by English Heritage, the quasi-independent agency that controls the monument, this is a clear exposition of the orthodox position, accepting some (but rejecting most) astronomical theories.

Barry Cunliffe and Colin Renfrew, eds., *Science and Stonehenge* (Oxford: Oxford University Press, 1997). A collection of essays that grew out of a conference held after the appearance of *Stonehenge in Its Landscape;* includes the latest entries in the bluestone and astronomy debates.

Chapter 3

Why Did the Pharaohs Build the Pyramids?

In about 450 B.C. Herodotus recounted a story about Khufu, a pharaoh so wicked that when he'd spent all his treasure, he sent his daughter to a brothel with orders to procure him a certain sum. Loyal daughter, she did so. But, hoping to be remembered for something besides the number of men she slept with, she also demanded from each man a present of a stone. With these she built one of the huge pyramids that still stand on the Gaza plateau, near the Nile River.

At the time Herodotus wrote, the pyramids were already a couple of millennia old. Yet the 2,000-plus years since haven't stemmed the flow of crackpot theories about the origins of the pyramids.

Some medieval writers believed they were the biblical granaries Joseph had used to store corn during Egypt's years of plenty. More recently, the pyramids have been described as sundials and calendars, astronomical observatories, surveying tools, and anchors for alien spacecraft.

Yet even Herodotus knew that the most widely accepted theory was that the pyramids were tombs for the pharaohs. Most reputable Egyptologists still believe that, and for good reason. The pyramids are ranged along the western bank of the Nile, which Egyptian myths tie to both the setting of the sun and the journey to an afterlife. Archaeologists have uncovered nearby ceremonial funeral boats in which the pharaohs were to sail to the afterworld. And the pyramids are surrounded by other tombs, presumably belonging to members of pharaohs' courts.

Most telling of all, many of the pyramids contained stone sarcophagi, or coffins. By the nineteenth century, some of the hierographic inscriptions on or near the sarcophagi were identified as spells to help the pharaohs pass from one world to the next.

The tomb theory lacked one critical piece of evidence, however: a body. During the nineteenth and early twentieth centuries, explorers and then archaeologists entered pyramid after pyramid. (There are more than eighty in various states along the Nile Valley, and perhaps others buried under the desert sand.) They would find what appeared to be the pharaoh's coffin, they would breathlessly open it, and—again and again—they would find it empty.

The most widespread explanation for the empty tombs has always been that the pyramids were robbed. Of course, most robbers were more interested in finding the pharaohs' treasures than their bodies, but they certainly weren't likely to take any time to make sure the latter were properly preserved. Nor were they likely to leave behind any mummy covered in pure gold.

The first tomb robbers were probably ancient Egyptians themselves, judging from the elaborate efforts to foil them. At the pyramid of Amenemhet III at Hawara, for example, the entrance leads to a small empty chamber, which leads to a narrow passage going nowhere. In the roof of that passage was a huge stone weighing more than twenty-two tons. Slid sideways, it revealed an upper corridor, again seeming to lead nowhere. A hidden brick door in one wall led to a third passage, then there were two more sliding ceiling blocks before reaching an antechamber and finally the burial chamber.

Yet it was all in vain; the Egyptian tomb robbers could not be thwarted. Their determination frustrated not just archaeologists but also later treasure hunters, such as the ninth-century Arab ruler Abdullah Al Mamun. He left a detailed report on what he thought was the first expedition into Khufu's Great Pyramid.

After leading his party through a series of false passages and plugged entrances, he finally reached the burial chamber, where he found nothing but an empty sarcophagus.

The European explorers who arrived in Egypt after Napoleon's conquest were more interested in carved stone than jewels, but they were only marginally more respectful of the pharaoh's monuments than their Egyptian and Arab predecessors. In 1818 Giovanni Belzoni, an Italian circus strongman turned explorer, used battering rams to get through the walls of the pyramid of Khufu's son, Khafre. Belzoni was busy stocking up for his upcoming exhibit in London, but he stopped long enough to check for bodies in what appeared to be the burial chamber. The only bones to be found belonged to a bull, perhaps some sort of offering thrown into the sarcophagus by some earlier intruders who'd made off with the pharaoh's body.

The search—for treasure and bodies—paid off in 1923, when the British archaeologist Howard Carter unearthed the tomb of Tutankhamen. "King Tut" is now probably the best-known pharaoh, and rightly so, given the magnificent and intact treasure Carter found. This included a solid gold coffin and a golden mask on the pharaoh's body.

Alas, the discovery proved nothing about pyramids, for Tutankhamen wasn't buried in one. His tomb had been cut right into the rocks of Egypt's Valley of the Kings.

Even more disturbing for Carter's crew was the death of the earl of Carnarvon, a rich amateur archaeologist who funded the expedition. Soon after arriving at the Valley of the Kings, Carnarvon was found dead in Cairo. Two others who had entered the tomb died soon after—first the head of the Louvre's department of Egyptian antiquities, then the assistant keeper of Egyptian antiquities at New York's Metropolitan Museum of Art.

Inevitably this led to all sorts of absurd speculation about a curse. One report had it that Carter found a tablet in the tomb inscribed, "Death will slay with his wings whoever disturbs the peace of the pharaoh."

∽

Curse or no curse, the search continued.

If the pyramids were built as tombs for the pharaohs, they were certainly expensive ones. As Rudyard Kipling wrote: "Who shall doubt the secret hid/Under Cheops' pyramid/Is that some contractor did/Cheops out of millions?" Pictured here is the Great Pyramid of Cheops. Library of Congress.

In 1925, just two years after the discovery of Tutankhamen's tomb, a team of American archaeologists under George Andrew Reisner was working near the foot of Khufu's Great Pyramid. A photographer trying to set up his tripod accidentally nicked out a piece of plaster from a hidden opening cut into the rock. That revealed part of a hundred-foot-deep shaft filled with masonry from top to bottom. It took two weeks to reach the bottom.

There Reisner found the coffin of Queen Hetepheres, Khufu's mother. Since the tomb had been so well hidden, Reisner hoped he might find an intact burial, but the sarcophagus was empty. Only after they'd gotten over their disappointment did archaeologists notice a plastered area on the wall of the chamber, behind which they found a small chest. Inside that were the embalmed viscera of the queen.

Reisner's guess—and he admitted it was only that—was that the queen must once have been buried elsewhere. Then, after robbers removed her body to get at jewels under its wrappings, her remains must have been reburied near her husband and son.

The hope of finding an intact burial in a pyramid was revived in 1951, when an Egyptian Egyptologist, Zacharia Goneim, uncovered the remains of a previously unknown pyramid at Saqqara, about six miles south of Giza. The pyramid had never been noticed before, since its builders never got beyond the foundation, which was then covered by the Sahara sands. At first, Goneim assumed an unfinished pyramid was unlikely to hold much of importance, let alone a pharaoh's remains. But his expectations rose as he followed a shallow trench into a tunnel. As he dug through three stone walls, he became even more excited; after all, no robber was likely to have taken the time to reseal a tomb on his way out. Jewels found in the pyramid seemed a further indication that here, at last, was a tomb the robbers never found.

Finally Goneim reached the burial chamber, which he identified as that of Sekhemkhet, a pharaoh about whom little was known, but a pharaoh nonetheless. When Goneim spotted a golden sarcophagus, he and his colleagues danced and wept and embraced each other. A few days later, in front of an audience of scholars and reporters, Goneim ordered the coffin opened.

To his shock, it was empty.

The failure to find a pharaoh in his tomb has spawned numerous theories, many based on the mathematical regularities that Egyptologists saw in the pyramids. In the nineteenth century, for example, the Scottish astronomer Charles Piazzi Smyth "discovered" that the Great Pyramid had just enough "pyramid inches" to make it a scale model of the circumference of the earth. Unfortunately, Piazzi Smyth's careful calculations were based on measurements taken when massive mounds of debris still covered the base of the pyramid.

In 1974, physicist Kurt Mendelssohn contended that the pyramids were public works projects rather than tombs, and that their purpose was to create a national Egyptian identity for what had been scattered tribes. Mendelssohn's theory explained not just the lack of bodies but also another disturbing problem with the tomb theory, namely that many pharaohs appeared to build more than one of them. For example, Khufu's father, Snefru, had three pyramids, and it's hard to imagine he intended his remains to be divided among them. Khufu himself had only one pyramid, but it has three rooms that seem to have been designed as crypts.

Another theory that's gained many followers is that the pyramids were cenotaphs—monuments to the dead pharaohs but not their actual tombs, which were hidden elsewhere to keep them safe from robbers. That would explain why they were full of funereal trappings but no bodies.

Still, the majority of Egyptologists continue to believe that the pyramids were built primarily as tombs, even if they served some other purpose as well. They're surrounded by other tombs, albeit of lesser officials. Even if ancient and not-so-ancient robbers have stolen most every trace of them, the pharaohs' bodies once lay there.

The pyramids, in the consensus view, can best be understood as part of an architectural progression that began with rectangular, flat-topped tombs of mud brick, today called *mastabas* (in which bodies *have* been found). Then architects started placing one flat-topped structure on top of another, creating what became known as the "step pyramids," the most famous of which still stands south of Cairo at Saqqara. Finally, someone had the idea of filling in the steps, and the familiar slope of the pyramid was born, probably at Meidum, about forty miles south of Saqqara.

The architectural development coincided with theological changes. Texts found in mastabas indicate a belief that the pharaoh would climb to heaven on its steps. Later texts from the period of the true pyramids reflect a cult of the sun god, and describe the pharaohs rising on the rays of the sun. The sloping sides of the pyramid, resembling as they do the shape of the sun's rays shining down, were the new pathway to heaven.

Did the cult of the sun inspire Egyptian architects to design the pyramids? It seems at first glance unlikely that so many extra tons of stones had to be quarried, transported, and hauled into place just because a staircase was no longer considered an effective way to get to heaven. But, difficult as it is for us to understand it some four and a half thousand years later, the Egyptian people considered it well worth the effort. (And, in spite of the popular misconception that Hebrew slaves built the pyramids, it was Egyptians who did it.)

Almost everything that has lasted of Egyptian civilization has to do with death. It appears to have been the defining force in their religion, their literature, their art. For the pharaohs, the afterlife was a very real goal, whether via staircase or sunbeam. It's completely appropriate, therefore, that the monuments that define their civilization for posterity were also, almost certainly, designed to house their dead.

To investigate further

Herodotus, *The Histories*, trans. Aubrey de Selincourt (Middlesex, Eng.: Penguin, 1954). He's been called both the "father of history" and the "father of lies"; either way, his tales still rank among the most entertaining ever.

Richard Proctor, *The Great Pyramid* (London: Chatto & Windus, 1883). Khufu's pyramid as an astronomical observatory.

Howard Carter, *The Tomb of Tutankhamen* (New York: E. P. Dutton, 1954). How does it feel to find yourself face to face with a pharaoh from three thousand years ago? Carter captures the awe and excitement of his history-making discovery. Originally published in 1924.

I. E. S. Edwards, *The Pyramids of Egypt* (Middlesex, Eng.: Viking, 1947). Still the classic history of the pyramids and their cultural and religious significance.

Peter Tompkins, *Secrets of the Great Pyramid* (New York: Harper & Row, 1971). A fascinating but too uncritical compendium of alternative explanations for Khufu's tomb.

Kurt Mendelssohn, *The Riddle of the Pyramids* (New York: Praeger, 1974). The pyramids as a political statement.

Brian Fagan, *The Rape of the Nile* (New York: Charles Scribner's Sons, 1975). Tomb robbers, tourists, and archaeologists in Egypt through the ages, with a special focus on Belzoni: "the greatest plunderer of them all."

Paul Johnson, *The Civilization of Ancient Egypt* (New York, Athenaeum, 1978). Its rise and fall, in one fact- and opinion-packed volume.

Robert Bauval and Adrian Gilbert, *The Orion Mystery* (New York: Crown, 1994). The latest case for an astronomical explanation; specifically, that the Giza pyramids were positioned to represent the three stars of Orion's belt.

Mark Lehner, *The Complete Pyramids* (London: Thames & Hudson, 1997). Pyramid by pyramid, everything you wanted to know about each.

Chapter 4

Who Was Theseus?

Theseus's exploits were legion: he brought democracy to Athens, joined Jason and the Argonauts in their quest for the Golden Fleece, and fought (to a draw) the fierce women warriors known as the Amazons. But all of this paled before his greatest deed, the slaying of the minotaur. The story, which was told most fully by Plutarch in the first century A.D. but which was clearly known well before then, went this way:

The powerful King Minos, who ruled Greece from his palace in Crete, was married to Pasiphae, who fell in love with a beautiful bull. Pasiphae had the inventor Daedalus build her a wooden cow, so she could hide inside and mate with the bull. She then gave birth to the monstrous minotaur—half man, half bull, and unfortunately fond of human flesh.

Minos turned to Daedalus, who built a huge labyrinth to hold the minotaur. Into this labyrinth, every nine years, the king sent fourteen Athenian youths, at once feeding the minotaur and avenging the death of Minos's son, Androgeos, at the hands of the Athenians. None of the youths ever returned—at least until Theseus, the son of the Athenian king Aegus, volunteered to go. He promised his father he'd return, flying a white sail to celebrate his success.

Back in Crete, Minos's daughter, Ariadne, fell in love with the courageous youth and handed him a ball of thread. Theseus slew the minotaur, then followed the unwound thread out of the labyrinth. Thus ended the cruel sacrifice of the Athenian youths, and with it the dominance of Crete over Athens.

It was not so happy an ending for Ariadne, whom Theseus abandoned on his way back to Athens, or for Aegus, who threw himself off a cliff when he spotted his son's ship still rigged with a black sail. (Theseus had forgotten to make the switch.) But that at least had the benefit of hastening Theseus's ascension to the throne.

Plutarch's story, filled with supernatural elements, obviously belongs to the realm of mythology. But early historians wondered whether the myth might not have preserved some memory of a Cretan empire that, in a prehistoric age, ruled Greece. In 1900 Arthur Evans, the director of the Ashmolean Museum at Oxford, arrived in Crete. What he found convinced him, and many others, that Crete had not only been the center of a great empire, but also that the story of Theseus was not nearly as fantastic as it once seemed.

Evans was ideally suited to excavate at Crete. A third-generation academic, he was an expert on ancient writing, in search of which he first went to Crete. He was also a supporter of Cretan independence, which stood him in good stead after the island was liberated from Turkish rule in 1899. Best of all, Evans had inherited a fortune from his father's paper business. This allowed him to bypass the usual tricky negotiations, and simply buy the land where he wanted to dig. Local tradition was clear about the site of Knossos, Minos's palace, being in the Kairatos Valley, and that's where Evans began digging.

Within weeks, it was clear that this was a remarkable site. Luckily, it had not been built over in Greek or Roman times, so workmen almost instantly reached the remains of a Bronze Age palace. And what a palace! It extended for many acres, and with its numerous dark rooms and passages, it immediately conjured up a labyrinth. Evans couldn't help but imagine ancient Athenian visitors returning home to tell tales of having been trapped in a

"Everywhere the bull!" wrote Arthur Evans of his discoveries at Knossos. The most famous and startling was this fresco, which portrayed a man vaulting over a charging bull and led archaeologists to wonder whether there might not be some truth to the story of Theseus slaying the minotaur. Copyright Wolfgang Kaehler/CORBIS.

seemingly endless maze. In the middle of the palace was a large courtyard. Could this have been the home, Evans wondered, of the creature mythologized as a minotaur?

Still in 1900, Evans made his most sensational discovery of all: a painting depicting a male youth in the act of somersaulting over the back of the bull, while two female youths stood by, apparently either spotting their companion or waiting their turn. More images of bulls and bull-leapers soon were found, some on engraved seals and some in the form of bronze or ivory statuettes.

An amazed Evans consulted with the obvious experts—Spanish bullfighters. He asked them whether the type of bull-leaping portrayed in the Cretan art was possible. The bullfighters responded that it couldn't be done, at least if the bull-leapers hoped to survive. But the evidence was overwhelming that some form of bull-leaping had taken place here. Whatever artistic license might have been taken by the Cretan artists and by the Athenian storytellers, bulls were clearly an integral part of this culture. Perhaps the youths pictured were Greek captives trained for the arena like the gladiators of ancient Rome.

Evans named the culture "Minoan," after its legendary (or perhaps not so legendary) king. He was convinced that the Minoans had, as the Theseus story recalled, once ruled over Greece, dominating the mainland politically and artistically. It was the Minoans, Evans believed, who laid the foundations on which were built the later achievements of the classical Greeks. The poetry of Homer, the philosophy of Plato, the architecture of the Parthenon—all these were foreshadowed in the Minoan culture.

Evans's confidence in his ideas was bolstered by his discovery at Knossos of a number of clay tablets. It was to search for ancient writing, you'll recall, that Evans initially went to Crete. The tablets, written in alphabets that came to be known as Linear A and Linear B, clearly confirmed Evans's belief that the Minoans were not only artistic but also literate.

To preserve the glories of Minoan civilization, Evans in 1901 began to reconstruct the palace at Knossos. He rebuilt the long-gone upper walls and columns, as well as part of the palace roof. He hired a Swiss artist, Émile Gillieron, to restore the frescoes. The result was completely unlike any other archaeological site of his time or ours; instead of looking at mere foot-high remains, even tourists with no historical background could get a clear sense of the full scope and grandeur of Minoan art and architecture.

Evans's critics accused him of creating a postcard version of history. It was no longer possible, they argued, to tell how much of Minoan civilization he'd discovered and how much he'd invented. By later archaeological standards, his critics were undoubtedly right; no archaeologist today would allow a reconstruction on the actual site of an excavation. But in fairness to Evans, it ought to be added that he was far more careful about preserving a precise and photographic record of what he found than were many of his contemporaries. And, reluctant as critics might be to admit this, he also created a site so dramatic that visitors ever since could not help but share in his passion for the Minoans.

∽

A more fundamental problem with Evans's view of Greek history emerged as other archaeologists, primarily Alan Wace in the 1920s and Carl Blegen in the 1930s, excavated sites on the Greek mainland. There they found evidence of a culture that was flourishing at the same time that the Minoans ruled Crete. This "Mycenaean" civilization was clearly independent of the Minoans, and at least as powerful if not as sophisticated as its neighbors to the south. Indeed, Wace and Blegen argued, the Mycenaeans may very well have conquered the Minoans and taken over Knossos, probably sometime after 1500 B.C.

In a way, this seemed further confirmation that the Theseus legend had some basis in history. The Athenians, like the Mycenaeans, were Greeks, so Theseus's triumph could stand for some actual battle or series of battles during which the Mycenaean Greeks defeated the bull-headed Cretans. Evans, however, would have none of this. So convinced was he of the Minoans' superiority that he insisted that only a natural catastrophe—perhaps an earthquake—could have ended their rule. And if some such disaster enabled the Mycenaeans to dislodge the Minoans from Knossos, there was still no question in Evans's mind that it was the Mycenaean military might, not their culture, that prevailed.

Evans's position became increasingly difficult after 1939, when Blegen, still excavating on the mainland, discovered more clay tablets written in Linear B, the same alphabet Evans had found at Knossos. True, the discovery might be interpreted to mean that the Minoans had brought their writing north and introduced it to the Greeks. But it also raised the possibility that Linear B— and writing in general—was a Mycenaean and not a Minoan invention.

Evans died in 1941, never having figured out what was written on his precious tablets. Eleven years later, Michael Ventris, an amateur cryptologist utilizing techniques developed during World War II, finally broke the code. The words written on the tablet were something of a disappointment; far from being great poetry or philosophy, they were mostly lists of goods that had been stored at Knossos and elsewhere. But Ventris's discovery was nonetheless extremely significant, for Linear B, it turned out, was a system of writing *Greek*—an archaic and difficult Greek, to be sure, but Greek nonetheless.

That meant that writing had come to Crete from Greece and not, as Evans had always maintained, the other way around. It remains possible that the Minoans had a writing of their own—Linear A, which has still not been decoded, may turn out to be Minoan—but after Ventris's breakthrough it was impossible to picture Mycenae as a mere outpost of Cretan civilization. On the contrary, the Mycenaean Greeks clearly had a powerful civilization of their own. And at some point, much earlier than Evans thought—and perhaps even led by a prince named Theseus—these Greeks had come to Crete, and conquered it.

Linear B did not, by any means, spell the end of the controversies surrounding the Minoans. By the 1960s, most archaeologists agreed that the Mycenaeans had conquered Crete, but there was no consensus on how they'd done so. And some archaeologists, notably Spyridon Marinatos, remained convinced that a natural catastrophe had so weakened the Minoans that it opened the door for the Mycenaeans.

That catastrophe, Marinatos believed, was the eruption of a volcano on the island of Thera, about seventy miles north of Crete. In 1967 Marinatos went to Thera, seeking proof. He soon uncovered more than he'd hoped for: preserved under a layer of volcanic ash was an entire Bronze Age town. There was no need for Evans-style restoration here; these houses were still remarkably intact, and many were filled with Minoan-style art and artifacts indicating that this had been a Cretan colony. The only thing missing were the people, who apparently had had enough time to flee before the volcano erupted.

This was an extraordinary discovery—a Cretan Pompeii but twice as old. But could a volcanic eruption on Thera have ended Cretan civilization? Marinatos believed so. He argued that the volcano may have been set off by earthquakes, which in turn caused tsunamis that devastated Crete. At the very least, he maintained, the earthquakes and tsunamis did enough damage to give the Mycenaeans their opening. Had he lived, Evans certainly would have felt vindicated by Marinatos's arguments.

Most archaeologists and other scientists, however, were not persuaded. For one thing, the dates didn't match. Most volcanologists placed the Thera eruption between 1600 and 1700 B.C., more than a hundred years before the estimated date of the Minoan collapse. Moreover, in spite of the obvious volcanic damage at Thera, there were no significant deposits of ash on Crete. Nor was there evidence that water from tsunamis had reached Knossos, let alone damaged it. In fact, the archaeological evidence on Crete seemed to indicate that fire, not ash or water, had caused much of the destruction there.

So most scientists—though by no means all—have denied the Thera volcano a significant role in the downfall of Minoan civilization.

Does that mean that Theseus played the role instead? That Theseus (or the Greeks he came to represent) slew the minotaur (or rather the Minoans the monster came to represent)? These are questions that can't be fully answered, given the centuries that separate us from Plutarch's time, and Plutarch from Theseus's time. But that certainly doesn't mean that no progress has been made in answering them; on the contrary, the discoveries of the past hundred years have filled in some very believable details about what once seemed an entirely fictional story.

To investigate further

Arthur Evans, *The Palace of Minos* (London: Macmillan, 1921–1936). Evans's own account of the discoveries at Knossos, in four volumes.

Anne Ward, ed., *The Quest for Theseus* (New York: Praeger, 1970). Essays on how the Theseus legend originated and developed in art and literature, from the classical era to the present.

Hans Wunderlich, *The Secret of Crete*, trans. from German by Richard Winston (New York: Macmillan, 1974). Wunderlich argues, provocatively but ultimately unconvincingly, that Knossos was never lived in, but was, like the Egyptian pyramids, a royal tomb.

Sylvia Horwitz, *The Find of a Lifetime* (New York: Viking, 1981). A readable biography of Evans, with a balanced presentation of the controversies until its publication.

D. A. Hardy et al., *Thera and the Aegean World III* (London: Thera Foundation, 1990). These proceedings of a major international conference, held in Thera in 1989, include more than a hundred papers by archaeologists and other scientists. The clear consensus was that the Theran eruption was *not* responsible for the end of Minoan civilization.

J. Lesley Fitton, *The Discovery of the Greek Bronze Age* (Cambridge, Mass.: Harvard University Press, 1996). An authoritative account of the excavations at Troy, Mycenae, Knossos, Thera, and other Greek Bronze Age sites.

Rodney Castleden, *Atlantis Destroyed* (New York: Routledge, 1998). Other Greek legends besides Theseus's may be rooted in Minoan Crete. Of these, the best known is undoubtedly that of Atlantis, which Plato (writing in the fifth century B.C.) described as a great island civilization that, following earthquakes and floods, was swallowed up by the sea. Many writers have speculated that Crete was Atlantis, destroyed by the Thera volcano and accompanying earthquakes and floods. This is an argument that faces many obstacles, and not just those cited in this chapter. For example, Plato described Atlantis as having been in the Atlantic, though Crete is clearly in the Mediterranean. And Plato put the destruction nine thousand years before his time, while the actual span was closer to nine hundred years. Castleden is the latest to make the case for Crete as Atlantis, and he's also one of the most reasonable, but it remains an unlikely scenario. Sometimes myths are just myths.

Chapter 5

Was There Really a Trojan War?

J ust a few miles from the Dardanelles, on the Asian side of the narrow strait that separates Greece from Turkey, stands a small hill known as Hisarlik.

This, according to Herodotus, Xenophon, Plutarch, and various other classical Greek and Roman writers, was the site of Troy, the Troy of Homer's *Iliad* and *Odyssey*. The classical Greeks were not sure whether Homer had ever actually seen Troy, but they had no doubt that the battles he described had taken place. Nor did they doubt that they'd taken place in and around Hisarlik.

In a world where humans were like gods (and gods were all too human), this was where the greatest of both clashed. It was to Troy that Paris, the son of Troy's King Priam, brought Helen, the most beautiful woman of the world, after he kidnapped her from her Greek home. It was to Troy that the Greek king Agamemnon led his troops to win her back. And it was at Troy that Achilles, the greatest of the Greek warriors, slayed Hector, Paris's brother. In the final scene of the *Iliad*, Priam met with Achilles to negotiate the return of his son's body, and a truce between the Greeks and the Trojans.

But, as readers of the *Odyssey* knew, the story didn't end there. With a fatal blow to Achilles' heel, Paris avenged his brother's death. And with the help of a giant wooden horse, the Greeks sneaked inside the Trojan walls and ultimately destroyed the city. So ended the golden age of Troy—and not so long after, the golden age of Greece as well.

The belief that all this actually happened—and happened at Hisarlik—drew later conquerors to the site. In 480 B.C., the Persian king Xerxes sacrificed a thousand bulls near Hisarlik, right before crossing the Dardanelles into Greece. A century and a half later, when Alexander the Great led his troops in the opposite direction, he honored Achilles with sacrifices near the same spot. Through the Middle Ages and the Renaissance, travelers continued to visit Hisarlik, convinced this was Troy.

Starting in the eighteenth century, however, scholars began to take a more skeptical approach. Many doubted there was a war at Troy, let alone the monumental clash of Homer's epics. Some even doubted there was a Homer, or at least a single man rather than a series of poets. After all, they noted, hundreds of years separated Herodotus from Homer, and hundreds more lay between the poet and the alleged golden age.

By the second half of the nineteenth century, only a minority of scholars believed that that the *Iliad* and the *Odyssey* recalled events that really happened. Even fewer believed that Troy, if it existed at all, was at Hisarlik. To most, the *Iliad* and the *Odyssey* were great literature, not history.

One man who remained convinced that Troy existed was Frank Calvert, the U.S. consul to the region and an amateur archaeologist. In the mid-1860s Calvert made a few preliminary excavations at Hisarlik, uncovering the remains of a temple from classical times and a wall from Alexander's time. This was encouraging, but it also convinced Calvert that there were many layers of history beneath Hisarlik and that the type of excavation necessary would require more money than he had.

Then, in 1868, Calvert invited to dinner Heinrich Schliemann, a visiting German millionaire with a passion for Homer. Schliemann, too, became convinced that Hisarlik was Troy. And, unlike Calvert, Schliemann had the money to do something about it.

In 1870, he and his crew began digging.

Schliemann believed that Homer's Troy was so ancient that it could only be found by burrowing deep into Hisarlik. So he opened up an enormous area of the hill, reaching straight down to solid bedrock. As he dug, he was disturbed to find various Stone Age objects, for these ought logically to be found beneath the Bronze or Iron Age city that Homer described. In May 1872 Schliemann admitted in his diary that he was "perplexed." Still, he kept digging.

Then, in May 1873, he struck gold—literally. As he later told the story, Schliemann feared how his workmen might react to the sight of gold. Telling them he'd just remembered it was his birthday, he said they should all take a break. Then he called his wife, Sophia, who secreted away the gold in her shawl. Only later did the couple examine their treasure, which surpassed Schliemann's dreams. There were exquisite works of gold and copper, including 2 gold crowns made of thousands of tiny pieces of threaded gold, 60 gold earrings, and 8,750 gold rings.

This must be, Schliemann concluded, the treasure of King Priam, including the jewelry of Helen. He later speculated that a member of the royal family had scooped up the treasure chest as the Greeks ransacked the city. The unfortunate Trojan was then buried under debris as the chest and the city went up in flames. A copper key found near the jewels must once have opened the chest, Schliemann surmised.

Still concerned for the treasure's safety, Schliemann sneaked it across the border into Greece. This did not sit well with the Turkish authorities, who took him to court. In 1875 Schliemann agreed to pay the Turkish government fifty thousand francs. In return, the Turks conceded that he was now the owner of a unique and undeniably valuable treasure.

But was it *Priam's* treasure, as Schliemann so quickly dubbed it? Privately, Schliemann admitted some doubts. Grand though the treasure was, it didn't explain the lack of other signs that Hisarlik was Homer's Troy. Schliemann had found remnants of a small prehistoric settlement, but none of the wide streets or towers or gates the poems had led him to expect.

He was determined to dig further, but the Turks, still furious about his smuggling the treasure out of their country, refused to

Sophia Schliemann, wearing some of the Trojan treasures that, according to her husband, were smuggled out of Turkey in her shawl. Gennadius Library, American School of Classical Studies.

grant him a permit. So Schliemann, never one to sit around, decided to continue his search for the Trojan War elsewhere.

If he couldn't get to Priam's kingdom, he decided, he would go to Agamemnon's instead. Here, too, the classical writers offered directions, this time to Mycenae, located below Corinth on Greece's Argolic Peninsula. Mycenae was long thought to be the burial place of ancient Greek kings, and unlike Hisarlik, Mycenae boasted some visible and impressive ruins.

Schliemann's inspired idea was to dig outside the Mycenae walls, where no one had looked before. The results were even more spectacular than at Hisarlik. He found five graves with the remains of nineteen men and women and two infants, all covered in gold. The graves also contained bronze swords and daggers with gold- and silverwork, gold and silver cups and boxes, and hundreds of decorated gold pieces. The men's faces were covered with distinctive gold masks that seemed to be portraits. Schliemann, with his customary flair for the dramatic, announced that he had stared into the face of Agamemnon himself.

Now Schliemann was more convinced than ever that Homer had described real people and real battles. But the sumptuous cemetery at Mycenae made the small town at Hisarlik seem even less imposing, and the contrast nagged at Schliemann. Finally, in 1890, in return for a large cash payment, the Turks granted Schliemann a permit to continue his excavation of Hisarlik.

This time Schliemann dug near the western border of the hill, about twenty-five yards outside the city where he'd found Priam's treasure. There he uncovered the remains of a large building. This, finally, was a structure worthy of Homer's heroes; perhaps, Schliemann thought, this was Priam's palace. Better still, within the building's walls workers found remains of pottery with unmistakably Mycenaean shapes and decorations. This provided Schliemann with the link he'd sought between Mycenae and Troy. If they hadn't fought with each other, then they must at least have traded with each other.

Ironically, the 1890 finds also confirmed Schliemann's worst fears, for the new discoveries were found much nearer to the surface than the town Schliemann had excavated in the 1870s. This indicated that Homer's Troy had been built centuries later than the small settlement where Schliemann had found the treasure, so the treasure couldn't have belonged to Priam, or any other figure from the *Iliad*. Worse still, it meant that Schliemann, in his eagerness to quickly reach the bottom of the hill, had cut right through the remains of Homer's Troy. In doing so, he almost certainly destroyed some of the remains of the city he so desperately wanted to find.

Schliemann died in 1890, so it was left to his onetime assistant, Wilhelm Dorpfeld, to continue the excavations. Dorpfeld assumed that the large house uncovered earlier that year was part of the Bronze Age city that Schliemann had sought, and he continued to dig to the west and the south of the original town. Over the course of 1893 and 1894 he found more large houses, a watchtower, and three hundred yards of the city wall. He also found lots more Mycenaean pottery.

Dorpfeld concluded that *this* was Homer's Troy. Indeed, the tower, the large houses, and the wide streets were much more in keeping with the poet's descriptions than any of the buildings Schliemann had uncovered. Dorpfeld's analysis of the layers at Hisarlik led him to conclude that Schliemann's small settlement was the second built at Hisarlik, and that it dated back to about 2500 B.C. Dorpfeld's Troy was the sixth city built on the same site, and was built between 1500 and 1000 B.C. The dating, though imprecise, put Dorpfeld's finds close enough to the traditional date for the Trojan War—about 1200 B.C.—to deepen his conviction that he had found Homer's Troy.

Dorpfeld's views prevailed for about forty years, when an American expedition under the direction of Carl Blegen arrived at Hisarlik. Blegen's digs, which lasted from 1932 to 1938, pointed to some serious problems with Dorpfeld's hypothesis. The destruction of the sixth Troy, Blegen determined, could not have been the result of a Greek invasion. At one part of the wall the foundation had shifted, while other parts seemed to have collapsed entirely. Blegen believed that type of damage couldn't be manmade—even by men with godlike qualities. He attributed it to an earthquake.

According to Blegen, it was the next settlement at Hisarlik—
and the seventh overall—that was Homer's Troy. After the earthquake, the Trojans rebuilt their city, but in dramatically different
ways. The large houses of the sixth Troy were now partitioned
into small rooms, and the wide streets crammed with tiny houses,
each with large storage jars sunk into their floors. All this indicated to Blegen a city under siege; with the Greeks outside the
Trojan gates, every available space had to be filled by refugees
and their goods. Blegen concluded that the seventh city fell soon
after the sixth, so it still fit the traditional date for the Trojan
War.

∽

First Schliemann, then Dorpfeld, then Blegen: all three archaeologists believed they found Homer's Troy at Hisarlik, albeit at different levels.

All three would have been heartened by the work of subsequent scholars and archaeologists. Some of the most tantalizing
evidence came from the remains of the Hittite civilization, which
flourished in Turkey until sometime after 1200 B.C. During the
1970s and 1980s, scholars deciphered clay tablets found there,
some of which listed the names of foreign kings and diplomats
with whom the Hittites dealt. Some of these scholars have suggested that among the names were Hittite translations of Priam
and Paris.

Back at Hisarlik, in the mid-1990s, the German archaeologist
Manfred Korfmann used new remote sensing technology to trace
the walls of the Dorpfeld-Blegen city well beyond the earlier lim-
its. Korfmann's Troy was, even more than his predecessors', a
citadel worthy of Homer's heroes. Korfmann's analysis also indicated that the Trojan walls would still have been visible in the
eighth century B.C., when Homer might have visited the site.

Still, the majority of scholars today have been wary of jumping to any conclusions—or at least to conclusions as dramatic as
those of Schliemann, Dorpfeld, or Blegen. The Hittite tablets,
they've stressed, are subject to a variety of interpretations and
certainly don't constitute proof that there ever was a Paris or
a Priam, let alone a Hector or a Helen, or an Achilles or an
Agamemnon.

Most scholars admit that they can't say for sure whether the Trojan War ever took place. The *Iliad* and the *Odyssey* were the products of a longing for a long-lost golden age, as well as a poet's very vivid imagination, and as such they certainly can't be considered a reliable historical account. But, just as Schliemann suspected, there can no longer be any doubt that the hill at Hisarlik was once a great city, as was the citadel of Mycenae. And though historians can't be certain about the names or the deeds of the the people who lived at either, they consider it very likely that each knew a great deal about the other.

The people of Troy and the people of Mycenae talked with each other, traded with each other, and, quite conceivably, fought with each other. At least to that extent, Schliemann—and Homer—were right.

To investigate further

Heinrich Schliemann, *Troy and Its Remains* (London: John Murray, 1875). Schliemann's own account of his 1871–1873 excavation, including the discovery of Priam's treasure.

Carl Blegen, *Troy and the Trojans* (New York: Praeger, 1963). Blegen's version, based on his 1932–1938 excavations.

John M. Cook, *The Troad* (Oxford: The Clarendon Press, 1973). A study of the archaeology in and around Hisarlik, including a comprehensive survey of pre-Schliemann theories. Many of these theories located Troy near the Turkish village of Pinarbasi, and Schliemann himself dug there before turning to Hisarlik.

Michael Wood, *In Search of the Trojan War* (New York: Facts On File, 1985). A companion to a BBC program, this provides a good introduction to Troy historiography, along with an intriguing and provocative look at the Hittite evidence.

William Calder III and David Traill, *Myth, Scandal, and History* (Detroit: Wayne State University Press, 1986). A collection of essays portraying Schliemann as a pathological liar, a thesis more fully developed in Traill's 1995 biography.

David Traill, *Schliemann of Troy* (New York: St. Martin's Press, 1995). An extremely controversial, all-out attack on Schliemann, accusing him of—among other things—cheating his business partners; lying to gain American citizenship; failing to give credit to Frank Calvert; and, most devastating of all, making up the story of how and where he found Priam's treasure. According to Traill, Schliemann lied about hiding the treasure in his wife's shawl to conceal the fact that he'd actually gathered the objects in the treasure from a variety of places in and around Hisarlik, then bunched them together so he could pretend he'd made a dramatic discovery. Traill's damning evidence includes the indisputable fact that Schliemann's wife was in Athens at the time of the discovery. Traill's critics argue that it would have been impossible for Schliemann to bring together so many objects, all of which were later shown to come from the same period. They also point out that the vast majority of his archaeological notes have turned out to be largely accurate. But Traill's defenders (and other Schliemann detractors) counter that the evidence of Schliemann's lying in his other business and personal dealings is overwhelming. Schliemann, they contend, couldn't be a Dr. Jekyll at Hisarlik while being a Mr. Hyde elsewhere. The book is well worth reading, but don't lose sight of the fact that the questions raised are largely irrelevant to the larger question of what happened at Troy. After all, even Schliemann eventually conceded that the part of Troy he first excavated dated back to well before the Trojan War and that Priam's treasure could not, therefore, have belonged to Priam or any of his contemporaries.

Caroline Moorehead, *Lost and Found* (New York: Viking, 1996). As riveting as the history of Troy is the mysterious fate of Priam's treasure, entertainingly revealed in Moorehead's book. Schliemann left the treasure to the German government, which displayed it at Berlin's Museum for Prehistory. In 1945 the treasure disappeared, apparently lost forever. Then, in 1991, a Russian art historian and a curator at the Pushkin Museum in Moscow broke the story that the entire treasure was buried in the museum's vaults, having been seized by Soviet troops at the end of World War II.

Vladimir Tolstikov and Mikhail Treister, *The Gold of Troy,* trans. from the Russian by Christina Sever and Mila Bonnichsen (New York: Abrams, 1996). In 1994 the Russians admitted they had the treasure and agreed to make it available to scholars and the public. This is the catalog of the first public exhibition in almost fifty years. It includes essays defending Schliemann (and the treasure) against Traill's accusations.

Susan Allen, *Finding the Walls of Troy* (Berkeley: University of California Press, 1999). Schliemann, who didn't want to share the spotlight, later minimized Calvert's contribution; here Allen moves Calvert out of the more famous man's shadow.

Chapter 6

Did Jesus Die on the Cross?

It's a classic "locked door" mystery.

A man is executed: he is crucified, then a lance is plunged into his chest to make sure he's dead. His body is buried in a tomb, by some accounts guarded by experienced centurions.

Two days later, the body is gone. More mysterious still, people who knew the man well report seeing him and talking to him. At first they suspect it's some sort of dream or hallucination, but they touch him and eat with him, Finally, they conclude the man has come back to life.

The man, of course, is Jesus of Nazareth. And his resurrection is not just the basis of Christianity but also a mystery that's intrigued historians for nearly two thousand years.

Compared to most people of his period, Jesus had a pretty well documented life.

The Roman historian Tacitus, writing early in the second century, mentioned that "Christus" had been sentenced to death by the Roman governor Pontius Pilate. Tacitus added that his death hadn't stopped the "pernicious superstition" of his followers.

Jewish sources were equally curt, with the exception of the first-century historian Josephus. Josephus recounted how, after Pilate condemned him to be crucified, Jesus "appeared . . . restored

to life, for the prophets of God had prophesied these and count-
less other marvelous things about him." The phrasing was bla-
tantly that of a believer, so most historians concluded that some
later Christian copyist must have added it. Still, most also
assumed that Josephus's original text must have made some mention of Jesus' death.

The Roman and Jewish sources offered mere mentions. To
learn more about Jesus' "passion" or suffering, historians turned
to the New Testament, in particular the gospels of Mark,
Matthew, Luke, and John. The earliest extant versions of the
gospels date from the fourth century, but most historians believe
the originals were written between 70 and 110, or between 40
and 80 years after the resurrection. They tell the same basic story,
including the last supper with his disciples; the betrayal by one of
them, Judas Iscariot; the arrest, trial, crucifixion, and resurrection.

Beyond that, there are all sorts of inconsistencies. In Mark,
which most historians think is the earliest of the gospels, three
women find a young man in a white robe in the tomb; he turns
out to be a messenger sent to tell them Jesus has been raised. A
decade or so later, Matthew adds an earthquake, a dazzling light,
and an actual appearance of Jesus before the women; then Jesus
appears, on a mountain in Galilee, before his eleven disciples.
(The twelfth, Judas, has hanged himself.) In Luke, written about
the same time as Matthew, the number of women at the tomb is
unspecified, two angels appear at the tomb, and the first appearance of the resurrected Jesus is not to the women but to two people on the road to Emmaus. And in John, one woman goes to the
tomb, and Jesus makes a number of appearances.

Why can't the gospel writers get their stories straight? They
disagree on the number of appearances, the people to whom
Jesus appeared, the times and places of the appearance, as well as
other details.

For many, the inconsistencies were reason enough to completely discredit the gospels as historical documents. More funda-
mentally, all of the resurrection stories—like those of Jesus' other
miracles—defied rational belief. As early as the second century,
the philosopher Celsus described the resurrection as a fantasy of

disciples who were "so wrenched with grief at this failure that they hallucinated him risen from the dead."

By the eighteenth and nineteenth centuries, with rationalism replacing religious belief among most educated Westerners, variations of Celsus's view were standard, especially among the liberals who staffed the leading theology departments at German universities. In 1782, for example, Karl Friedrich Bahrdt came up with the "two nails" theory of the crucifixion: he concluded that Jesus' hands but not feet had been nailed to the cross, enabling him to walk after he was taken down. Bahrdt speculated that Jesus' followers supplied him with drugs to alleviate the pain and induce a deathlike faint; they then hid their leader and nursed him back to health. In 1835 David Friedrich Strauss dismissed as myth just about every gospel story. Strauss explained the resurrection as mass hysteria.

In America, too, rationalism reigned. In 1804, Thomas Jefferson decided to extract from the gospels what was genuine; what was left in the "Jefferson Bibles" were plenty of sayings and parables and a mere skeleton of the original narratives. No miracles, no proclamations of Jesus' divinity, and certainly no resurrection.

All this seemed reasonable in what was, after all, the "Age of Reason." By the twentieth century, even religious Christians were mostly satisfied to leave the history of Jesus to rationalist historians. What emerged was sort of a truce: Christians could concern themselves about faith, historians about history. For the former, there was Christ; for the latter, Jesus. And neither had to pay much attention to the other.

The truce held until the second half of the twentieth century.

A number of factors revitalized the quest for the historical Jesus. Biblical scholars started moving from seminaries and church colleges to secular institutions, where they were free to take a new look at Jesus. Scholars from other disciplines, in particular cultural anthropology and the social sciences, became interested in the history of religion. But most significant of all was the discovery of a set of ancient documents. These would dramatically change how historians viewed the life and death of Jesus.

In December 1945, in an area of Upper Egypt known as Nag Hammadi, an Arab peasant named Muhammad Ali al-Samman was searching for some soft soil to fertilize his crops. He stumbled on a red earthenware jar. Breaking it open, he found thirteen papyrus books, bound in leather, along with some loose papyrus leaves. Some of these straw leaves he used to kindle a fire, but the rest eventually made their way to the Coptic Museum in Cairo.

Among the documents Muhammad Ali al-Samman found was one titled "the Gospel According to Thomas." Early church documents had mentioned Thomas's gospel (mostly disparagingly), but historians assumed it was lost forever. Yet here it was, in its entirety and almost perfectly preserved by the dry air of the Egyptian desert. Radiocarbon dating placed the papyrus leaves between 350 and 400, but some scholars, noting that Thomas consisted almost entirely of Jesus' own words, suspected that it was written closer to the time of Jesus himself, perhaps as early as the 50s. That would make Thomas earlier than Mark, Matthew, Luke, or John.

What did Thomas have to say about the resurrection?

Absolutely nothing.

Now, a dead body coming back to life is hardly a minor biographical detail. It's hard to imagine Thomas wouldn't have heard about it, or would forget to mention it. Many historians concluded, therefore, that the resurrection was an invention, not of Jesus or his disciples, but of later Christians, probably Mark.

Thomas tuned modern scholars in to a debate that apparently raged throughout the first two centuries after Jesus' death. On the one side were the orthodox Christians who insisted (along with Mark, Matthew, Luke, and John) that Jesus had risen. Not only that, he rose bodily; the canonical gospels go to great length to stress that the risen Jesus didn't just appear before his followers. He talked to them; he ate with them; he invited them to touch them; he explicitly told them (in Luke) that he was "not a ghost."

Against this orthodox view stood the "Gnostics," of which Thomas represented just one variant. They, too, believed Jesus lived on—but not literally. For the Gnostics, Jesus appeared in

A fifth gospel—that of Thomas—was discovered in 1945. Thomas didn't mention the resurrection, leading some scholars to speculate that it was an invention of later Christians. Photo by Jean Doresse, courtesy of the Institute for Antiquity and Christianity.

ecstatic revelations, in visions, and in dreams. Much like Martin Luther more than a thousand years later or various pentecostal congregations today, Gnostics believed that Jesus could inspire any individual at any time.

Why did orthodox Christians insist on a literal view of resurrection? Why did they so vehemently reject Gnosticism as heresy?

One leading Gnostic scholar, Elaine Pagels, has suggested that the answer had more to do with politics than religion. Resurrection, she argued, served to legitimize the power of the men who'd inherited the church leadership from the disciples who'd seen the risen Christ. If anyone could experience Christ on their own, that totally undercut their power. So, according to Pagels, it was crucial for the church leaders to stress (as Luke did) that the resurrected Lord stayed on earth for forty days, then ascended to heaven. And any sightings of Jesus *after* those forty days . . . well, they just didn't count.

          ✑

By the 1980s and 1990s, a new and much more liberal consensus had replaced the previously dominant view of Jesus. With the resurrection reduced to a political ploy (albeit a brilliant one), theologians felt free to focus on Jesus' sayings rather than his death. Freed of his image as Messiah, Jesus emerged in a variety of guises: a peasant, a sage, a rabbi, a Buddha, a revolutionary, even a comic firing off one-liners.

Many of those who painted these portraits came together in 1985 in the "Jesus Seminar." Here members didn't just discuss or debate the historicity of the gospels; they voted on them. Playing on the tradition of printing Jesus' words in red ink, the scholars took turns dropping beads into a container. A red bead meant the particular piece of the gospel was "authentic." Pink meant "maybe." Gray: "probably not." And black was "definitely not."

The voting guaranteed publicity, as well as quite a bit of ridicule. Members welcomed the attention; for many, the historicity of Jesus was of more than academic interest. Founder Robert Funk saw the Jesus Seminar as a direct and intentional challenge to the Christian Right, an attempt to take control of the religious discourse away from the Pat Robertsons and the Jerry Falwells.

Yet Funk and his followers, unlike Robertson and Falwell, were serious scholars, and that presented them with an intellectual problem. There was plenty of evidence in the gospels for their view of Jesus as a sage wandering around the countryside, sort of a Jewish Socrates. Yet they couldn't just quote his sayings and parables and then ignore everything in the gospels, including Jesus' own words, about his death and resurrection.

So they took a variety of tacks. Some, like Burton Mack of the Institute for Antiquity and Christianity in California, argued that the passion was nothing but an invention of later orthodoxy: there was no incident in the Temple, there was no last supper, Jesus probably didn't even die on a cross. John Dominic Crossan, a former priest who became a professor at DePaul University in Chicago, conceded there was a last supper but quipped that "everyone has a last supper—the trick is knowing about it in advance." Crossan concluded that the body of a crucified Jesus was unlikely to have escaped the fate of other crucified bodies— namely, to be eaten by wild dogs.

Not surprisingly, the Jesus Seminar generated a backlash, with conservative scholars accusing it of misleading readers into thinking that literary or historical analysis of the gospels could reveal the real Jesus. Many conservative scholars emphasized the extent to which gospels are imbued with foreshadowings of the crucifixion and resurrection, but for liberals these were just further examples of the inventiveness of the gospel writers.

By and large, variations of the liberal consensus hold sway in academic circles, where even feminist and gay Jesuses have poked up. Like Martin Luther, Robert Funk of the Jesus Seminar has taken his theses and nailed them—or perhaps taped them—to the church's door. Whether they'll stick remains to be seen.

To investigate further

The New Testament. A best-seller for almost two millennia. While you're at it, you might want to read the Old Testament, too.

James Robinson, ed., *The Nag Hammadi Library in English* (San Francisco: Harper & Row, 1988). Translations from the Coptic, including the Gospel of Thomas.

David Freidrich Strauss, *Life of Jesus Critically Examined* (Philadelphia: Fortress Press, 1972). Originally published in German in 1835 and still a classic of rationalism.

Albert Schweitzer, *The Quest of the Historical Jesus* (New York: Macmillan, 1955). Originally published in German in 1906, Schweitzer's book offered a thorough historiography up to then. Schweitzer devoted his life to practicing medicine on the disease-beset coast of Africa, convincing many that he had much in common with the subject of his book.

Edmund Wilson, *The Dead Sea Scrolls* (New York: Oxford University Press, 1969). The 1947 discovery of these documents near the shore of the Dead Sea created even more furor than the Nag Hammadi find. Many, including Wilson, believed the texts would change our view of Christian origins by shedding light on a sect that had much in common with Jesus' early followers. Scandalously long delays in publishing the scrolls convinced many, again including Wilson, that church leaders were suppressing evidence because it challenged the uniqueness of Christianity. In the 1990s, after Wilson's death, the scrolls were finally opened to all scholars, and most concluded that they confirmed his basic claim that Christianity grew out of first-century Judaism. They've been a disappointment, however, to those who hoped to find a direct connection to Jesus. The first part of Wilson's book was originally published in 1955.

Hugh Schonfield, *The Passover Plot* (Dorset, Eng.: Element, 1965). Paints Jesus as a political revolutionary who deliberately provoked the authorities, then arranged to be taken down from the cross alive so he could "rise" again.

Elaine Pagels, *The Gnostic Gospels* (New York: Random House, 1979). The politics of early Christianity as revealed through the Nag Hammadi documents.

John Dominic Crossan, *The Historical Jesus* (San Francisco: HarperCollins, 1991). Jesus as Jewish peasant. Crossan writes clearly and passionately, making his later, more pop distillations of this work (of which the most notable is his 1995 book *Jesus: A Revolutionary Biography*) largely unnecessary.

Barbara Thiering, *Jesus and the Riddle of the Dead Sea Scrolls* (San Francisco: HarperCollins, 1992). A dissident scholar's view of the Dead Sea Scrolls as cryptograms about Jesus that reveal that he did not die on the cross but was later revived and traveled around the Mediterranean in the company of Peter and Paul.

A. N. Wilson, *Jesus: A Life* (New York: W. W. Norton, 1992). Wilson's theory is that the man who appeared as the resurrected Jesus was one of his brothers, probably James, who took the opportunity to seize control over Jesus' movement.

Robert Funk, Roy Hoover, and the Jesus Seminar, *The Five Gospels* (New York: Macmillan, 1993). When the votes were in, only 18 percent of the words ascribed to Jesus in the gospels passed as authentic; postpublication votes moved on from his words to his deeds and, not surprisingly, the resurrection lost the election.

E. P. Sanders, *The Historical Figure of Jesus* (London: Allen Lane, 1993). Jesus as a Jewish prophet who believed the world was about to end.

John Shelby Spong, *Resurrection: Myth or Reality?* (San Francisco: HarperCollins, 1994). An Episcopal bishop's intellectual journey from a literal to a more symbolic belief in Easter.

Burton Mack, *Who Wrote the New Testament?* (San Francisco: HarperCollins, 1995). Mack goes farther than most modern scholars, even secular ones, in exposing how the gospels were fictional mythologies only distantly related to the historical Jesus.

Robert Funk, *Honest to Jesus* (San Francisco: HarperCollins, 1996). The latest work from the founder of the Jesus Seminar; as always, he's provocative and readable.

Luke Timothy Johnson, *The Real Jesus* (San Francisco: HarperCollins, 1996). A sharp attack on the Jesus Seminar and the "misguided" quest for the historical Jesus.

Russell Shorto, *Gospel Truth* (New York: Riverhead Books, 1997). A journalist's entertaining survey of the most recent searchers for the historical Jesus, in particular the members of the Jesus Seminar.

Charlotte Allen, *The Human Christ* (New York: The Free Press, 1998). A thorough account of the search for the historical Jesus, though sometimes colored by Allen's Catholicism.

Chapter 7

What Were the Nazca Lines?

In September 1926, two archaeologists scrambled up the rocky slopes near the town of Nazca, in south-western Peru. The Peruvian, Toribio Mejia, and the American, Alfred Kroeber, intended to check out a nearby cemetery. Then, as they stopped for a moment and looked down on the flat, stony desert, they noticed a series of long, straight lines stretching to the horizon. Both scholars assumed the lines were some sort of irrigation system, and neither gave them much thought beyond that.

It was not until the 1930s, when commercial airlines began flying over the desert, that pilots and passengers realized there were many more of these lines—and lots more to their origins. From the air, they could see hundreds of lines, many radiating outward from central points, some of them miles long and perfectly straight. There were also other forms, including triangles, rectangles, trapezoids, spirals, and several animal shapes. As anthropologist Anthony Aveni wrote, the view from the sky resembled an unerased blackboard at the end of a busy geometry class.

Back on the ground, archaeologists examined the lines and shapes and saw that they'd been made by simply brushing aside the pebbles that covered the desert. Underneath was a light sand that stood out all the more clearly because the darker pebbles now formed a border alongside the lines and shapes. Archaeologists also realized that, once created, these drawings could remain in their original condition indefinitely; the desert around Nazca was so dry (receiving about twenty *minutes* of rainfall a year) and so windless that the lines might very well be centuries or even millennia old. Indeed, the remains of pottery found alongside some of the lines seemed to indicate that some were more than two thousand years old.

What, scientists wondered, could have inspired the artists of the period to choose such a difficult canvas? And why would they have drawn patterns so large that, from ground level, they couldn't even be recognized? Perhaps, some speculated, the ancient Nazcans may have known how to fly, using some sort of primitive gliders or hot air balloons. Or perhaps, according to the most notorious explanation for the lines and shapes, they hadn't been drawn by the Nazcans but by visitors from outer space; according to this theory, the lines were landing strips and the shapes were landing bays for extraterrestrial aircraft.

The extraterrestrial theory, made famous by Erich von Däniken's worldwide best-seller *Chariots of the Gods?*, was pure fantasy. It was based on nothing more than a very superficial resemblance between a small segment of the desert drawings and a modern airport. But von Däniken's book, like the theory that the ancient Nazcans could fly, at least offered some sort of explanation for the huge and mysterious etchings.

How else could scientists account for these lines that were drawn in the sand—but could only be seen from the sky?

༄

The first serious study of the Nazca lines came in 1941, when an American historian, Paul Kosok, visited the desert. Kosok, too, sought the mystery's solution by looking to the sky. His moment of inspiration came as he was watching the sun go down. Suddenly he noticed that it was setting almost exactly over the end of one of the long lines. A moment later, he realized that it was June 22, the shortest day in the year and the day when the sun sets farthest north of due west.

Since the Nazca lines—such as this massive hummingbird—could be seen only from the air, some scientists speculated that the ancient Peruvians may have known how to fly. Copyright Bettmann/CORBIS.

"With a great thrill we realized at once that we had apparently found the key to the riddle!" Kosok later recalled. "For undoubtedly the ancient Nazcans had constructed this line to mark the winter solstice. And if this were so, then the other markings might very likely be tied up in some way with astronomical and related activities."

Kosok had to leave the desert before he could conduct a more thorough study, so he enlisted the help of Maria Reiche, a German-born tutor of mathematics in Lima. By the end of the year Reiche had discovered that twelve other lines led to either the winter solstice or the summer solstice. The desert, Kosok and Reiche concluded, was "the largest astronomy book in the world."

By marking crucial astronomical positions on the horizon, it also served as a giant calendar.

Critics of Kosok and Reiche argued that with so many lines running in so many different directions, it could easily be just a coincidence that some of them lined up with the sun. What was needed was a more systematic approach.

In 1968 Gerald Hawkins arrived in Peru, intent on providing just that. Hawkins seemed just the man for the job. He was an astronomer rather than an archaeologist, and his computer-assisted analysis of the alignments at Stonehenge had convinced him that those ruins had once been an astronomical observatory. Hawkins started by assigning a crew to fly over the desert and take a series of photographs that were used to plot an accurate map of the lines. Then he fed into the computer the positions of the sun, moon, and various stars along the horizon, adjusted to take into account the changes that gradually occurred over the past two thousand years. Finally, he selected 186 lines from one particular section of the desert.

Hawkins found that 39 of the 186 lines matched an astronomical position. That might sound impressive, but with so many astronomical positions to choose from, it was actually a huge disappointment. About 19 lines could have been expected to match some alignment by chance alone, and many of the other matches were actually "duplicates"—where a single line led to a winter solstice in one direction and a summer solstice in the other. Moreover, more than 80 percent of the selected lines headed off in entirely random directions.

So Hawkins, the great champion of an astronomical explanation for Stonehenge, concluded that at Nazca, "the star-sun-moon calendar theory had been killed by the computer."

❧

In the early 1980s the Canadian archaeologist Persis Clarkson collected the fragments of pottery found along the lines, then compared them to pottery known to come from various eras of Peruvian prehistory. Her striking conclusion was that some of the fragments (particularly those near the drawings of animals) dated back to between 200 B.C. and 200 A.D., while others matched a style prevalent about a thousand years later.

The implications for those seeking an explanation for the lines were dramatic. If the drawings and lines had been created over such a lengthy period, and if they represented the work of people from very different eras, then they might also have served a variety of purposes. In other words, more than one explanation might apply to the lines. Or, to return to Aveni's metaphor, the blackboard may have been covered with the unerased work of not one, but many different geometry classes.

The explanations that followed in the late 1980s frequently had to do with water—not surprising, given its scarcity in the desert. Anthropologist Johan Reinhard argued that some of the lines may have connected particular points in the irrigation system with places of worship, perhaps as part of some fertility ritual. The many bird designs took on a new significance, especially since modern Nazca farmers interpret sightings of herons, pelicans, or condors as signs of rain; perhaps the bird and other animal drawings had been intended to invoke rain.

Two other anthropologists, Aveni and Helaine Silverman, noted that the lines correlated with various geographic benchmarks. Most of the lines were laid out in the same direction that water flowed after the rare desert rainstorm, and many had the same orientation as nearby gullies where water once ran. Aveni and Silverman didn't think the lines had been irrigation ditches—they were far too shallow for that—but they agreed with Reinhard that there was some sort of ceremonial link between the lines and water.

Aveni also teamed up with another anthropologist, Tom Zuidema, an expert on the Incas, who'd ruled much of Peru when the Spanish arrived. Zuidema recognized that Cuzco, the Inca capital, was designed as a network of straight lines emanating from the Temple of the Sun, in the center of the city. The radial layout had religious and social significance to the Incas, according to the early Spanish chroniclers. Zuidema and Aveni concluded that the radial layout of many of the desert lines indicated that the Nazcans had similar beliefs.

Another anthropologist, Gary Urton, looked for parallels in the practices of modern residents of mountain villages near Cuzco. Urton described how the villagers of Pacariqtambo, during certain festivals, took part in a ritual sweeping of long, thin strips of the plaza. To Urton, it didn't seem too much of a leap to imagine ancient Nazcans performing a similar ritual on the desert lines.

❧

Maria Reiche, meanwhile, continued to live in Nazca, acting as not just an expert on the lines but also their protector. After von Däniken's works turned Nazca into a tourist destination, Reiche used her own limited funds to hire security guards. Even as an old woman, she would patrol the desert in her wheelchair, shooing away tourists if she feared they'd damage the lines. In Nazca she was a local hero.

In the early 1990s Reiche and her sister, Renate Reiche, became a bit too vigilant, at least according to some researchers. Maria Reiche's guards temporarily stopped both Clarkson and Urton from working on the desert, accusing the former of stealing potsherds and the latter of willfully harming the plains. Perhaps, Maria Reiche's critics suggested, she was trying to preserve her astronomical theory as well as the lines.

If so, Maria Reiche, who died in 1998 at age ninety-five, might have taken some consolation from the latest astronomical analyses, conducted by Aveni and a British astronomer, Clive Ruggles. Like Hawkins, Aveni and Ruggles found that celestial alignments couldn't account for the majority of the Nazca lines. Unlike Hawkins, however, they concluded that there were too many alignments for all of them to be just a coincidence. Aveni also noted that some of the radiating lines at Cuzco lined up positions of the sun, moon, and stars, leading him to conclude that astronomy did have some role at Nazca, albeit a smaller role than Kosok or Reiche envisioned.

Von Däniken's readers, too, would undoubtedly be disappointed by the latest thinking about the lines. The range of overlapping theories—astronomical, agricultural, religious—don't provide the same kind of satisfaction that a single explanation would.

Alas, it's highly unlikely that any single explanation could ever account for all the lines and drawings.

Still, the recent findings of Aveni, Silverman, Urton, Zuidema, and others have a great deal more in common than it might at first seem. Each of these scholars began by looking for connections between the Nazcans and other Peruvian cultures, old or new. And each of these connections helped make sense of the Nazca lines.

The lines have been called a "wonder of the ancient world," implying they were something so remarkable that they could not be understood in the context of anything else known about South American antiquity. But for the most recent archaeologists, anthropologists, and historians of Nazca, the reverse holds true: if the lines are to be understood at all, it can only be in the context of their world.

To investigate further

Paul Kosok and Maria Reiche, "The Mysterious Markings of Nazca," *Natural History* (May 1947). The astronomical thesis, with which everyone who came after had to (and still has to) contend.

Erich von Däniken, *Chariots of the Gods?* (New York: G. P. Putnam's Sons, 1969). The Nazca lines make up just one element of von Daniken's case that aliens once visited Earth; his other "proof" includes the Easter Island statues and the pyramids of Egypt.

Gerald Hawkins, *Beyond Stonehenge* (New York: Harper & Row, 1973). In spite of his negative conclusions about Nazca, Hawkins makes a strong case for the astronomical sophistication of ancient humans.

Tony Morrison, *The Mystery of the Nasca Lines* (Suffolk, Eng.: Nonesuch Expeditions, 1987). A fine popular survey, though with a great deal of not particularly interesting biographical information about key researchers (especially Reiche). Superb photos.

Evan Hadingham, *Lines to the Mountain Gods* (New York: Random House, 1987). An excellent summary of others' theories, leading up to Hadingham's own speculation that the drawings were directed at the gods on whom the Nazcans depended for water.

Anthony Aveni, ed., *The Lines of Nazca* (Philadelphia: American Philosophical Society, 1990). A collection of essays by the leading researchers, including Clarkson, Urton, Silverman, Ruggles, and Aveni himself, all offering a pan-Andean approach to the lines.

Chapter 8

Who Was King Arthur?

The legend of King Arthur—in stark contrast to the actual man—is easy to track back to its origins. Much of the credit goes to an obscure Welsh cleric named Geoffrey of Monmouth, who taught at Oxford during the first half of the twelfth century. In about 1138 Geoffrey produced *The History of the Kings of Britain*.

The story, as Geoffrey tells it, moves toward its climax in the fifth century. Heathen Saxons, led by the brothers Hengist and Horsa, have invaded and destroyed much of the country. A young wizard, Merlin, arrives on the scene with prophecies of a king who will save Britain.

Meanwhile, King Uther falls hopelessly in love with Ygerna. Unfortunately, she's already married—to Gorlois, the duke of Cornwall. Merlin steps in to help out. He transforms Uther into an exact likeness of Gorlois, so the king can slip by the duke's guards and sleep with Ygerna. Thus is Arthur conceived.

Fast forward about fifteen years, when the young Arthur ascends to the throne. He routs the Saxons, confining them to a small section of Britain. Later he conquers the Picts, the Scots, the Irish, and, among many others, the Icelanders. When Roman ambassadors demand he pay tribute to the emperor, Arthur crosses the English Channel and defeats their armies in France.

While Arthur is abroad, his nephew, Mordred, crowns himself king and lives in adultery with Arthur's queen, Guinevere. Arthur returns and slays the traitor but is himself seriously wounded. He's last seen as he's carried off to the "isle of Avalon."

So goes the tale, as told by Geoffrey of Monmouth. Arthur's victory is only temporary, since the Anglo-Saxons eventually do conquer Arthur's Britons (thus making Britain into Angle-land, or England). But this only added to the story's appeal to the Britons, who yearned for a return to a golden age when they ruled the land. For them, Arthur was not dead; he was waiting for the right moment to return from Avalon.

That yearned-for golden age became even more golden in the imaginations of later medieval writers, who enhanced Geoffrey's legend. The French author Robert Wace introduced the Round Table, so that Arthur's knights could sit as equals. Another Frenchman, Chrétien de Troyes, brought to the fore Lancelot, Arthur's loyal knight (and Guinevere's passionate lover). The German Wolfram von Eschenbach added Parzival. By the end of the Middle Ages, Arthur's fifth-century foot soldiers had become knights on horses; his fortified hills had become grand castles; and his court had become Camelot, a chivalric utopia.

It was an Englishman, Thomas Malory, whose fifteenth-century *Morte d'Arthur* combined all these elements, giving his countrymen a mythic tradition to match any nation's. There was a certain irony to this, since the original story pitted Arthur's Britons against the Anglo-Saxon ancestors of the English, but such is the nature of classic myths. They can transcend almost any sort of border; witness the revival of the legend in the twentieth century in variations ranging from the feminist (most notably, in the novels of Marion Zimmer Bradley) to the musical (starring Richard Burton, in the Broadway version).

The yearning for a return to a golden age, it seems, is eternal. When journalist Theodore H. White, quoting from the musical, referred to the Kennedy years as "one brief, shining moment," the president's administration was quickly labeled "Camelot."

Yet lost amid his legend was Arthur himself. Even in Geoffrey of Monmouth's own lifetime, it was clear that his *History* was anything but. In about 1197, William of Newburgh called Geoffrey's work a "laughable web of fiction" and calculated that there weren't as many kingdoms in the world as Geoffrey had Arthur conquering.

Since then, historians following in William's footsteps have attempted to sift from the legend the "historical" Arthur—if, indeed, he really existed.

∽

Above all, that meant turning to the (very few) sources that preceded Geoffrey of Monmouth and were thus both closer to Arthur's time and less likely to have been corrupted by later mythologizing. These were mostly Welsh writings, since it was the Welsh who were descendants of the ancient Britons.

These Britons came to power after the fall of the Roman Empire, early in the fifth century. They had wielded considerable power under the empire, so it seemed natural (to them) that they take over after the Roman legions left. That was unlike other areas of the former empire, where the invaders who drove out the Romans seized power. Independent Britain was therefore still in many ways Roman; the Britons, or at least their upper class, saw themselves as the heirs to the imperial culture and civilization.

Unfortunately for them, they also inherited the Roman enemies. The Britons immediately found themselves under attack from groups they thought of as barbarians: the Irish from the west, the Picts from the north, and the Anglo-Saxons from across the North Sea. The invaders saw no reason to withdraw just because the Britons had replaced the Romans.

The situation the Welsh bards described was desperate— every bit as much as that faced by the British in Geoffrey of Monmouth's account. But if we can believe a Welsh monk named Gildas, in about the year 500 the Britons won a great victory at a spot called Mount Badon. In *The Ruin of Britain*, written only about fifty years after that, Gildas described the battle and the two generations of relative peace and prosperity that followed.

Was this interregnum of Gildas the brief, shining moment of Camelot? Perhaps. But, as skeptics have been quick to point out, nowhere does Gildas mention the name of Arthur. Frustratingly, Gildas never says who commanded the Britons.

That was left to Nennius, another Welsh cleric. In the *History of the Britons,* which Nennius compiled sometime early in the ninth century, there's no doubt about the identity of the hero: it is "the warrior Arthur." According to Nennius, Arthur defeated the Saxons in twelve battles, at one point slaying 960 of the enemy in a single charge.

But can Nennius be trusted? Such obviously impossible deeds as single-handedly killing 960 of the enemy clearly belong to the traditions of epic poetry, not history. His notoriously disorganized material didn't help, either; the cleric himself described his approach as "making one heap" of all he found. Some historians found comfort in that, arguing that someone unable to organize anything probably also couldn't invent anything, but others just found it frustrating.

Welsh writers who followed Nennius also credited Arthur with the victory at Mount Badon. But, like Nennius, they were all writing at least three hundred years after the actual events. It was impossible to tell whether the oral tradition they recounted was the actual history of fifth-century Britain.

Clearly, the Welsh writings alone would not convince the skeptics. What was needed was some harder evidence that Arthur existed, and that seemed to materialize in 1191 (or, according to some, 1192). That was when the monks of Glastonbury Abbey announced that they had discovered the bodies of Arthur and Guinevere.

✑

The discovery was described by a Gerald of Wales, writing just a couple of years later. Gerald told how the bodies were found at Glastonbury, "deep in the earth, enclosed in a hollow oak." He added that a leaden cross was found "under a stone, not above, as is the custom today."

The inscription on the cross read: "Here lies buried the famous King Arthurus with Wennevereia his second wife in the isle of Avallonia."

Was Glastonbury the isle of Avalon?

Glastonbury Abbey, where twelfth-century monks claimed to have found the bodies of Arthur and Guinevere. Library of Congress.

There's no clear consensus among historians, but most are inclined to disbelieve the bones were Arthur's and Guinevere's. For one thing, the town of Glastonbury, which is in Somerset, is almost entirely surrounded by meadows. These meadows may once have been swamps, but it's still a bit of a stretch to imagine them as the "isle" of Avalon.

Skeptics also noted that the leaden cross with the engraving was written in a style of letters common in the tenth or eleventh century, not the fifth or sixth—when Arthur supposedly died. This seemed to point to a fraud.

Worse, the monks had a definite motive to fake the discovery. Much of the abbey had recently burned down, and Arthur's grave site would (and did) draw plenty of pilgrims to the abbey. The pilgrims brought with them much-needed funds for rebuilding.

The abbey's defenders have countered that if the monks had wanted to forge an inscription, they would have known enough to choose a properly ancient one. They argued that Arthur's body had first been found in the years after 945, when the abbey demolished a mausoleum on the grounds. Arthur, they surmised, must have been reburied at that point, along with a new cross in contemporary tenth-century letters.

Archaeologist C. A. Ralegh Radford bolstered the monks' story a bit in 1962 and 1963 when he found indications that someone had indeed dug where the monks said they did. But that proved nothing about what they found, and the reburial hypothesis depended on buying into a whole chain of events, each part of which was unproven.

So, barring some dramatic new archaeological discovery, Glastonbury seems unlikely to provide any definite answers about Arthur. Neither the bones nor the cross can be subjected to any modern scientific analysis; the former disappeared sometime during the sixteenth century, and the cross somewhat later.

After finishing his search for Arthur's burial place, Radford turned to his birthplace. Geoffrey had said it was at Tintagel Castle, on the Cornish coast, that Uther and Ygerna had conceived Arthur, and it was there that Radford next dug. Underneath the late medieval castle there, he was delighted to find fragments of imported pottery from the fifth of sixth century. This proved nothing about Uther or Ygerna or Arthur, of course, but it suggested that people of considerable wealth lived there at about the right time.

Even more tantalizing were the results of the search for Arthur's headquarters, the legendary Camelot. Cadbury Castle, just a short distance from Glastonbury, had been been associated in popular legends with Camelot since at least the sixteenth century. Between 1966 and 1970, archaeologists under the direction of Leslie Alcock dug for clues.

Under the high ground known locally as "Arthur's Palace," Alcock uncovered the foundations of a large hall, built with timber and showing signs of skilled workmanship. Alcock also found the remains of an unmortared stone wall enclosing part of the hill, and a gate tower.

All this pointed to a major fortress dating back to about 500. An exultant Alcock wrote that "with every justification, we can think of Arthur and his troops feasting and carousing . . . in a hall similar to that at Cadbury, and riding out to battle through a gate tower like that at the southwest entrance."

Of course, that didn't prove Cadbury was Camelot, as Alcock readily admitted. This was more a fortified hill than a real fort, let alone the castle of the medieval romances. Moreover, nothing found at Cadbury linked the fort with Arthur's name. It could have been the headquarters of any sixth-century military leader.

Radford and Alcock couched their findings carefully, stressing that they'd revealed more about Arthur's Britain than about Arthur himself. Yet their discoveries inevitably placed Arthur at center stage, and some of the media reports on them were quick to equate Cadbury and Camelot.

That, in turn, generated a backlash among academics, who reiterated all of the limitations of the Welsh sources as well as the archaeological finds. Skepticism still prevails among the majority of academics, one of whom described the pro-Arthur case as nothing more than saying there's no smoke without fire.

But smoke there was. Sometime in the fifth or sixth century, we can be pretty sure, there was a brief resurgence of the Britons. At someplace called Mount Badon, someone led the Britons to victory. The Welsh bards, writing at a time closer to the actual events than any subsequent historians, called the Britons' leader Arthur.

So can we.

To investigate further

Richard White, ed., *King Arthur in Legend and History* (New York: Routledge, 1997). A handy collection of excerpts from the early sources, including Gildas, Nennius, Geoffrey of Monmouth, William of Newburgh, and Wace.

E. K. Chambers, *Arthur of Britain* (New York: Barnes & Noble, 1927). This thorough study initiated the modern quest for the historical Arthur; quite reasonably, Chambers remained an agnostic on the subject of Arthur's existence.

Robin G. Collingwood, *Roman Britain and the English Settlements* (Oxford: Clarendon Press, 1937). Arthur as a wide-ranging general and cavalry leader.

Kenneth Hurlstone Jackson, "The Arthur of History," in *Arthurian Literature in the Middle Ages*, ed. Roger Sherman Loomis (Oxford: Clarendon Press, 1959).

Responding to arguments that Arthur couldn't have been a major figure because all his battles were in the North, Jackson's linguistic analysis of place names attempted to show he could have fought in southern Britain as well.

Geoffrey Ashe, ed., *The Quest for Arthur's Britain* (New York: Praeger, 1968). Includes archaeological reports from Radford at Tintagel and Glastonbury, and Alcock at Cadbury.

Leslie Alcock, *Arthur's Britain* (Middlesex, Eng.: Penguin, 1971). The case for Arthur as a genuine historical figure and a great soldier.

Leslie Alcock, *"By South Cadbury Is That Camelot"* (London: Thames & Hudson, 1972). The excavations of Cadbury Castle between 1966 and 1970.

John Morris, *The Age of Arthur* (New York: Charles Scribner's Sons, 1973). A history of the British Isles from 350 to 650, notable for its breadth of scholarship and its acceptance of Arthur as a historical figure.

David N. Dumville, "Sub-Roman Britain: History and Legend," *History* 62, no. 205 (June 1977). For an academic paper, this is a surprisingly savage attack on Alcock's and Morris's tendency to make too much of the limited evidence of Arthur's existence. Wrote Dumville: "We must reject him from our histories and, above all, from the titles of our books."

Geoffrey Ashe, *The Discovery of King Arthur* (Garden City, N.Y.: Anchor Press, 1985). A clever if not entirely convincing attempt to prove that Arthur led an army of Britons into Gaul, where he was known to Continental sources as Riothamus.

Norma Lorre Goodrich, *King Arthur* (New York: Franklin Watts, 1986). Based on a close reading of Geoffrey and other late medieval texts—an extremely dubious approach—Goodrich locates Arthur and his kingdom near what's now the border between England and Scotland.

Chapter 9

Why Did Mayan Civilization Collapse?

All was mystery, dark, impenetrable mystery." So wrote John Lloyd Stephens, a best-selling travel book writer, after coming upon the ruins of Copan in 1840. Stephens had traveled by mule and canoe, then hacked his way through the rain forest of Honduras in the hope of finding the lost cities of the ancient Mayans. He would discover more than forty other ruins during the next three years, spent in southern Mexico and Central America. Here, hidden in the jungle, were sprawling complexes of palaces and pyramids, along with monumental stone sculptures carved with a hieroglyphiclike script. These were the remains, Stephens clearly saw, of a remarkable civilization.

The archaeologists who followed Stephens agreed, especially after they were able to decipher some of the markings on the monuments. These turned out to be numbers, and they revealed that the Mayans were sophisticated mathematicians. They'd created calendars stretching back millions of years, and they'd meticulously charted complex astronomical movements. From this, the leading archaeologists deduced that the Mayans, or at least their rulers, were a profoundly intellectual people.

They were also a uniquely peaceful people, as portrayed by Sylvanus Morley, writing in 1946, and J. Eric Thompson, in 1954.

These two prominent archaeologists noted that there were no visible fortifications around the Mayan ruins. They must have been sacred places, Morley and Thompson concluded, where priestly kings contemplated the mathematics of the universe, interrupted only by occasional visits of peasants who brought them their food and depended on them for their wisdom.

The numbers carved on the monuments also revealed when the Mayan civilization ended. The last date recorded at Copan was (translated from the Mayan calendar) A.D. 820, and other Mayan cities followed like dominoes: for Naranjo it was 849, Caracol 859, Tikal 879. But the question remained: *Why* did the civilization end? Unlike the Aztecs of Mexico or the Incas of Peru, who were destroyed by the Spanish conquistadors, the Mayans abandoned their cities by 900—almost 600 years before Columbus sailed. Nor were there any signs that another Native American civilization—such as the warlike predecessors of the Aztecs—had destroyed the Mayan cities. And wars between the cities themselves seemed inconceivable, at least to Morley and Thompson, whose image of the peaceful Mayans dominated archaeological thinking.

So, at least until the past few decades, the demise of Mayan civilization seemed every bit as impenetrable as the jungle that engulfed it.

⟋⟋

Many scholars assumed that the problem must have been environmental. Morley, for example, speculated that the Mayans kept clearing away the forest for farms until finally they ran out of land. Others assumed that the Mayan farmers wore out the soil. Still others argued for a natural catastrophe, perhaps an earthquake or a hurricane or a prolonged drought. Malaria and yellow fever also were blamed, especially since disease definitely played a destructive role after the Spanish conquest.

The problem with all these theories was that there was no real evidence to back up any of them. Maybe they couldn't be disproven, but an environmental catastrophe that could topple a civilization like the Mayans' ought to have left some signs in the archaeological record—and that just didn't seem to be the case.

How the Mayan city of Copan may have looked during the eighth century. Copyright Peabody Museum, Harvard University.

Thompson's theory was that some less civilized people, perhaps from central Mexico or from the Gulf Coast, moved into the northernmost Mayan cities on the Yucatán Peninsula and overthrew the rulers there. This was more of a cultural invasion than a military one, he believed, but it nevertheless disrupted the established Mayan political and religious order there, and to the south as well. That in turn may have led to a revolt of Mayan peasants, who'd been perfectly content to serve their own priestly elite but who balked at paying tribute to barbarian outsiders.

There was at least some evidence for Thompson's theory. Central Mexican–style orange pottery, dating to the tenth century, was found in some Mayan cities on the Yucatán Peninsula, and Gulf Coast–style architecture started showing up there soon after. The problem was that the Mayan heartland to the south showed no sign of foreign influence. As for the pottery and architecture, that could have come from perfectly peaceful commerce. And even if the outsiders had forced their way into the North, the dating of the pottery and architecture was not precise enough to tell whether they'd come before or after the Mayan collapse. Foreigners might very well have done no more than fill a vacuum already vacated by the Mayan rulers.

Still, in the absence of any more viable alternatives, the ideas of Thompson and Morley continued to dominate Mayan scholarship. That lasted until the 1960s and 1970s, when linguists were finally able to decipher words as well as numbers from the ancient Mayan script. The translated texts did more than call into question Thompson's and Morley's ideas about the collapse. In fact, they completely transformed the scholarly view of Mayan civilization.

∽

Had it not been for Thompson, the scripts would probably have been translated years or even decades earlier. Thompson was certain that they contained only esoteric mathematical concepts and calendars, like those that had already been translated. Anyone who suggested that the Mayan monuments might be inscribed with words or letters as well as numbers or pictures was met with such scorn that he or she quickly abandoned any effort to decipher the script.

So influential was Thompson that scholars largely ignored the work of Diego de Landa. Landa was a Franciscan missionary who traveled through the remains of the Mayan cities in the mid-1550s—almost three hundred years before Stephens arrived at some of the same ruins. Landa made some crude attempts to match the Mayan symbols with letters—incorrectly, it turned out—but he was on the right track. Alas, Landa was a more devoted missionary than scholar; after determining that the Mayan books he'd collected contained nothing but "superstition and lies of the devil," he burned them all.

Only four books survived the combined destructive forces of Spanish missionaries and the soggy tropical environment. One of these ended up in the National Library of Berlin. At the end of World War II, when the library went up in flames, this book almost was reduced to ashes, too. Fortunately, a Soviet soldier named Yuri Knosorov rescued it and took it home with him.

There, far away from Thompson's intellectual tyranny, Knosorov went to work. In 1952 he announced that he'd broken the code: the Mayan script was neither all letters (as Landa thought) nor all numbers and pictures (as Thompson thought); rather, Knosorov wrote, it was a mix of syllables and words.

Thompson, true to form, mocked Knosorov's work. "This could be an authentic example of the effects of strict Party cooperation . . . in Russia," he wrote in his typically contemptuous tone. "For the good of the free world, it is hoped that it is so, as far as military research is concerned."

Gradually, however, other scholars began to question Thompson, and to build on Knosorov's insights. By the time Thompson died in 1975, the general principles of Mayan grammar and syntax were understood, and scholars could get down to translating the Mayan works.

There was still a great deal of work to be done, for though only four books had survived, there were thousands of Mayan texts carved or painted onto stone monuments, as well as on Mayan pottery and building walls. And what was written on these various media, once translated, shattered the image of the Mayans presented by Morley and Thompson. On monument after monument, the translators found detailed accounts of military strategies, of bloody battles, of gruesome sacrifices of enemy prisoners. Gone were the peaceful intellectual-priests; the Mayan rulers, it turned out, were bloodthirsty warriors. Most of the writing documented their military victories.

No longer bound by the Morley-Thompson perspective, archaeologists now started turning up other evidence of Mayan militarism. In Tikal, for example, there were long, narrow ditches and ridges that could have been moats and parapets; at Becan there were walls that could very well have been defensive; at Caracol there were burn marks on buildings and an unburied child on the floor of a pyramid. At Bonampak, vivid murals that were once thought to portray some sort of ritual could now be viewed as real battle scenes.

With the new, militaristic image of the Mayans established, archaeologists could now incorporate it into new explanations for the civilization's collapse. Arlen and Diane Chase found weapons

at a site in Belize and concluded that uncontrolled warfare between Mayan cities caused the collapse of the civilization there.
Arthur Demarest found mounds of decapitated heads during a dig
in northern Guatemala and came to a similar conclusion. He estimated that after 820 or so the Mayan population there fell to just
5 percent of its previous level.

"The collapse," Demarest said, "was due to Bosnia-like en-
demic warfare."

⌒∾⌒

Just as archaeologists seemed to be reaching a consensus about
the impact of intercity wars, new evidence surfaced, reviving one
of the old environmental explanations for the collapse. In 1995,
paleoclimatologists examining sediments at the bottom of Lake
Chichancanub in central Yucatán found that those from the period between 800 and 1000 were especially rich in calcium sulfate.
Calcium sulfate tends to settle to the bottom only when there is
too little water in the lake—usually during a drought. This particular drought was so severe, argued David Hodell and his colleagues, that it caused crop failures, famine, and disease, all of
which contributed to the Mayan collapse.

Did that put scientists right back where they started?

Not quite.

For one thing, Hodell didn't argue that the drought was the
only cause of the collapse; instead, he argued that it was the trig-
ger that set off a whole series of environmental and cultural crises.
Similarly, many of those who believed warfare was to blame also
presented it as just one of many factors. Indeed, since the 1970s,
scientists on all sides of the issue have been increasingly open to
explanations that take into account a variety of interrelated factors—including environmental stresses and warfare, whether with
an outside enemy or between Mayan cities. Many different factors could have weakened the Mayans, leaving them increasingly
vulnerable to some final crisis. The nature of that final crisis may
have varied from city to city.

The past few decades have also seen archaeologists broaden
their focus from the Mayan heartlands in the South to the civilization's more northerly outposts on the Yucatán Peninsula. Some

of these cities, though nowhere near as grand as those to the south, outlasted their neighbors by hundreds of years; a few even survived until the Spanish conquest. Perhaps some of these northern cities were bolstered by refugees fleeing whatever crisis befell the Mayan heartland to the south.

The latest thinking is that the different Mayan cities suffered many ups and downs, perhaps inevitably, given their constant fighting. The collapse of the great southern cities prior to 900, along with the rise of cities to the north, may have been part of this continuing process, albeit an extreme example of it. Some archaeologists, most notably E. Wyllys Andrews, have even gone so far as to argue that Mayan civilization didn't collapse, but merely moved north.

Most archaeologists wouldn't go that far. The extent of the southern collapse, after such extraordinary architectural and artistic achievements, was unprecedented in Mayan history, perhaps in all history. That the northern cities subsequently rose to prominence may help explain what happened, but it certainly doesn't fully explain what set it off, or why the Mayans never fully recovered. Those questions remain a mystery—by no means as dark or as impenetrable as it seemed to Stephens back in 1840—but a mystery nonetheless.

To investigate further

Sylvanus Morley, *The Ancient Maya* (Stanford, Calif.: Stanford University Press, 1956; originally published in 1946). A dated but impressively thorough survey of Mayan culture.

J. Eric Thompson, *The Rise and Fall of Maya Civilization* (Norman, Okla.: University of Oklahoma Press, 1966; originally published in 1954). Many of Thompson's ideas have been eclipsed by those of later archaeologists, but the book is still very much worth reading. If only Thompson's successors had shared his talent for popular writing.

T. Patrick Culbert, ed., *The Classic Maya Collapse* (Albuquerque, N.M.: University of New Mexico Press, 1973). A collection of papers from a 1970 conference that was important both in reflecting and in advancing the emerging consensus according to which a series of interrelated factors caused the collapse.

Linda Schele and David Friedel, *A Forest of Kings* (New York: William Morrow, 1990). Based on their translations of the writings at various Mayan centers,

Schele and Friedel present the histories of a number of dynasties. The kings emerge as both sophisticated and brutal.

Michael Coe, *Breaking the Maya Code* (London: Thames & Hudson, 1992). Coe turns the incredibly technical story of the deciphering into a narrative that's understandable and dramatic, even a bit gossipy.

Jeremy Sabloff and John Henderson, eds., *Lowland Maya Civilization in the Eighth Century* (Washington, D.C.: Dumbarton Oaks Research Library, 1993). A collection of papers from a 1989 conference that included many of the leading thinkers and theories.

Gene and George Stuart, *Lost Kingdoms of the Maya* (Washington, D.C.: National Geographic Society, 1993). A lavishly illustrated view of the Maya by a husband-and-wife team of archaeologists. The Stuarts' son, David, who first visited Meso-america at age three, later became a leading scholar of Mayan anthropology.

David Hodell, Jason Curtis, and Mark Brenner, "Possible Role of Climate in the Collapse of Classic Maya Civilization," *Nature* (June 1995). The case for drought.

Chapter 10

Who Built the Statues on Easter Island?

For sheer remoteness, hardly any place on earth comes close to Easter Island. South America is forty-three hundred miles to the east, Tahiti twenty-three hundred to the west. Yet somehow, though seemingly isolated from more technologically advanced civilizations, the inhabitants of the island carved hundreds of huge monolithic statues in the shape of men, many of them higher than a three-story building. Somehow these same islanders then transported these *moai* throughout the land, erected many of them on stone platforms, and topped them off with giant blocks of red stone.

The statues were still standing in 1722 when the Dutch explorer Jacob Roggeveen spotted the island on Easter Sunday (thus the name). Wrote Roggeveen: "These stone images at first caused us to be struck with astonishment, because we could not comprehend how it was possible that these people . . . had been able to erect such images, which were fully thirty feet high and thick in proportion."

Just over fifty-two years later, Captain James Cook stopped briefly at Easter Island while searching for a long-suspected (but nonexistent) continent in the southern Pacific. Cook, too, was amazed: "We could hardly conceive how these islanders, wholly unacquainted with any mechanical power, could raise such stupendous figures, and afterwards place the large cylindric stones upon their heads."

Who built the Easter Island moai, and why?

Most scientists assumed it must have been Polynesian immigrants, who reached shore after a long but not impossible trip from some island to the west, perhaps in the Marquesas. Few took seriously Thor Heyerdahl, a Norwegian scientist who, in the late 1940s, formulated a theory that South American Indians had settled on Easter Island and built the moai.

To prove he was right, Heyerdahl decided to build a primitive raft and cross the Pacific himself.

∽

Heyerdahl first came to his theory after noting similarities between the legends of the Easter Islanders and the ancient Incas of Peru. The islanders hailed a white chief-god Tiki as the founder of their race, while the Incas told of a white chief-god Kon-Tiki, whom their forefathers had driven out of Peru onto the Pacific.

Heyerdahl recalled that the first Europeans who visited the island in the eighteenth century were struck by the mysterious presence there of some white-skinned inhabitants who stood out from the normally brown-skinned Polynesians. Tiki and Kon-Tiki had to be one and the same, and the white natives of Easter Island must have been his descendants.

Other oral traditions on the island seemed to buttress Heyerdahl's theory. The islanders spoke of a race of "long-ears" who pierced their ears and put heavy weights into the lobes until they were artificially lengthened. The long-ears ruled the island until, the story went, the short-ears got fed up with them and overthrew them. Since the moai had ears hanging down almost to their shoulders, Heyerdahl naturally assumed that they were built by the long-ears. And where did the long-ears come from? The islanders' stories left no doubt: from the east, toward which there was only ocean . . . and South America.

If the long-ears, and Tiki or Kon-Tiki, could cross the Pacific in a balsawood raft, Heyerdahl thought, so could he.

So he headed to the Ecuadoran jungle, where he and his crew felled the biggest trees they could find. Then they peeled off

Easter Island moai, their backs (as always) to the Pacific. Copyright Wolfgang Kaehler/ CORBIS.

the bark, Indian-style, and lashed nine big logs together with ordi-nary hemp ropes, using neither nails nor metal in any form. Atop the raft they added an open bamboo cabin, two masts, and a square sail.

The party smashed a coconut against the bow and christened the boat *Kon-Tiki*. In April 1947, joined by five men and a parrot, Heyerdahl set sail from the coast of Peru.

Heyerdahl's was a sea adventure to rival *Moby Dick*. With just harpoons, his crew fought off a whale shark so huge that when it swam under the raft, its head was visible on one side while the whole of its tail stuck out on the other side. The drinking water became brackish after two months, but rains replenished the sup-plies. Breakfast often consisted of the bonitos and flying fish that had landed on deck during the night.

The ocean currents and trade winds pushed the raft farther and farther to the west, well beyond Easter Island, in fact. After 101 days at sea, the raft crashed into an uninhabited South Sea island east of Tahiti. All six men had survived the trip, though a large wave had washed away the parrot.

Heyerdahl was exultant: the *Kon-Tiki* expedition proved it was possible for a simple raft to cross the Pacific. But just because it *could* have happened didn't mean it *did* happen. To prove that South Americans settled on Easter Island, Heyerdahl needed more evidence.

✍

In 1955, Heyerdahl again set off for Easter Island, this time in a converted trawler and accompanied by a crew of professional scientists. Ironically, the scientists who first came under Heyerdahl's aegis, along with those who followed, ended up largely discrediting his theory.

For one thing, their radiocarbon dating placed people on the island by the fifth century A.D., with the earliest moai going up some time between 900 and 1000. Yet the Tiahuanaco culture in the highlands of Peru and Bolivia, where Heyerdahl believed the islanders originated, didn't extend its influence to the South American coast until about A.D. 1000. How could these South Americans cross the ocean before they even descended the mountains?

Moreover, the expedition found no trace on Easter Island of pottery or textiles, the two most characteristic products of Peruvian culture. In contrast, archaeologists on the Galapagos, a chain of Pacific islands far closer to South America, found numerous fragments of pots, at least some of which were clearly the same kind made by the pre-Inca South Americans.

Studies in other disciplines further undercut Heyerdahl. Botanists determined that the island's totora reed was distinct from the kind found in Peru. Sweet potatoes on the island, which Heyerdahl made much of as a link to South America, could have come from elsewhere in Polynesia.

Linguistic analyses also pointed to the west. Many of the islanders' words appeared to be similar to their Polynesian equivalents, and the discrepancies could easily be attributed to the long years of isolation. The island's "Rongorongo" script was also determined to have more in common with Polynesian writing than Peruvian.

Measurements of skeletons, too, showed the islanders had more in common with Southeast Asians than South Americans, and most scientists concluded the early European visitors' descriptions of fair-skinned people must have been exaggerated. After all, only some of the early accounts of Easter Islanders mentioned white skin; others, such as the famously observant Captain Cook, wrote that "in colour, features, and language, they bear such affinity to the people of the more western islands, that no one will doubt that they have had the same origin."

As for the old tales of Tiki and Kon-Tiki, these were just stories, according to most scientists. All of them had to be taken, in the words of Paul Bahn, "with a large pinch of marine salt." Bahn criticized Heyerdahl for his selective use of oral traditions, which allowed him to emphasize those that supported his theory while ignoring other stories—for example, that Hotu Matua, the island's first king, came from an island called Hiva. That's a commonplace name in the Marquesas, twenty-one hundred miles northwest of Easter Island.

Even the dramatic *Kon-Tiki* voyage wasn't spared from the sober inquisitions of science. Pre-Inca Indians used paddles, not sails, some argued, and the desert coast of Peru had none of the light woods needed for rafts or canoes. Moreover, the *Kon-Tiki* had been towed fifty nautical miles from shore, thus avoiding the currents that would have carried Heyerdahl somewhere up the coast to Panama, rather than anywhere near Polynesia.

The onslaught of scientific analyses that began with Heyerdahl's 1955–1956 expedition led to an even stronger consensus that Polynesians were Easter Island's first settlers. Unlike the South American Indians, the Polynesians had extensive experience on the seas, colonizing other islands such as Hawaii and New Zealand. Some scientists went so far as to contend that any evidence of a mingling of South American and Polynesian cultures (such as some Easter Island–style spearheads found in Chile) could be attributed to Polynesian sailors who may have ventured to the New World and then returned home.

That was little consolation to Heyerdahl, who continued to maintain that the discoverers were sailing west, not east. He continued to fight the historiographic tide, revisiting the island and defending his thesis even as fewer and fewer listened.

That should not diminish his achievements, however. It was Heyerdahl who arranged for the first scientific expedition to Easter Island and who allowed the scientists who accompanied him to conduct their research free of bias. And it was Heyerdahl's much-publicized expeditions that inspired other scientists to go there themselves and to continue the search for the moai's sculptors.

The consensus view that Polynesians first settled Easter Island provides at least a partial explanation for the giant statues. Ancestor worship was common throughout Polynesia, so the moai may have been some sort of monument set up by the island's tribes or families to honor their dead. The red stone blocks that topped the largest of the moai could have evolved from the Marquesas tradition of placing a stone on the image of a dead man as a sign of mourning.

Yet there was another mystery about these moai, which Cook had noticed during his brief visit. Many of the statues had been toppled from their platforms, and some had apparently been deliberately beheaded.

Why would a people who devoted such a colossal effort to their moai deliberately topple them? What happened between Roggeveen's 1722 visit, when they were apparently still standing, and Cook's arrival in 1784?

Heyerdahl blamed Polynesian immigrants, who he said arrived before the Europeans and went to war against the descendants of the original South American settlers. He turned again to the island's traditions, which recounted a revolt of the "short-ears" against the island's long-eared rulers. Perhaps the short-ears overthrew both the long-ears and their statues, he speculated.

Again, though, the lack of archaeological evidence has undercut Heyerdahl's theory. There are no architectural or artifactual traces of a sudden influx of new cultural influences at that point in Easter Island history, or at any other point, for that matter.

Archaeologists did find large quantities of spearheads and daggers dating from the period prior to the European discovery, leading many to conclude that warfare must have played a part in toppling the moai and the culture that worshiped them. The appearance in rock art of the period of "birdmen" seems also to indicate a new cult that may have replaced ancestor worship.

Most scientists believe an ecological crisis led the islanders to fight for ever scarcer resources. Overpopulation and deforestation were already serious problems by the sixteenth century, when some of the largest moai were erected. Some archaeologists have suggested that the building spree may have been spurred by an increasingly desperate desire for divine intervention. When their ancestors failed to help, the islanders may have lost faith in them and angrily toppled the statues.

Instead of the islanders' ancestors or gods, it was, of course, the Europeans who soon intervened. By the nineteenth century, missionaries and slave traders had virtually eradicated what remained of the original Easter Island culture and religion. Yet Europeans (and Americans) also deserve credit for their efforts, albeit belated, to preserve the original Easter Island culture. In the 1960s, scientists, including some members of Heyerdahl's expedition, restored several toppled moai to their stone platforms. There they still stand, looking over the islanders (and nowadays, plenty of tourists as well).

Right beyond them, as always, is the Pacific Ocean.

To investigate further

John Dos Passos, *Easter Island* (Garden City, N.Y.: Doubleday, 1971). A useful anthology of excerpts from accounts of the early European visitors to the island, including Roggeveen and Cook. Dos Passos's own visit, which concludes the book, is of much less interest.

Thor Heyerdahl, *Kon-Tiki* (Chicago: Rand McNally, 1950). When it comes to adventures on the sea, Melville has nothing on Heyerdahl.

Thor Heyerdahl, *Aku-Aku* (Chicago: Rand McNally, 1958). A colorful narrative of the 1955–1956 expedition, no less enjoyable because of the author's iconoclastic views, though slightly marred by his patronizing attitude toward the islanders.

Thor Heyerdahl and Edwin Ferdon, Jr., eds., *Archaeology of Easter Island* (Chicago, Rand McNally, 1961). Reports from Heyerdahl's team, many of whom disagreed with their leader.

Thor Heyerdahl, *Easter Island* (New York: Random House, 1989). Heyerdahl's most recent defense of his hypothesis did little to convince skeptics, but his account of how the islanders moved the statues is interesting and the volume is beautifully illustrated.

Paul Bahn and John Flenley, *Easter Island, Earth Island* (London: Thames & Hudson, 1992). The most recent and best popular account of the pro-Polynesian, anti-Heyerdahl position. The book's only flaw is that the authors insist on treating Easter Island's ecological crisis as a metaphor for the earth's, an approach that makes for admirable environmentalism but potentially dubious history.

Steven Roger Fischer, ed., *Easter Island Studies* (Oxford: Oxbow, 1993). A useful if specialized collection of essays on the island's natural history, settlement, archaeology, traditions, language, script, and arts.

Jo Anne Van Tilburg, *Easter Island* (Washington, D.C.: Smithsonian Institution Press, 1994). A thorough but somewhat academic overview of the island's archaeology, ecology, and culture.

Steven Roger Fischer, *Rongorongo* (Oxford: Clarendon Press, 1997). How Fischer (sort of) cracked the code of the island's mysterious hieroglyphiclike script.

Chapter 11

What Was Joan of Arc's "Sign"?

The Hundred Years War might never have lasted that long had a seventeen-year-old peasant girl not introduced herself to the heir to the French crown. In 1429, when Joan of Arc met the future King Charles VII, the on-again, off-again wars between France and England had been going on a mere ninety years, and the end seemed near. The English had routed the French army at Agincourt, then formed an alliance with the duke of Burgundy that gave them effective control of half of France. Paris was in Anglo-Burgundian hands, the Parlement was in exile in Poitiers, and Orléans, the last French stronghold north of the Loire River, was surrounded by British troops.

To make matters worse, Charles was an extremely reluctant champion of his own cause. After his father's death in 1422, Charles had taken the title of king of France, but he'd never been formally crowned, and he continued to be known as the "dauphin," or crown prince. His own mother, Queen Isabeau, had effectively disowned him when she'd joined the Burgundian side. Never decisive, Charles was now paralyzed by doubts about his own legitimacy; he seemed uncertain both about whether he was truly his father's son and about whether he could rule France.

Into this desperate situation stepped France's savior, Joan of Arc. The young maid in armor appeared at the king's castle in Chinon and quickly won his trust and rallied his troops. In May she forced the English to retreat at the Battle of Orléans, and two months later she escorted Charles to Reims for his triumphant coronation.

For Joan, the victory was short-lived. She was captured by the Burgundians, sold to the English, tried and condemned as a heretic, and in May 1431, burned at the stake. But she had saved France: though the Hundred Years War would drag on until 1453 (lasting 116 years, to be precise), the British would never again threaten to overrun the entire nation.

But how did Joan do it? And, first and foremost, what had convinced the wary Charles to entrust his fate to her—a mere seventeen-year-old, a peasant with no military experience, and a girl to boot? Contemporaries told tales of a "sign" that Joan had shown the dauphin, something that immediately gained his trust. Ever since, historians have been determined to figure out what that sign was.

The sign was a subject of immediate interest at Joan's 1431 trial for heresy. The official record of the court, of which three copies have survived, indicates that her prosecutors and judges questioned her repeatedly about it.

At first Joan refused to answer, saying the sign was a matter between her king and herself. But this trial was run under the auspices of the Inquisition, and her inquisitors knew how to wear her down. By the trial's seventh session, on March 10, Joan gave in and answered their questions: an angel had given the sign to the king, she told the court. Pressed further, Joan continued to duck questions about what, exactly, the angel had brought. Two days later, she added that the angel had told the king that he should put Joan to work for his army.

At the trial's tenth session, on March 13, Joan was again questioned about the sign. "Do you want me to risk perjuring myself?" she asked, almost as if to warn the court that what would follow would be a lie. Then she launched into a much more detailed description of how a number of angels—some with wings, some with crowns—brought the king a crown of fine gold. One of the angels handed the king the crown and said, "Here is your sign." The crown was now in the king's treasury, Joan added.

Most historians have been understandably reluctant to believe Joan's testimony. The techniques of the Inquisition were hardly conducive to eliciting honest answers; though Joan was never tortured, she was overmatched by more than seventy churchmen and lawyers. Joan's question about perjuring herself indicated she had decided to stop resisting them and to give them what they wanted—namely, evidence that she was in touch with supernatural forces. Once Joan admitted that, it was up to her inquisitors to determine whether these were angels or devils—and there was no doubt they'd choose the latter. Her fate was sealed.

Twenty-five years after Joan's death, a second court overturned its verdict, and these records also survive. Like the original verdict, this one was pretty much predetermined. Charles, who wanted to eliminate any taint of heresy from his reputation, ordered an investigation into the first trial in 1448. The hearings stretched on until 1456, when the second court pronounced the first one "contaminated with fraud, calumny, wickedness, contradictions, and manifest errors of fact and law." Joan was, the court said, "washed clean."

It was at this second trial, which became known as the "trial of rehabilitation," that a now-famous version of Joan's first meeting with the dauphin emerged. Two witnesses recalled that when Joan entered the castle of Chinon, Charles hid himself among his courtiers. Yet Joan, though she'd never before laid eyes on the dauphin, immediately recognized him. Joan then spoke privately with the dauphin, after which he appeared "radiant," according to the witnesses.

The story of the hidden king, later embellished to include Joan's refusal to address a courtier posing as the king, appealed to historians, since it could be explained without recourse to any supernatural power on Joan's part. Many historians noted that even if Joan had never before seen the king, she could have picked him out based on someone else's description. The story was also appealingly theatrical, and it proved irresistible to, among others, Shakespeare, Schiller, Twain, and Shaw.

The hidden-king story may very well be true, but it still left unanswered questions. Would Charles have trusted Joan just because she picked him out of a crowd? Wouldn't Charles have realized that someone could have described him to Joan? And what did Joan say to him or show him that made him so "radiant"?

To those questions, none of the witnesses at the trial of rehabilitation had an answer.

ℒ

One theory, which first appeared in print in 1516, was that Joan told the dauphin about a prayer he'd recently made. According to a chronicle written by Pierre Sala, who claimed to have heard the story from an intimate friend of Charles VII, Charles had asked God to grant him his kingdom if he was the true heir, or to let him escape death or prison if he wasn't. When Joan told Charles that she knew about his prayer—a prayer he'd confided to no one—he took it as a "sign" to trust her.

Like the hidden-king story, the prayer story could easily be true. It, too, could be explained without resorting to the supernatural. Joan would not have had to be extraordinarily intuitive to figure out that Charles was insecure about his parentage. The court was full of gossip that he was illegitimate, especially since his mother had disowned him as part of her alliance with the Burgundians and the English. Charles himself must have heard the widespread rumor that his real father was Charles VI's brother, the duke of Orléans. So Joan could easily have guessed that he'd turned to prayers, and Charles would certainly have been relieved that someone had arrived to answer them.

But the problem with the secret-prayer story is the same as with the hidden-king story. Even if true, is it enough to explain Charles's decision to put his fate in the hands of an unknown teenager? Charles may have been weak and indecisive, but he was neither stupid nor naive. He would have been as capable as later historians of seeing how Joan might have known what he looked like, or what his prayers were. The appeal of the hidden-king and secret-prayer stories—that a rational, modern historian can make sense of them—is also their weakness, for if Joan's sign could easily be explained away, why did it so sway Charles?

What was required, clearly, was a more dramatic sign, one that could impress the dauphin yet one that didn't involve angels or devils or other supernatural phenomena. In 1805, Pierre Caze came up with a theory that fit the bill: it was Joan, not Charles, Caze wrote, who was the illegitimate offspring of Queen Isabeau and the duke of Orléans. By this account, the infant Joan was smuggled out of Paris to save her from her father's enemies. She was handed over to Jacques d'Arc, who raised her (and who in this version of Joan's story was a country gentleman, not a peasant). The sign she gave Charles at Chinon, then, was some proof that she was his half sister, perhaps a ring or a document or some inside knowledge of their family.

Caze's theory solved all sorts of problems. It explained why the dauphin trusted her. It also explained how Joan had gotten in to see the dauphin in the first place, and how she learned military tactics and strategy. This was no ordinary peasant girl; this was a princess born to command, with royal blood and royal contacts. The theory caught on, especially among monarchists who were never entirely comfortable with the idea of a peasant saving the kingdom. It also appealed to those who liked conspiracies, and it reemerged in various forms during 1960s and 1970s.

The problem—and neither Caze nor any of his followers could ever overcome this—is that the theory was based on no evidence whatsoever. In fact, it presumed that a good deal of the evidence from both of Joan's trials was somehow falsified. The testimony about Joan's birth came not just from her parents but also from numerous other relatives and neighbors who said they either witnessed her birth or knew her from the day she was born. For Joan to be the king's sister, all of these witnesses—indeed, much of her hometown—must have committed perjury, as part of a grand conspiracy to conceal her royal birth.

Caze's theory, though ingenious, simply isn't credible.

✑

Others proposed conspiracies that were less grand, less royal. In 1756, Voltaire suggested that the dauphin's ministers sought out a peasant girl and trained her, in the hope that her dramatic appearance at Chinon would inspire the cowardly Charles and his dejected soldiers to strike back at the English. In 1908, Anatole France's biography of Joan implicated church leaders in the same type of conspiracy. To those who shared their skeptical attitude toward either church or state, such conspiracy theories were very appealing; alas, neither Voltaire nor France had any evidence to back them up.

Another way to explain Joan's influence was to argue that it was never as great as it seemed, and for this position there was some evidence. Charles may have been deeply moved by Joan's sign, but he didn't instantly turn over his troops to her. Instead, in typically bureaucratic style, he appointed a commission to examine her more rigorously. The commissioners met for three weeks at Poitiers. Their report has been lost, but apparently they believed Joan's story, since she then proceeded to Orléans.

Many historians have also disparaged Joan's military contributions, even at the Battle of Orléans. Anatole France, for example, pictured her as little more than a mascot for the French army: brave and inspiring, yes, but with no real role in the battle's planning or execution. And none of the testimony at either of Joan's trials indicated that she was ever in command of the troops at Orléans. There was no point in arguing about how Joan did what she did, some historians argued, since she didn't do all that much anyway.

Such belittling positions had always to compete, of course, with the legend of the savior of France, the young woman whose death at the stake seemed sometimes to rival Christ's on the cross. Through the centuries, Joan became the symbol of France, embraced by all, regardless of their political or religious beliefs. She has stood with revolutionary republicans and Catholic monarchists alike, among others. Most recently, Jean-Marie Le Pen's ultraconservative nationalists have made her one of their own.

Not surprisingly, these groups have all been quicker to extol her powers than to offer any credible explanation of them. Yet most historians, though less biased, haven't done much better. Most believe, unlike Anatole France, that Joan was a significant

A victorious Joan of Arc, from an 1833 painting. Library of Congress.

factor in the war, and that she held great sway over the king, at least for a while. But almost all reject any form of a conspiracy theory, whether it be the result of Joan's royal blood or plots of Charles's ministers. That has left historians without any generally agreed-upon explanation for Joan's achievements, starting with her sign to the king.

So, in one sense, after more than five hundred years of historiography, historians are asking the same questions as Joan's inquisitors: Were there angels at work here? Or devils?

To a historian, of course, the answers must be no. But to return to these questions is perfectly appropriate, for to the people of the fifteenth century—and these included Joan and Charles and the French soldiers, as well as the lawyers and churchmen who condemned her—angels and devils were very real. So were the "voices" that Joan believed she heard and that she attributed to St. Catherine and St. Margaret. It was because the French soldiers believed she had saints and angels on her side that they followed her into battle. And it was because Joan's judges believed she had devils on her side that they condemned her to death.

Charles, though a highly educated and sophisticated courtier, was also a man of his times. He may very well have believed that Joan's voices or angels had come to save his kingdom. And that belief, more than anything she said or did at Chinon, was the true "sign" of her power.

To investigate further

Wilfred Jewkes and Jerome Landfield, *Joan of Arc* (New York: Harcourt, Brace, & World, 1964). Includes the relevant sections of the original trial and the trial of rehabilitation.

Jules Michelet, *Joan of Arc,* trans. Albert Guerard (Ann Arbor: University of Michigan Press, 1957). The French original, published in 1841, transformed Joan into a republican heroine by stressing that her devotion was to the kingdom, not the king.

Anatole France, *The Life of Joan of Arc,* trans. Winifred Stephens (New York: John Lane, 1908). Joan as the dupe (albeit heroic) of priests who heard about her hallucinations and decided to make use of them.

Vita Sackville-West, *Saint Joan of Arc* (Garden City, N.Y.: Doubleday, Doran, 1938). Both a biography and a meditation on the nature of religious belief.

Regine Pernoud, *Joan of Arc,* trans. Edward Hyams (New York: Stein & Day, 1966). Joan, as seen through her own words and those of the other witnesses at her trial.

Maurice David-Darnac, *The True Story of the Maid of Orléans,* trans. Peter de Polnay (London: W. H. Allen, 1969). In this latest version of the bastardy theory, Joan proves her royal birth by showing Charles a gold ring engraved with the arms of the House of Orléans. She also manages to escape the stake.

Edward Lucie-Smith, *Joan of Arc* (London: Allen Lane, 1976). A psychological approach to Joan that's sometimes insightful, often not.

Frances Gies, *Joan of Arc* (New York: Harper & Row, 1981). A straightforward biography, clear and unbiased, though offering no new interpretations.

Marina Warner, *Joan of Arc* (New York: Alfred A. Knopf, 1981). How Joan fitted into traditions of thought about women, in her own time and after.

Anne Barstow, *Joan of Arc* (Lewiston, N.Y.: Edwin Mellen Press, 1986). Compares Joan to other late-medieval mystics and heretics.

Regine Pernoud and Marie-Veronique Clin, *Joan of Arc,* trans. and rev. Jeremy du Quesnay Adams (New York: St. Martin's Press, 1998). Pernoud is the leading French scholar on Joan, but it's unclear whether she meant this to be a narrative history or an encyclopedia.

Chapter 12

Who Invented Printing?

Y ou wouldn't think there could be much question about an event that was almost immediately recognized as one of the major turning points of world history. Besides, who could question the primacy of Johann Gutenberg? His title as inventor of printing has been so universally accepted that Marshall McLuhan didn't hesitate to refer to the culture he spawned as the "Gutenberg galaxy."

Yet questions abound.

For a figure of such historic import, Gutenberg has always been somewhat shadowy. And even in his own times, Gutenberg was by no means the only name put forward as the inventor of printing.

The earliest reference to the invention of printing comes in a letter dated 1472, just four years after Gutenberg died. It's from a Sorbonne professor named Guillaume Fichet. Writing to a friend, Fichet mentioned that not far from the city of Mainz, "there was a certain Johann who bore the surname Gutenberg, who first of all men thought out the art of printing, by which books are made, not written with a reed . . . nor by pen . . . but by metal letters."

Other early references place the invention in Strassburg, sometimes crediting Gutenberg but at other times another printer, named Johann Mentelin. Claims were also made on behalf of printers in Venice and Milan. Many of these claims seem motivated by little more than local pride.

Something more than that seems to be operating in Avignon, in France, judging from two court documents there. According to two contracts dated 1446, a Prague silversmith named Procopius Waldvogel agreed to teach the secret of "artificial writing" to some local citizens. One of the contracts refers, tantalizingly, to "two alphabets of steel and forty-eight forms of tin, and other forms as well." Could these letters be types for printing, à la Gutenberg's? Waldvogel was undoubtedly working toward a comparable invention, but most scholars have concluded that he had a way to go. The likeliest scenario is that Waldvogel's letters were used for some sort of variation of the traditional woodcut technique—closer perhaps to a manual typewriter than to true typography.

More persistent was the claim on behalf of Laurens Coster of Haarlem, first put forth by a Dutch scholar in 1588. Coster came up with the idea for printing in 1440, according to Hadrian Junius, while Coster was cutting some letters for his grandchildren from the bark of a beech tree. Later Coster exchanged the beechwood characters for lead and then tin. His printing business soon flourished.

Alas, Junius wrote, the growth of Coster's business led him to take on assistants, one of whom—"a certain Johann"—turned out to be unscrupulous. After learning the secrets of the trade, Johann waited until Christmas Eve, when everyone else was at church. Then he stole all the type and equipment and headed off to Mainz, where he set up his own operation.

The Coster story spread beyond the Netherlands, with support coming over the years from French, English, and American scholars. Partly this was because of a substantial body of early though undated Dutch printed works, some from metal type and some from wood blocks. In Haarlem's market square a statue of Coster, "inventor of the art of printing," still stands.

In the past few decades, however, the story has been largely discredited. More precise analyses of the type, inscriptions, and paper have shown that most of the evidence of early Dutch printing

dated from after 1465—and ten years after the earliest books
known to have been printed at Gutenberg's hometown of Mainz.

The storybook quality of the Coster tale is also suspicious. It's
a bit hard to buy that Coster so easily jumped from the idea of
cutting letters for his grandchildren to printing books and estab-
lishing a flourishing business—all within the six months prior to
the Christmas Eve theft.

One reason the Coster legend lasted so long was that it named
the villain, "Johann," thus directly answering the claims on behalf
of Gutenberg. Waldvogel, too, had some alleged links to Gutenberg: Walter Riffe, who was at one point an acquaintance of
Gutenberg, visited Avignon while Waldvogel lived there.

These connections are at best tenuous and serve mostly to
indicate that even in the fifteenth century most people associated
the invention of printing with Gutenberg. Yet until the eighteenth century, very little was known about Gutenberg's own
activities. That changed between 1727 and 1770 as a series of documents pertaining to lawsuits involving Gutenberg surfaced in a
variety of archives.

From these emerged a much clearer picture of Gutenberg as
well as a new—and by far the most serious—threat to Gutenberg's claim to be the inventor of printing.

The first crucial documents to surface record a lawsuit brought
against Gutenberg in 1439, when he lived in Strassburg. Gutenberg, whose inventing ambitions extended beyond printing, had
apparently invented some new method of manufacturing mirrors.
He'd entered into a partnership with one Andreas Dritzehn to
produce and sell them to pilgrims on the way to Aachen, but
the deal fell apart. Apparently the partners got wrong the date of
the pilgrimage, which was due to take place not in 1439 but a
year later. They decided they didn't want to wait a year for the
mirror sales, so Dritzehn then suggested that Gutenberg should
instead teach him another—and unspecified—art. Gutenberg and
Dritzehn drew up a new contract to cover Gutenberg's "art and
adventure."

Was this the art and adventure of printing? The documents are very vague; clearly both parties in the lawsuit intentionally avoided giving away the secret. The documents offer only glimpses, but these include the mention of the purchase of lead and other metals, and of a press and certain "forms."

Whatever Gutenberg was up to, others were convinced it could pay off big. According to testimony from the trial, a woman had visited Andreas Dritzehn one night, and she expressed some reservations about how much he'd invested. Dritzehn conceded he'd mortgaged his inheritance, but he confidently told the woman: "We shan't fail. Before a year is out we shall have recovered our capital and then we shall be in bliss."

Dritzehn's brothers also thought the invention was worth a lot of money, and that's what led to the lawsuit. The contract contained a clause that in the event of the death of one of the parties, his heirs would *not* take his place. Still, when Dritzehn died in 1438, his brothers wanted in on the deal. Gutenberg refused, and the court found in his favor. As a result, Dritzehn's brothers never learned the secret art his brother was learning from Gutenberg, nor can we know for sure what it was.

The next crucial document is more explicitly about printing. It dates from October 1455, by which time Gutenberg had returned from Strassburg to his hometown of Mainz. Again, Gutenberg faced a lawsuit. (He faced many, perhaps inevitably for an inventor in a prepatent era.) The record of this one has become known as the Helmasperger Instrument, after the notary who signed it, Ulrich Helmasperger.

The plaintiff was Johann Fust, another partner of Gutenberg's and in the minds of some historians the true inventor of printing.

This much is clear from the Helmasperger Instrument: Fust loaned Gutenberg a large sum of money for what was described as "the work of the books." Later Fust sued for the principal and interest, most of which the court awarded him. The Helmasperger Instrument doesn't say exactly how much, nor whether Gutenberg could pay. Nonetheless, many historians concluded that the decision bankrupted Gutenberg and enriched Fust, who may have taken over the former's printing shop.

Whether in Gutenberg's shop or in one he set up for himself, Fust then went on to become a successful printer. Fust's name, along with that of a new partner, Peter Schöffer, appears on the *Mainz Psalter* of 1457, of which ten copies still exist. The *Psalter* is the first printed book whose place, date, and printer is unquestioned, and Fust's supporters cite it as evidence that their man, not Gutenberg, completed the press and first put it to use.

But did Fust actually contribute to the invention of the press, or did he merely capitalize on Gutenberg's invention? Was the *Psalter* the first book printed, or merely the first book printed with a place, date, and printer?

And what about the Gutenberg Bible? It's the Bible and not the *Psalter* that many still view as not just the first printed book but also as one of the most beautiful. Who printed that? And when?

✍

About the Bible the Helmasperger Instrument offers no definitive answers. Nor do the extant copies of the book itself, which contain no printer's name, no place of printing, no date. But other clues point to Gutenberg as the printer—and an earlier date than that of the *Psalter*.

A note in a copy now at the Bibliothèque Nationale in Paris informs us that the binder and the tinter finished work in August 1456. Working backward, that makes it likely the sheets were printed in 1454 or 1455—*before* Fust could have taken over Gutenberg's press.

Further evidence surfaced in 1947, in the form of a March 1455 letter from Aeneas Silvius Piccolomini (who later became Pope Pius II) to a Spanish cardinal. Piccolomini described seeing sheets from the Bible printed by this "astonishing man" in fall 1454. The letter didn't say whether the astonishing man was Gutenberg or Fust, but by confirming the earlier print date it made stronger the case that the printer of the Gutenberg Bible was, in fact, Gutenberg.

For most historians, the note and the letter secured Gutenberg's claim to fame.

That's not to deny Fust an important place in the history of printing, however. For centuries Fust has been portrayed as the

The Gutenberg Bible contains no printer's name, no place of printing, no date. Library of Congress.

villain of the story, the evil capitalist who took advantage of Gutenberg, the classic head-in-the clouds inventor. Fust, according to this view, waited until Gutenberg had invested all of their funds in the production of the soon-to-be-famous Bible. Then, knowing there was no way Gutenberg could pay him back, he called his loan and seized the assets of the business. Fust's name didn't help his reputation, either: it was sometimes spelled Faust, which encouraged some early historians to incorporate elements of the Faust legend into the story.

Modern historians have been kinder to Fust. For one thing, many have noted that Fust grew up in a family of goldsmiths. Even if the invention was Gutenberg's, therefore, Fust ought not to be dismissed as a mere money-hungry exploiter with no interest in a craft.

Nor is it likely that the Mainz judges would have upheld his claim if it hadn't had some merit. It's very possible that, just as

Fust claimed, Gutenberg took some of the money that was supposed to go toward their joint Bible project and used it instead to
print other works, such as calendars and grammars. Fust had no
share in the profits from the other publications, so it's understandable that he'd be angered by the diversion of his funds.

So Fust was no devil and Gutenberg no saint. Perhaps Fust
even made some minor technical improvements to the press.
Similarly, Gutenberg may have learned some techniques from
Waldvogel and Coster, or from others in France or Italy or Germany. He also may have gotten some ideas from the Far East,
where some form of metal letters had been in use for centuries
and where paper—not to mention silk, gunpowder, and porce-
lain—was invented. Increasingly, historians have seen all these
places, all these artisans and inventors, as part of a gradual process that led to the invention of the printing press.

Still, it was the genius of Johann Gutenberg that synthesized
all the trends and trials of the times. Drawing no doubt on others'
work, he brought together paper of the right quality, ink of the
right consistency, a press adapted for both, and above all a type-
casting instrument that could make types by the thousand available at short notice.

Exactly when it all came together is still a mystery. Some have
interpreted the Dritzehn lawsuit to mean Gutenberg pulled it off
in Strassburg, perhaps in about 1440. The consensus among historians, however, is that it was in Mainz during the 1450s, not
long before the printing of the Bible that's rightly remembered by
his name.

Whenever it was, Gutenberg created a method of producing
more to read in a day than scribes could write in a year. After
that, the world was never the same.

To investigate further

Karl Schorbach, ed., *The Gutenberg Documents* (New York: Oxford University
Press, 1941). The key documents in translation, including the records from the
Helmasperger Instrument and the suit brought by Dritzehen's brother.

Pierce Butler, *The Origin of Printing in Europe* (Chicago: University of Chicago
Press, 1940). The case against Gutenberg.

Victor Scholderer, *Johann Gutenberg* (London: The British Museum, 1963). Not much more than a pamphlet, but the closest thing to an English-language biography.

Frederick Goff, *The Permanence of Johann Gutenberg* (Austin: University of Texas Press, 1970). A brief summary of some of the controversies surrounding Gutenberg.

Elizabeth Eisenstein, *The Printing Revolution in Early Modern Europe* (Cambridge: Cambridge University Press, 1983). Not much about Gutenberg, but plenty about how he changed the world.

Albert Kapr, *Johann Gutenberg* (Aldershot, Eng.: Scolar Press, 1996). Completed in East Germany in 1986 but not translated until ten years later, this is the most recent biography; generally admirable, though it suffers somewhat from having been written prior to the fall of the Berlin Wall, which deprived the author of access to some articles in English and French journals.

Janet Ing, *Johann Gutenberg and His Bible* (New York: Typophiles, 1988). A clear and concise historiography.

Chapter 13

Did Richard III Kill the Princes in the Tower?

E very tale condemns me for a villain," Shakespeare has Richard III complain shortly before his death. And what a villain he makes! Here was a man who didn't hesitate to murder the saintly Henry VI and his youthful heir Edward . . . or to drown his own brother George (in a vat of Malmsey wine) . . . or to marry the widow of one of his victims, then poison her when another and better-connected potential bride appeared on the scene. Most heinous of all, and what guaranteed Richard's infamy, was the kidnapping and murder of "the princes in the Tower." They were just children, and they were Richard's own nephews, but they stood between their uncle and the throne.

Yet, if Shakespeare's Richard had good reason to worry about his reputation, the real king could take comfort in knowing that he would have more than his share of defenders. Five hundred years after his death, the murder of the princes in the Tower continued to inspire mystery writers, most notably Josephine Tey, author of the best-selling *The Daughter of Time*. The Richard III Society has more than three thousand members dedicated to clearing his name.

To his defenders, Richard was the victim of a propaganda campaign organized by Henry VII, the first of the line of Tudor

kings who succeeded their hero. These "Ricardians" paint a strik-
ingly different portrait of Richard: a brave soldier, a concerned
king, a loyal brother. And they have their own ideas about who
killed the princes in the Tower.

⁓

More than Shakespeare, the man responsible for the traditional
view of Richard as evil incarnate was Thomas More. It was he
who set forth the basic plot that Shakespeare and other Tudor
writers followed. More wrote *The History of King Richard III*
between 1514 and 1518 and revised it in the late 1520s.

Richard of Gloucester, as he was known before he became
king, grew up in the shadow of his older brother, King Edward
IV. Even More conceded Richard was loyal to Edward, who in
turn repaid him with various titles and estates, primarily in northern England.

In April 1483 Edward died at age forty, after a life overly full
of food, drink, and women. He left two sons, twelve-year-old
Edward and ten-year-old Richard. The dying king's wish was for
his son to become King Edward V, with his brother serving as
"protector" until the boy was old enough to rule on his own.

This arrangement didn't satisfy Edward IV's queen, Elizabeth
Woodville. While Richard was up North, she managed to convince the royal council in London to reject his protectorship.
Then she sent an urgent message to her brother, Anthony, telling
him to bring the young Edward to London so he could be
crowned immediately.

On learning of the plot, Richard moved South quickly, inter-
cepting Anthony Woodville and Edward. After an evening of
feasting, Richard had Woodville arrested and sent North, where
he was soon beheaded. Richard then accompanied his young
nephew to London, where he installed him in the Tower of London—then a royal residence, not a prison.

Still, plans were proceeding for the coronation of the young
king, and Richard persuaded the queen to let her younger son
join Edward to attend the ceremony. Richard promised to return
the boy immediately after the coronation. More persuasive,

undoubtedly, were Richard's troops, who surrounded the queen's sanctuary at Westminster Abbey.

Meanwhile, Richard needed some pretext for claiming the crown for himself. That conveniently appeared in June, courtesy of Robert Stillington, bishop of Bath and Wells. Stillington disclosed to the royal council that Edward IV's marriage to Elizabeth Woodville was invalid because he had once been contracted to marry another lady, Eleanor Butler. Therefore the princes in the Tower were bastards . . . and bastards couldn't inherit the throne.

With Edward IV's other brother, George, already drowned in the aforementioned wine, the next in line was none other than Richard of Gloucester.

Richard now felt the crown was within his grasp. In late July or early August he sent a letter to Sir Robert Brackenbury, constable of the Tower, ordering him to kill the princes. Brackenbury refused.

So Richard turned over the job to James Tyrell, an ambitious supporter who enlisted two henchmen. According to More's account, Tyrell waited outside while the others sneaked up to the sleeping princes, "suddenly lapped them up among the clothes," and forced the "featherbed and pillows hard unto their mouths." Then the three men buried the bodies "at the stayre foot, metely depe in the grounde under a great heape of stones."

If Richard was the villain of More's history, the hero was Henry VII, who in 1435 slew Richard on Bosworth Field, bringing to an end the bloody War of the Roses and founding the happy line of Tudor monarchs.

Or so More wrote. But was it true?

✍

It was difficult, even for Richard's supporters, to question the integrity of Sir Thomas More. This was, after all, the man executed in 1535 because his conscience wouldn't let him go along with Henry VIII's plan to divorce Catherine of Aragon and marry Anne Boleyn. More was a writer, a philosopher, and (after his 1935 canonization) quite literally a saint.

Early portraits of Richard show no signs of the hunchback or withered arm that More and Shakespeare used to represent his moral as well as physical deformity. Library of Congress.

Yet question they did. As early as 1768, Sir Horace Walpole described More as "an historian who is capable of employing truth only as a cement in a fabric of fiction." Undeniably, he got certain facts wrong, among them his description of Richard's deformities. The hunchback and withered arm appeared in no other contemporary reference.

Ricardians also questioned More's sources. More was only five when Richard took the throne and only seven when he died, so he obviously wasn't writing about anything he witnessed personally. One source may have been Cardinal John Morton, in whose household More lived as a boy. A more biased source could hardly be imagined: Morton was both imprisoned and exiled by Richard III.

Besides, Ricardians noted, More neither finished nor published the *History*. Perhaps, they surmised, he'd dropped the project as he'd learned the truth about Richard and Henry.

Above all, Ricardians argued that More's account didn't make sense. If the royal council had already ruled the princes were bastards and so couldn't inherit the throne, why would Richard have to kill them? If Henry found the princes missing when he took over the Tower in 1485, why didn't he rant and rave about that, or at least search for the bodies?

To Ricardians, all this pointed to Henry as the culprit. His motive was at least as strong as Richard's, they argued. As a fairly distant cousin of both Richard and the princes, his claim to the throne was much weaker than Richard's . . . and pretty much hopeless if either of the princes were still alive.

To all these questions, traditionalists had answers. Sure, Richard's council had declared the princes illegitimate, but Richard knew that Henry VII could just as easily persuade *his* council to reverse the decision. As long as they were alive, the princes could always be a rallying point for Richard's enemies and a threat to his crown.

As for Henry, there were several reasons why he might not have done anything about the princes after taking over. Perhaps he didn't know for sure what happened to them. Perhaps he assumed everyone blamed Richard. Perhaps he feared that if he admitted he didn't know where the princes were, it would lead to uprisings on their behalf.

Indeed, that fear was borne out. Twice during Henry's reign, anti-Tudor forces coalesced around leaders claiming to be the princes. The "Edward" who led a 1487 uprising turned out to be Lambert Simnel, the son of an Oxford joiner and organmaker. In 1491 a man claiming to be the younger prince was revealed to be Perkin Warbeck. He may have gained some useful knowledge from his father, who had once earned a living by supplying carpets to the royal court.

So the arguments for and against both Richard and Henry went round and round for centuries, with the prestige of More and Shakespeare generally giving weight to the traditionalists but Richard getting a strong defense, even as early as 1619, from a revisionist history by Sir George Buck. Only one thing seemed sure: the same facts could lead to different conclusions.

Then, in the 1930s, the facts changed.

In 1933, Westminster Abbey finally gave in to pressure from the Ricardians to open the tomb in which the remains of the princes were supposedly interred. Back in 1674, following the instructions of Charles II to clear a site near the White Tower, workmen discovered a chest containing two small skeletons. The location immediately conjured up More's description of the burial site, and Charles concluded that the bones were those of the princes. Velvet found amid the bones lent credence to the conclusion, since it was worn only by persons of the highest rank.

Charles ordered the bodies reinterred at Westminster Abbey, where they remained for another 259 years.

The 1933 study by Lawrence Tanner, Westminster's archivist, and William Wright, president of Great Britain's Anatomical Society, was too early for carbon dating, let alone DNA technology. But Tanner and Wright were able to use dental evidence to estimate that the the elder child was twelve or thirteen and the younger nine to eleven. Edward had been twelve and Richard ten when they disappeared.

This was not absolute proof that Richard was a murderer, but it did corroborate at least one aspect of the traditionalists' story.

A year later, more evidence surfaced, this time in the Municipal Library of Lille. This was a report written in 1483 by Dominic Mancini, an Italian monk. Unlike More, Mancini was in London during the critical months when Richard took the throne. The monk stated his intention up front: "to put in writing by what machinations Richard III attained the high degree of kingship."

Mancini described how the princes were moved to the inner apartments of the Tower and were gradually seen less and less, then not at all. As to the way the young king died, Mancini reported only that "already there was a suspicion that he had been done away with."

Ricardians made much of the fact that Mancini didn't come right out and accuse Richard of the murder. They also pointed out that what he reported may have been no more than gossip. Still, at the very least, the report was evidence that the stories about Richard's ruthlessness were not just inventions of later Tudor propagandists. Even in his own time, there were clearly plenty of people who suspected that Richard had killed the princes.

For the majority of historians, the twentieth-century revelations were enough to convict Richard. The evidence is entirely circumstantial, and few historians would deny the Ricardians their reasonable doubt. But history is not a court of law; historians must consider probabilities, not possibilities. Others had a motive to kill the princes, but none so compelling as Richard's. Others had opportunity, too, but so did Richard, and it's hard to imagine someone else doing away with the princes without Richard knowing about it.

Yet if most historians have concluded that Richard was probably guilty of the murder, Ricardians can take some solace in a consensus that he was by no means the incomparable monster portrayed by More and Shakespeare. In killing the princes, Richard was following a well-established precedent. Edward II was murdered on the orders of his wife, who took over in the name of her son Edward III. Richard II was starved to death by Henry IV. And Henry VI was killed on the orders of Edward IV.

Richard recalled all of these deaths. Medieval England was no time to be a deposed king, and that's most likely how Richard saw his nephews. Shakespeare's "bottled spider" was very much a man of his times.

To investigate further

Dominic Mancini, *The Usurpation of Richard III* (Oxford: Clarendon Press, 1969). Mancini may have filled his report with bias and gossip; nevertheless, he was there. Translated and with an introduction by C. A. J. Armstrong, who discovered the document.

Paul Kendall, ed., *Richard III* (New York: W. W. Norton, 1965). Brings together the two most prominent early antagonists in the debate, with the full texts of More's *History of King Richard III*, first published in 1543, and Horace Walpole's *Historic Doubts on the Life and Reign of King Richard the Third*, first published in 1769.

Lawrence Tanner and William Wright, "Recent Investigation Regarding the Fate of the Princes in the Tower," *Archaeologia* 84 (1935). If only they conducted a DNA test . . .

Josephine Tey, *The Daughter of Time* (New York: Macmillan, 1951). A 20th-century Scotland Yard inspector concludes that Richard was framed in a novel that's a fine detective story but less convincing as history.

Paul Kendall, *Richard the Third* (New York: W. W. Norton, 1955). A readable and sympathetic biography that points the finger at the duke of Buckingham.

Elizabeth Peters, *The Murders of Richard III* (New York: Warner Books, 1986). A moderately entertaining English country house mystery, originally published in 1974, in which a bunch of Ricardians dress up as their heroes, then find themselves living through—or rather, dying through—reenactments of his crimes.

Charles Ross, *Richard III* (Berkeley: University of California Press, 1981). A comprehensive portrait of Richard's life and his very bloody times.

Alison Weir, *The Princes in the Tower* (New York: Ballantine Books, 1992). The most recent and one of the most persuasive cases against Richard.

Bertram Fields, *Royal Blood* (New York: Regan Books, 1998). Fields, a Hollywood lawyer, would definitely have gotten his client off on the grounds that there's reasonable doubt about his guilt, but he's less convincing when he tries to prove Richard's innocence.

Did Columbus Intend to Discover America?

C ontrary to popular mythology, Christopher Columbus had no trouble at all convincing the king and queen of Spain—or anyone else—that the world was round. This was common knowledge among educated Europeans long before 1492. The resistance to Columbus's plan had to do with a different and much more radical idea—that he could discover a new route to Asia by sailing west from Europe.

The standard wisdom was that, if Asia was to be reached by sea, it would be by rounding Africa and heading east across the Indian Ocean. Since Asia was, in fact, east of Europe, this was a perfectly logical plan, and it paid off in 1499 when the Portuguese explorer Vasco de Gama arrived in India. Columbus's "Enterprise of the Indies," in contrast, made no sense. For even if the Indies (as Asia was then called) lay somewhere across the Atlantic, it was far too long a trip for a fifteenth-century mariner. The geographer most sympathetic to Columbus, Paolo del Pozzo Toscanelli, estimated that the Indies were more than 3,500 miles west of the Canary Islands, and most scholars were convinced they were a lot farther.

But, as everyone knows, Columbus was not to be dissuaded. He calculated that only 2,760 miles of open water separated Europe and Asia, and he persuaded Ferdinand and Isabella of

Spain that it would be worth their while to finance his voyage. So, in September 1492, the *Niña,* the *Pinta,* and the *Santa María* set sail from the Canaries. A mere five weeks later—at just about the spot he'd predicted he'd find land—Columbus stepped ashore.

The irony of Columbus's triumphant landing, of course, was that he was nowhere near Asia. The standard wisdom was in this case entirely correct: Asia was a good 6,000 miles farther west than the Bahamian island on which Columbus now stood. Had there not been two continents and numerous other islands between Europe and the Indies, Columbus and his crew would almost certainly have vanished into the seas.

For more than four hundred years this was the story of Columbus told on both sides of the Atlantic, the story of the determinedly heroic, albeit grossly mistaken, discoverer of America. But, starting at about the turn of the twentieth century, the story has come under increasingly skeptical scrutiny.

How, many historians have asked, could Columbus have been so wrong? And how, in the face of the overwhelming evidence that the lands he found were not China or Japan, could he continue to maintain that they were the Indies and that their people were "Indians"? Some historians have concluded that Columbus never intended to go to Asia at all and that his "Enterprise of the Indies" was just a ruse to throw other explorers off the track. They maintain that from the start, Columbus's goal was to discover a New World.

That Columbus was heading for the Indies is certainly what the explorer told the world, and contemporary chroniclers believed him. The most prominent of these was Bartolomé de las Casas; he not only wrote the most comprehensive history of Columbus's voyages but also included in it parts of Columbus's own journals. (The originals have been lost.) The prologue to Columbus's journal, as recorded by Las Casas, seems as straightforward a description of Columbus's intentions as anyone could want. "Your Majesties," the explorer wrote to Ferdinand and Isabella, "decided to send me, Christopher Columbus, to those lands of

THE FIRST SIGHT OF THE NEW WORLD
Columbus Discovering America

How could the most famous navigator of all time, here getting his first sight of the New World, have no idea what he was looking at? Library of Congress.

India to meet their rulers and to see the towns and lands and their distribution, and all other things . . . and you ordered me not to go eastward by land, as is customary, but to take my course westward, where, so far as we know, no man has traveled before today."

In Columbus's October 21 journal entry, after he landed on what he described as an outlying island, he reported that he was still determined to reach the Asian mainland to deliver to the "Great Khan"—the Chinese emperor—letters of introduction from Ferdinand and Isabella. And on his way back to Spain, Columbus wrote to Ferdinand and Isabella that the fort he'd established would be convenient "for all kinds of trade with the nearest mainland as well as with . . . the Great Khan."

None of this would seem to leave any room for doubt about where Columbus was headed, or where he thought he ended up.

The second most important contemporary chronicler was Ferdinand Columbus, the explorer's son, and he was equally adamant about his father's intended destination. Ferdinand not only wrote the first biography of Columbus but also preserved his father's books—including marginal notes that were invaluable to future historians. These indicate that Columbus learned about Asia by reading the works of medieval writers such as Marco Polo and John Mandeville. He also apparently consulted Aristotle and Seneca, both of whom discussed the possibility of sailing west to the Indies. Two medieval books in the Columbus library—Pierre d'Ailly's *Imago Mundi* and Pope Pius II's *Historia Rerum*—venture various guesses about how narrow the ocean might be, and the relevant passages are duly underlined, presumably by Columbus himself.

Ferdinand's biography also included copies of the correspondence between his father and Toscanelli, the Italian geographer whose estimates of the distance between Europe and Asia provided Columbus with additional support for his theory. Toscanelli's letter, Ferdinand wrote, "filled the Admiral with even greater zeal for discovery." More dramatically, Las Casas wrote, it "set Columbus' mind ablaze."

But, though neither Las Casas nor Ferdinand Columbus had any doubts about Columbus's intended destination, both included a story that cast a very different light on Columbus's "Enterprise." The story first appeared in print in 1539, in Gonzalo Fernandez de Oviedo's history of the discovery of America. As Oviedo told it, a ship en route from Portugal to England ran into bad weather and was blown far to the west, ultimately reaching some islands inhabited by naked people. On the return trip, all but the pilot died. He washed ashore on the island of Madeiras, where Columbus lived on and off during the early 1480s. The pilot, too, soon died, but just before his death he drew a map of where he'd been and gave it to Columbus.

If the story of the "unknown pilot" is true, then Columbus did not set off into the great unknown bolstered only by an untested theory. If he had a map, he had a pretty good idea where he was going—and a pretty good reason to suspect it wasn't the Indies. But Oviedo, the first to tell the story, concluded that it probably wasn't true, and Ferdinand Columbus didn't believe it either. Las Casas was somewhat more credulous, noting that the story was widely circulated, but it certainly didn't shake his belief that Columbus was seeking the Indies. Later historians followed their lead, dismissing the story if they mentioned it at all.

It was not until the turn of the twentieth century that the unknown pilot found his champion.

∽

Henry Vignaud's startling thesis, boldly stated in a number of volumes published early in the twentieth century, was that Columbus never intended to go to the Indies. The unknown pilot had told Columbus about America, and he wanted those lands for himself. So, knowing full well that the Indies were beyond his reach, he concocted his "Enterprise" merely to make sure no one else would beat him to America. And once the Columbus myth had been established, Vignaud maintained, historians dared not challenge it, for fear that "the great undertaking which, as Columbus averred, he had organized for the purpose of carrying out a scientific idea . . . would have been reduced to the proportions of a vulgar voyage of discovery."

In other words, Columbus was a liar. And, according to Vignaud and his followers, the unknown pilot wasn't the only thing he lied about.

The journal, for one thing, was a fake, or at least sufficiently rewritten and falsified (by either Columbus or Las Casas) to conceal Columbus's true motive. The Toscanelli correspondence was also forged (either by Columbus or his son); after all, the only evidence of their letters to each other was in Ferdinand's biography, an authorized bio if ever there was one.

Skeptics such as Vignaud also brought to the fore some documents of their own, hitherto ignored or at least brushed aside. The most important of these was the contract between Columbus and the Spanish king and queen known as the "Capitulations." The Capitulations went into great detail about what would be Columbus's share of the profits from his trip, but they never mentioned the Indies. Most suspicious of all, the Capitulations empowered Columbus to "discover and acquire" any islands he came upon, a phrase the emperor of China would certainly not have appreciated. Indeed, it is difficult to imagine the emperor handing over any island to three lightly armed Spanish ships. Much more likely, Vignaud believed, was that Columbus (and Ferdinand and Isabella) had in mind the discovery and acquisition of some new, and to Europeans unknown, territory.

Traditionalists rose to Columbus's defense. Led by Samuel Eliot Morison, whose reputation as a sailor added tremendously to his credibility as a historian, the traditionalists responded that even though the Capitulations didn't mention the Indies explicitly, the references to Columbus's share of pearls, precious stones, and spices—all products of Asia—clearly indicated that was his destination.

As for the story of the unknown pilot, Morison scoffed at the landlubbers who'd swallowed it hook, line, and sinker. Here the historian's sailing expertise proved handy; he argued that the story was meteorologically impossible, since the prevailing winds wouldn't blow a vessel across the Atlantic from east to west.

Sure, Morison conceded, Columbus may have heard tales of islands to the west, and of exotic flotsam washing ashore on islands under Portuguese control. The explorer may very well have been influenced by some of the sea stories he heard. But there was no secret map or unknown pilot; Oviedo's story demonstrated nothing more, Morison wrote, than the "unfortunate tendency to pluck at the laurels of the great."

Morison's reputation and scholarship ensured that Columbus would not be toppled from his pedestal. But Vignaud and his followers did succeed in creating a great deal of doubt about the traditional story, especially as it pertained to Columbus's later voyages.

Columbus's voyage of discovery was just the first of four trips he made to the New World; he returned in 1493, and then again in 1498 and 1502. Somewhere along the way, Vignaud's followers asserted, he must have noticed that the islands he found had little in common with anything described by Marco Polo and John Mandeville. Where were the great empires of China and Japan? Where were the streets of marble and the roofs of gold? Here were only primitive villages.

It was on his third voyage, perhaps, that Columbus came closest to recognizing the truth. In July 1498 he reached what is now known as Venezuela's Paria Peninsula, and he began to suspect that this was more than just an island off the coast of China. He looked at the broad delta of the Orinoco River and deduced, correctly, that such an enormous volume of fresh water could only come from a mainland of considerable size. In his journal, as recorded by Las Casas, Columbus wrote, "I believe this is a very great continent, until today unknown."

But after this brief moment of clarity, Columbus leaped to a conclusion far more preposterous than his original "Enterprise of the Indies." The new continent must be, he decided, the "Terrestrial Paradise," the legendary Garden of Eden. His subsequent letter to Ferdinand and Isabella was a strange mix of theology and geography: "I am completely persuaded in my own mind that the Terrestrial Paradise is in the place I have said," he explained, because it is "just above the Equator, where the best authorities had always argued Paradise would be found."

Then came an even stranger concept: the earth was not round, Columbus explained, but it "has the shape of a pear, which is all very round, except at the stem where it is very prominent . . . and this part with the stem is the highest and nearest to the sky." It was at this point nearest the sky that Columbus had found Eden.

Had Columbus lost his mind? Perhaps; he was under a great deal of pressure, and he was ill at the time. But it's more likely, in the opinion of most historians, that his "Terrestrial Paradise" grew out of his long-held conviction that his voyages were divinely inspired. Moreover, Columbus's belief that he'd found Paradise in no way contradicted his claim to be en route to Asia. As he wrote to the Spanish monarchs, Paradise was just where the authorities said it would be; indeed, several medieval Christian writers quoted in *Imago Mundi,* one of the well-read books in

Columbus's library, located the Garden of Eden at the farthest point of the Far East.

In any case, Columbus later abandoned the idea of a Terrestrial Paradise. In 1502, during his fourth and final voyage to the New World, he proclaimed that he was searching for a strait by which he could pass through this new continent to reach Asia.

Most historians, still following Las Casas and Ferdinand Columbus and Morison, stressed that Columbus never realized the extent of this new continent, never, in fact, thought of it as a true continent. Rather, in Columbus's mind, it was an extension of the Malay Peninsula. It was, to be sure, larger than he'd anticipated, but Asia lay right beyond it, if only he could find a way through or around.

Most probably Columbus died believing that he'd reached the Indies. If so, Columbus was extraordinarily stubborn and single-minded; otherwise there's no way he could have ignored the evidence of his later voyages—or even, for that matter, his initial voyage. Then again, it took an extraordinarily stubborn and single-minded man to convince Ferdinand and Isabella to finance his voyage, and to sail into the unknown.

To investigate further

John Cummins, *The Voyage of Christopher Columbus* (New York: St. Martin's Press, 1992). The most recent translation of Columbus's journal is especially interesting because it incorporates the sections recorded by Ferdinand Columbus as well as those preserved by Las Casas.

Ferdinand Columbus, *The Life of The Admiral Christopher Columbus by his Son Ferdinand,* trans. Benjamin Keen (New Brunswick, N.J.: Rutgers University Press, 1959). Ferdinand, known as a somewhat bookish man, had a tendency to overemphasize the scholarly basis of his father's Enterprise of the Indies, sometimes at the expense of his father's more businesslike qualities. But he's still a remarkable biographer as well as son. The book was first published in 1571, thirty-one years after Ferdinand's death.

Henry Vignaud, *The Columbian Tradition on the Discovery of America* (Oxford: Clarenden Press, 1920). Columbus was a fraud, and historians were his dupes.

Samuel Eliot Morison, *Admiral of the Ocean Sea* (Boston: Little, Brown, 1942). Still the definitive biography.

Samuel Eliot Morison, *The Great Explorers* (New York: Oxford University Press, 1978). The section on Columbus includes a summary of the traditional view on Columbus's intended destination. While you're at it, read the rest of the book; there was no better historian of the sea than Morison.

Kirkpatrick Sale, *The Conquest of Paradise* (New York: Alfred A. Knopf, 1990). Sale offers one of the latest (and best) presentations of the Vignaud position as part of a more general attack on Columbus, in which he blames the explorer for just about everything that went wrong with America, from enslaving blacks and Indians to destroying the environment. Not always convincing, but always lively and provocative.

John Noble Wilford, *The Mysterious History of Columbus* (New York: Alfred A. Knopf, 1991). An absorbing survey of the ways historians from Columbus's time on have mythologized, debunked, and otherwise interpreted the man and his journeys.

Valerie I. J. Flint, *The Imaginative Landscape of Christopher Columbus* (Princeton, N. J.: Princeton University Press, 1992). A fascinating, though somewhat academic, interpretation of the medieval sources of Columbus's view of the world; here is, Flint writes, "not the New World Columbus found, but the Old World which he carried with him in his head."

William D. Phillips Jr. and Carla Rahn Phillips, *The Worlds of Christopher Columbus* (Cambridge, Eng.: Cambridge University Press, 1992). A balanced history of the explorer's life and times, especially strong on his time in Spain.

Miles H. Davidson, *Columbus Then and Now* (Norman: University of Oklahoma Press, 1997). A provocative but poorly organized critique of Columbus biographies.

Chapter 15

Did Martin Guerre Return?

The story of Martin Guerre generally begins with his marriage, in 1538, to Bertrande de Rols. This was meant to consummate a union between the Guerres and the Rols, two prosperous peasant families in the village of Artigat, in southwestern France. But the marriage got off to a rocky start.

The problem, though both families blamed sorcery, was most likely the ages of the bride and the groom: Bertrande was only nine or ten; Martin, fourteen. It took eight years to consummate the marriage, a delay that was undoubtedly humiliating to Martin. So was a huge family fight—in 1548—during which Martin's father accused him of stealing some grain. Soon after, the young man abandoned his wife and disappeared without a trace.

Eight years later, after the death of both his parents, Martin Guerre returned to Artigat. He explained that he'd crossed the Pyrenees, joined the Spanish Army, and fought in the Netherlands. The experience, it seemed, had changed him: he was a more confident figure, easily adapting to his role as the family's new patriarch, and he was a kinder and more loving husband. His family and his wife were delighted to have him back.

Then, late in 1558, Martin asked his uncle, Pierre Guerre, for his share of the profits from the family farm during his absence. This did not sit well with Pierre. He angrily pointed out that for the eight years Martin was gone, he'd not just run the farm but also taken care of his nephew's wife and son. Pierre's distrust of the prodigal son increased the next year, when two soldiers passing through the village said they'd served with Martin Guerre and that he'd lost a leg during the war. Yet the Martin in Artigat clearly had both legs.

Pierre was now convinced that his adversary was not only greedy but also an impostor. The dispute led to a series of trials, culminating in an appeal before the Parlement of Toulouse in 1560. One of the judges there, Jean de Coras, wrote a book about the case that remains the primary source for most of what historians know about it.

The Toulouse proceedings were extraordinary. Most of the inhabitants of Artigat and many from surrounding villages were called as witnesses. Among those who testified against the defendant were Pierre, Pierre's sons, Bertrande's mother (who had since married Pierre), and the village shoemaker (who declared that the "new" Martin's feet were inexplicably smaller than the "old" Martin's). Also highly damaging was the testimony of a number of inhabitants from the nearby town of Le Pin; they recognized the defendant as a former fellow townsman, a scoundrel named Arnaud du Tilh, alias Pansette.

There was also plenty of testimony on behalf of the defendant. Martin's four sisters stated that the man on trial was without a doubt their brother. The defendant himself answered all questions with confidence, recalling in detail events from his childhood and adolescence. Above all, Bertrande—though she had joined Pierre in signing the complaint that led to the trial—now refused to swear that the accused was not her husband.

The judges, Coras included, were perplexed. But they noted that the financial dispute between Pierre and the defendant created a strong motive for a false accusation by the uncle. They were also swayed by the defendant's perfect recall and by the fact that Bertrande, the one who knew him best, had backed away from her accusation. The judges, Coras wrote, were "more disposed to the advantage of the prisoner and against the said Pierre Guerre."

Then came a denouement that would have left John Grisham shaking his head. As the judges were about to announce their decision, in walked a man with a wooden leg. He said his name was Martin Guerre.

The defendant objected strenuously. He claimed Pierre must have bribed someone to play the part, and he barraged the newcomer with questions, some of which the witness seemed less sure about than the defendant. But the defendant's case was collapsing around him. Martin's sisters deserted him, hugging the newcomer. Then Bertrande was brought into the courtroom, and after one look, she began to tremble and weep. She ran to embrace the newcomer and begged him to forgive her for having been fooled by the impostor.

Coras and his fellow judges were no longer in doubt. Arnaud du Tilh, alias Pansette, was found guilty of "imposture and false supposition of name and person" as well as adultery and was sentenced to be hanged. The sentence was carried out in Artigat on September 16, 1560.

Just before he died, Arnaud du Tilh confessed. He said the idea for the crime had first come to him when some acquaintances of Martin's had mistaken him for Guerre, and that he then learned as much as he could about him. Once Bertrande accepted him, he was able to learn even more from her, though she was entirely unaware of what he was doing.

Even so, questions remained. How could Arnaud have fooled an entire village, including Martin's wife and family? Was Bertrande as completely duped as she claimed? And what prompted Martin's timely return just when Pierre's case seemed lost?

Coras's explanation to the first two questions was that Arnaud was a remarkably talented trickster, and his account of the trial reveals a grudging admiration for the story's villain. "It was truly a tragedy for this fine peasant," the judge wrote, "all the more because the outcome was wretched, indeed fatal for him." Bertrande's gullibility was also easily explained, given "the weakness of her sex, easily deceived by the cunning and craftiness of men." Moreover, Coras believed, she would have put aside any doubts because of her loyalty to the man she believed was

FIGVRA COMMISSIONIS TESTIVM.

A courtroom scene from the trial of Martin Guerre, a sixteenth-century peasant whose story has raised more questions than that of any prince of the period. Courtesy of Special Collections Department, Harvard Law School Library.

her husband and, perhaps, because of her gratitude that he was back.

As for the timely appearance of the one-legged man, Coras admitted it seemed like a miracle. He concluded it was the work of God.

Coras's version of the events satisfied his sixteenth-century readers, of whom there were many. His book *A Memorable Decision* was reprinted five times in the six years after it was published, and several more editions in French and Latin appeared later in the century. An account by a young lawyer named Guillaume Le Sueur was also published in 1561 and presented a broadly similar account of the case.

Still, at least one contemporary commentator expressed some doubts about whether Coras had discovered the full story. This was the renowned essayist Michel de Montaigne. Montaigne suggested that Coras would have been better off following the example of the ancient Athenians who, when they found a case particularly difficult, told the parties to come back in a hundred years. In other words, Montaigne felt, the death sentence was very harsh, given the unanswered questions.

But it was Coras's account, not Montaigne's, that remained the standard for more than four hundred years. Then, in the 1980s, a French moviemaker and an American historian turned the traditional version on its head.

Natalie Zemon Davis, the author of the 1983 book *The Return of Martin Guerre,* was also a consultant to the screenwriters Jean-Claude Carriere and Daniel Vigne on the 1982 movie. In both the movie and the book, Bertrande is dramatically transformed. No longer Arnaud's dupe, she is now his full-fledged partner. She is now sort of a prefeminist heroine, a woman characterized by, in Davis's words, "a stubborn independence and a shrewd realism about how she could maneuver within the constraints placed upon one of her sex."

Bertrande, in Davis's version, knew that Arnaud was a fraud almost from the start. But she saw in him the chance to escape from her shaky and uncomfortable role as an abandoned woman, neither wife nor widow. That Arnaud turned out to be a much kinder man and a better lover than Martin made him "a dream come true, a man she could live with in peace and friendship . . . and in passion." So Bertrande filled in Arnaud on all the details of Martin's life he needed to know, and she made sure everyone else in the village knew that there was no doubt this was her husband.

Once Pierre turned on Arnaud, however, Bertrande's position was again in jeopardy, so she resorted to a delicate strategy. She pretended to side with Pierre by joining him in signing the complaint against Arnaud. That way, if Pierre won, she'd avoid his wrath. At the same time, she attempted—subtly, so Pierre couldn't tell—to undermine his case in court by refusing to swear that the defendant was not her husband. Pierre, like Coras, might attribute her hedging to a woman's weakness, but it was actually a calculated and brilliant performance.

In fact, had it not been for the untimely appearance of the real Martin, Bertrande's strategy might have succeeded, and she and Arnaud could have lived happily ever after. As it was, she recognized that the return of the real Martin Guerre doomed Arnaud, so she quickly abandoned her lover and embraced her husband.

What was most remarkable about Davis's inversion of the traditional account is that it did not depend on the discovery of some new account of the trial that contradicted Coras's. Though she drew upon various other court records, Davis's history was based largely on a careful rereading of Coras's book.

Davis found in Coras's work a profound ambivalence about the case that previous commentators had overlooked and that Coras himself had perhaps tried to suppress. For example, in explaining his reasons for finding Bertrande innocent of any collusion with Arnaud, Coras stressed the need to keep together husband and wife. "In doubtful situations the law commands that the presumption in favor of marriage triumph over any other," he wrote. This sounds more like a pardon than a resounding statement of Bertrande's innocence.

Davis also pointed out that the real Martin Guerre—the man with the wooden leg—was extremely skeptical about his wife's innocence. In response to Bertrande's plea that he forgive her for having fallen for Arnaud's trick, Guerre remained (this still according to Coras) "austere and fierce." Without even looking at his wife, he responded: "Don't excuse yourself by my sisters nor by my uncle: for there is neither father, mother, uncle, sister, or brother who must better know their son, nephew, or brother than wife must know her husband. And for the disaster that has befallen our house, no one has the wrong but you."

Underlying Coras's ambivalence about Arnaud and Bertrande, Davis believed, were religious doubts. Protestantism was spreading throughout southwestern France, and though the peasants of Artigat remained Catholics, Bertrande would have been attracted to the new religion's teaching that a wife deserted by a husband is free to remarry after a year. This was, of course, not her position at the trial, where she maintained Arnaud *was* her Martin. But privately, she and Arnaud may have drawn upon Protestant ideas to justify their actions.

Coras, too, though nominally a Catholic, was certainly sympathetic to Protestantism, and Davis believed that played a role in his initial impulse to find Bertrande innocent, even though he seemed to have considerable doubts. Coras's Protestant tendencies later became more overt—so much so that, in October 1572, in front of the same Parlement building in Toulouse where Arnaud du Tilh was condemned, Coras himself was put to death on a charge of heresy.

Davis's version of the story was not universally accepted. Some historians believed she was reading into Coras's text more than was there and that her book was more of a historical romance than a history. Others criticized both the traditional version and Davis's for too readily accepting that the man with the wooden leg was the real Martin Guerre. They, like Arnaud before the court, argued that Pierre could have found a one-legged man, and paid him to show up at just the right moment.

Overall, though, most scholars have accepted Davis's reinterpretation. One of the leading historians of the period, Emmanuel Le Roy Ladurie, said that *The Return of Martin Guerre* was a great book and an even better movie. Even one of her fiercest critics,

Robert Finlay, praised Davis's work as "imaginatively conceived, eloquently argued, and intrinsically appealing."

One of the most appealing aspects of Davis's work is that she herself concedes that her interpretation is open to doubt; indeed, her book is to some considerable extent a meditation on the difficulties historians face in trying to figure out what's true and what's not. Those doubts are compounded by a case like Martin Guerre's, where Arnaud and Bertrande and even Coras may have had very good reasons for concealing the truth.

The final words of Davis's book could just as easily apply to most of the other historians discussed in this book. "I think I have uncovered the true face of the past," she wrote, "or has Pansette done it again?"

To investigate further

Jean de Coras, *A Memorable decision of the High Court of Toulouse, containing the prodigious story of our time of a supposed husband, enriched by one hundred and eleven fine and learned annotations . . . "* An English translation by Jeannette K. Ringold appears in *Triquarterly* 55 (Fall 1982). The original was published in 1561.

Michel de Montaigne, "Of Cripples," in *The Complete Essays of Montaigne*, trans. from the French by Donald M. Frame (Stanford, Calif.: Stanford University Press, 1965). Montaigne's comments on the Guerre case appear, fittingly, in an essay on our limited ability to discern the truth. The essay was originally published in 1588.

Janet Lewis, *The Wife of Martin Guerre* (San Francisco: Colt Press, 1941). Lewis's quaint novel has little in common with Davis's historical account, except that it portrays an independent-minded woman.

Natalie Zemon Davis, *The Return of Martin Guerre* (Cambridge, Mass.: Harvard University Press, 1983). Who would have thought that a scholarly study of sixteenth-century peasant life could also be a tragic love story?

Robert Finlay, "The Refashioning of Martin Guerre," *American Historical Review* 93, no. 3. In Finlay's view, Davis has perpetrated a fraud almost as ingenious as Arnaud's. "The virtues of *The Return of Martin Guerre* are clear," he writes. "Unfortunately, none of the central points of the book—the knowing Bertrande, the devious court strategy, the tragic romance, the Protestant justification, the self-fashioning peasants, the conflicted judge, the 'multivalent' text— depend on the documentary record."

Natalie Zemon Davis, "On the Lame," *American Historical Review* 93, no. 3. Davis's response to Finlay.

Anthony Guneratne, "Cinehistory and the Puzzling Case of Martin Guerre," *Film & History* 20, no. 4. Guneratne suggests that Pierre may have worked with Arnaud in an effort to consolidate his landholdings. Later, after their falling out, Pierre may have found another impostor to stage the last-minute court-room drama.

Chapter 16

Did Mary, Queen of Scots, Murder Her Husband?

I t ought to have been easy for Mary Stewart to find a suitable husband.

She was young (twenty-two). She was beautiful ("a countenance," wrote Sir Walter Scott, "the like of which we know not to have existed"). And, unlike her cousin, England's Queen Elizabeth, she was conventionally feminine in her outlook, at least to the extent that she longed for a man on whom she could depend. Perhaps most attractive of all, to any potential suitor, was her dowry: since Mary was queen of Scotland, her husband would be a king.

Yet the man she married in July 1565—Henry Stuart, the earl of Darnley—was about as poor a husband as could be imagined. Superficially, to be sure, he had some fine traits. Like Mary, he was young, good-looking, and a cousin of Elizabeth. The last put Henry close behind Mary in line for the English throne, and Mary therefore had some reason to hope that the marriage would strengthen her own claim to be Elizabeth's successor.

Alas, as Mary quickly learned, Henry's good qualities were all on the surface. He turned out to be spoiled, lazy, and no help at all when it came to governing the country. By the end of 1565 Mary was ignoring her husband and leaning heavily on the advice of other advisers, particularly a onetime musician from Italy named David Rizzio.

Henry, for his part, deeply resented Rizzio's influence, as did many others in the Scottish nobility. That Rizzio was foreign and, like Mary, a Catholic, especially outraged many of the Protestant lords. In March 1566 a group of them broke into the queen's quarters, dragged out the screaming Rizzio, and stabbed him to death. Henry himself did not participate in the murder, but he was definitely part of the conspiracy; to leave no doubt about that, the murderers carefully left Henry's dagger in Rizzio's body.

Still, Mary continued to play the part of the dutiful wife. Even though Henry was suffering from syphilis, she persuaded him to return from his family's home near Glasgow. In February 1567 Henry moved to Kirk o' Field, a house on the outskirts of Edinburgh, where Mary dutifully nursed him back to health.

But the royal reconciliation was short-lived. On February 9 Mary left the house to attend a servant's wedding in the city, and a few hours later, Kirk o' Field blew up. Henry's body was found in the garden; he had apparently escaped the explosion, only to be smothered outside.

The man behind the assassination, most observers were convinced, was Henry's longtime enemy James Hepburn, the earl of Bothwell. It was no surprise, then, when Bothwell was indicted for murder in April. The more contentious question was Mary's role in the murder. Contemporary Catholic writers such as Bishop John Leslie instantly rose to her defense, portraying her as more innocent than the Virgin Mary. Protestant writers, most notably George Buchanan and John Knox, were equally vehement that she was guilty.

Mary herself denied that she had anything to do with her husband's death, and many seemed willing to accept her word. But her credibility soon plummeted. On May 15, just three months after the king's murder, the queen remarried. Her new husband was none other than the earl of Bothwell, the prime suspect in Henry's murder.

∽

The marriage to Bothwell, even more than the murder of Henry, spelled the end of Mary's reign. Bothwell was a powerful lord, but he didn't have the network of alliances with other nobles

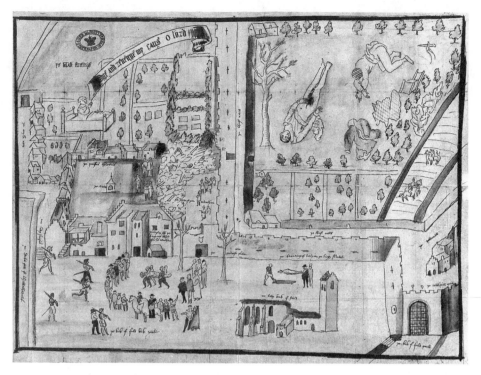

To her defenders, Mary was as innocent as the Virgin Mary . . . which made it hard to explain her marriage to the man accused of murdering her husband. A contemporary sketch of the murder scene is shown here. Public Record Office.

that was critical for a sixteenth-century Scottish king. As for Mary, her support among the Protestant lords, always tenuous, evaporated entirely after the marriage. In what many considered a desperate attempt to restore her reputation, Mary claimed that she married Bothwell because he abducted and raped her. Few believed the story.

In June 1567, with the support of much of the Scottish public, a band of disaffected nobles defeated the forces of Mary and Bothwell, and imprisoned the queen at Lochleven Castle. A month later, unable to withstand their threats, Mary agreed to abdicate. She turned over the throne to her infant son, James, whose government was led by Mary's half brother, James Stewart, the earl of Moray. A year later, Mary escaped from Lochleven and attempted to regain the throne, but Moray's forces again defeated hers, this time in a decisive battle near Glasgow on May 13, 1568. Three days later Mary fled to England, hoping to convince Elizabeth to help restore her to the throne.

For Elizabeth, however, Mary's presence created a quandary. On the one hand, the sight of any queen toppled from her throne could only make the queen of England uneasy. On the other hand, to restore Mary to power would require the defeat of the pro-Protestant, pro-English party in Scotland, something Elizabeth was also loath to see. Elizabeth decided to appoint a commission to investigate the whole affair, then report back to her.

The commission was the first chance both sides had to present their cases. (Bothwell's murder trial in April 1567 had shed little light on the crime; with the court surrounded by about two hundred of his armed supporters, his acquittal was assured and meaningless.) The English commissioners met throughout 1568 and 1569, first at York, then at Westminster, and finally at Hampton Court.

Moray himself arrived at Westminster in December 1568 to argue the case against Mary. But it was not so much his arguments as his evidence that electrified the proceedings. Moray brought with him what had up to then been only a rumor—a series of letters and sonnets, allegedly written by Mary to Bothwell, in which she expressed her passionate love for Bothwell and her equally passionate hatred for Henry.

To quote from the letters, Mary wrote to Bothwell that she wanted only to be "between your arms, my dear life." (And this while Henry was still alive.) She would do whatever he asked; he needed only to "send me word what I shall do." As for Henry, the sentiments expressed in the letter were clear: "Cursed be this pocky fellow that troubleth me thus much."

The letters were extremely incriminating, since they made Mary out to be both murderer and adulterer. But Mary denied the letters were hers, and her defenders were quick to label them forgeries. And, indeed, there was much about the letters that was suspicious. For one thing, Mary's supporters demanded to know, why were the letters kept secret until the commission met?

According to Moray, his government had been in possession of the letters since June 1567, when they captured Bothwell's servant, George Dalgleish. Dalgleish had led them to the silver "casket" that contained the documents. Yet, as Mary's defenders pointed out, Moray waited more than a year before making public this vital evidence. This would have given him plenty of time to forge the documents, then present them to the commissioners at the most opportune moment. Moreover, by the time Moray reached Westminster, Dalgleish—the only one who could contradict his story—had been conveniently executed for helping Bothwell murder Henry.

The content of the letters was also questionable. None was dated and none was signed, so there was no way to know for sure that the letters were written by Mary, as opposed to some other lover of Bothwell. The love sonnets were in a style wholly unlike Mary's known poetry, and the poetess, whoever she was, seemed impressed by Bothwell's wealth—an unlikely sentiment for the queen, who was far richer than Bothwell. All this convinced many of Mary's defenders that the Casket Letters were a mix of outright forgeries and actual documents that were doctored to appear to be Mary's.

Elizabeth's commissioners never ruled on the authenticity of the documents, nor did Elizabeth herself. Instead, they decided that there was no proof that either Moray or Mary had acted dishonorably. This was legally illogical, but it made political sense, at least for the short term. Moray could return to Scotland, where he could continue to rule as England's Protestant ally. Mary would remain in England, and in fact would remain in prison, but at least Elizabeth had not passed any judgment against her that would have offended Catholics at home or abroad.

In the long run, however, Elizabeth still had a problem. As long as Mary was alive, she could continue to be a focal point for Catholic plots to regain the British as well as the Scottish throne. Mary willingly participated in at least three such conspiracies, the last of which involved a plan to assassinate the British queen. This was the final straw for Elizabeth; faced with overwhelming evidence of Mary's role in the assassination plot, she reluctantly ordered her execution. Mary was beheaded on February 8, 1587.

As for Bothwell, his end was even grimmer. He sought refuge in Denmark, where the king was as unhappy to see him as Elizabeth was to see Mary. The king threw him into the fortress of Dragsholm, where the prisoner was chained to a pillar half his height. The cruel conditions drove Bothwell insane, and so he remained until his death in April 1578.

∽

As long as Elizabeth lived, Mary continued to be portrayed in starkly contrasting extremes. To Protestant writers, she was a papist plotter; to Catholics, an innocent martyr. Once Elizabeth died, and was succeeded by Mary's son James, these perspectives gave way to something of a compromise. What emerged was the image, still familiar today, of a romantic heroine brought down by bad luck and bad loves.

The new image served James well. As a Protestant king ruling two Protestant countries (England and Scotland), he could hardly allow a martyred Mary to continue to inspire Catholic hopes and dreams. At the same time, he would have found the venomous Protestant portraits of Buchanan and Knox equally objectionable; after all, this was his mother they were talking about.

Thus was born a convenient and neat compromise. But, though it may have satisfied the political needs of the moment, it ducked the question of whether the Casket Letters were genuine or forged. True to form, James tried to eliminate the question by eliminating the evidence. Sometime early in his reign, and while they were in the possession of his government, the letters disappeared—and they haven't been seen since.

That didn't stop subsequent historians from speculating about them. In the absence of any new evidence, most tended to repeat the same arguments that Moray and Mary raised before Elizabeth's commissioners. Most twentieth-century historians, citing the inconsistencies in the letters' styles and contents, have leaned toward thinking them some combination of outright forgeries and doctored documents. But with the originals gone, the mystery of the letters can't be definitively resolved.

Historians have been less reluctant to pass judgment on the more fundamental question of Mary's role in Henry's death, about which there is plenty of evidence besides the Casket Letters. And most of that evidence ties Mary to the murder. Her coaxing Henry to return to Edinburgh, in spite of his role in Rizzio's murder and his syphilis; her departure from the house just hours before the explosion; her marriage to Bothwell just months after the murder—all seem to indicate that Mary knew something was going to happen. Even if she wasn't aware of the particular plot to blow up Kirk o' Field, she must have known that something was going on. And her eager involvement in later plots to get rid of Elizabeth indicate that Mary had no qualms about political assassinations.

That's not to say she was the monster portrayed by Buchanan and Knox. Sixteenth-century royal politics were a dirty business, and Mary's behavior was no dirtier than those of many of her counterparts, Elizabeth included. The difference was that Elizabeth played the game well and won. Mary, for all her beauty and charm, never could keep up with her cousin.

To investigate further

George Buchanan, *The Tyrannous Reign of Mary Stewart*, trans. and ed. W. A. Gatherer (Edinburgh: University Press, 1958). Includes Buchanan's 1571 *A Detection of Mary Queen of Scots* and the relevant sections of his 1582 *History of Scotland*. A pretty good idea of Buchanan's attitude toward Mary can be gauged from his tale (completely invented) of how Mary's servant was ordered to haul a half-naked Bothwell up by a rope out of his wife's bed and directly into that of the queen.

James Emerson Phillips, *Images of a Queen* (Berkeley: University of California Press, 1965). How her contemporaries turned Mary into a symbol of everything good and everything evil.

M. H. Armstrong Davis, *The Casket Letters* (Washington, D.C.: University Press of Washington, D.C., 1965). The most recent book-length study of the letters, in which Armstrong Davis argues that they were forged to frame Mary. So certain is Armstrong Davis of Mary's innocence that he also argues, much less persuasively, that the Kirk o' Field explosion that killed the king was actually Henry's botched attempt to kill Mary.

Antonia Fraser, *Mary Queen of Scots* (New York: Delacorte Press, 1969). The best biography to date, at once scholarly and romantic.

Gordon Donaldson, *The First Trial of Mary, Queen of Scots* (New York: Stein & Day, 1969). A thorough study of the York, Westminster, and Hampton Court hearings, with a somewhat less sympathetic view of Mary than Fraser's.

Ian Cowan, ed., *The Enigma of Mary Stuart* (London: Victor Gollancz, 1971). A useful collection of too-short excerpts from various works on Mary, from the sixteenth century to the twentieth.

Jean Plaidy, *Mary Queen of Scots* (New York: G. P. Putnam's Sons, 1975). Not surprisingly, since Plaidy is also a best-selling writer of romance fiction (under the pseudonym Victoria Holt), this biography presents the Mary of romance, a woman who unwisely let her heart prevail over her head.

Jenny Wormald, *Mary Queen of Scots* (London: George Philip, 1988). A portrait of Mary as abject failure, so devoid of political judgment and will that she drove her opponents to take action against her.

Chapter 17

Who Wrote
Shakespeare's Plays?

Biographies of Shakespeare, wrote Mark Twain in 1909, were like the brontosaur that stands in the Museum of Natural History. "We had nine bones, and we built the rest of him out of plaster of paris."

Twain was exaggerating, as was his wont. But he had a point: for all the millions of words written about Shakespeare, not much was known about him. About the only things his biographers could say for sure were that he lived in the town of Stratford-on-Avon; that he was the son of a glovemaker; that he became an actor of bit parts; and that he invested, quite successfully, in a theater company known as the King's Men. There are records of his baptism, his marriage, his lawsuits, his taxes, his death. And that's about it; the rest, as Twain put it, was plaster of paris.

Nothing in the Stratford documentary record gives any indication that Shakespeare was a writer, let alone the world's greatest. There are no manuscripts in his hand, or even letters. There are no signatures, except for six shaky scribbles. There's no mention in his will of books or manuscripts or anything at all literary. There's no record that he attended grammar school in Stratford, or that he traveled abroad, or that he had any close connections to anyone in the queen's court. Yet, somehow, to judge from his plays and poems, Shakespeare acquired an extensive knowledge

Shakespeare, as shown in the 1623 Folio. The Folio includes no information about his life. By permission of the Folger Shakespeare Library.

of Italy, of royalty, of philosophy, literature, history, law, and medicine.

The one obvious link between the man from Stratford and the playwright was the name: Shakespeare. Yet even that raised doubts. In the Stratford documents, the name is spelled a variety of ways—as Shaxper or Shagsber or Shakspere. In the published versions of the works and in the contemporary references to them, it's always Shakespeare or Shake-speare.

To Twain, the explanation was clear: the playwright and the poet was not the same man as the glovemaker's son. Precisely who did write the plays Twain couldn't say for sure. But others could. Through the years, they've proposed scores of candidates, among them Queen Elizabeth, King James, Walter Raleigh, Christopher Marlowe, and (apparently based on the premise that "Sheik" sounds like "Shake") an Arab sheik known as El Spar.

∽

There may have been rumors about Shakespeare in the first two centuries after his death, but it was not until the 1800s that they created a serious stir. This was the heyday of the Romantics, for whom Shakespeare was the very embodiment of poetry, and the more they venerated his works, the harder it was for them to reconcile the plays and the poems with their author's mundane life in Stratford. Even as devout a Shakespearean as Coleridge was amazed "works of such character should have proceeded from a man whose life was like that."

As the century progressed, the anti-Stratfordians coalesced around a single candidate, Francis Bacon. Bacon had all the credentials that Shakespeare lacked: Bacon was a philosopher, a scientist, a lawyer, and a politician who frequented the courts of both Elizabeth and James. He found his most zealous champion in an American woman named Delia Bacon (no relation), who was convinced that papers proving her namesake's authorship were buried in a hollow space beneath Shakespeare's gravestone in Stratford. In September 1856 she showed up there, shovel in hand. At the last minute her nerve failed her, and she left Shakespeare's bones undisturbed. But she continued to preach the gospel to a growing audience of believers.

Later Baconians dropped the search for buried manuscripts and instead concentrated on the existing ones. It was a strangely narrow scrutiny, however. The Baconians focused almost entirely on the discovery of ciphers, cryptograms, and codes—all purportedly revealing that Bacon was Shakespeare—that were supposedly embedded in the texts. The leading decoder was Ignatius Donnelly, a congressman from Minnesota who took on all sorts of eccentric causes, Bacon's among them.

Much of Donnelly's 1888 book on the subject is too convoluted to follow, involving all sorts of calculations based on adding, subtracting, dividing, and multiplying the page, line, and word numbers of various words in the text, such as "Francis," "William," "shake," and "spear." A few of his findings are pretty straightforward, however; for example, Donnelly noticed that in the First Folio, a 1623 collection of Shakespeare's plays, the word "bacon" appeared on page 53 of the histories and also on page 53 of the comedies. For Donnelly, this couldn't be a coincidence; it had to be the author's way of revealing his true identity.

Others followed Donnelly's lead, apparently convinced that whoever wrote Shakespeare's plays and poems was primarily interested in creating elaborate brainteasers for future generations to solve. Walter Begley, for example, studied the last two lines of one Shakespeare's poem: "The Romaines plausibly did consent/ To Tarquins everlasting banishment." Begley pointed out that if you combined the first two letters of the last word in the last line (ba) and and the first three letters of the last word in the second-to-last line (con) you discovered the poem's true author. Like Donnelly, Begley ignored the role of chance; it apparently didn't occur to him that the letters in Bacon's name are all pretty common and could be found close together in plenty of other texts, Shakespearean and non-Shakespearean.

Inevitably, the cryptographers were especially drawn to a nonsense word used by a clown in Shakespeare's *Love's Labour's Lost*. The word—*honorificabilitudinatibus*—had enough letters to contain a jumbo assortment of secret messages. One of the best "solutions" came in 1910, when Edwin Durning-Lawrence rearranged the letters to spell "Hi ludi F. Baconis nati tuiti orbi." Translated from the Latin, that read: "These plays F. Bacon's offspring are preserved for the world." What Durning-Lawrence conveniently ignored was that *honorificabilitudinatibus* was a word that had been around for a while before it appeared in *Love's Labour's Lost*, so Bacon couldn't have designed it to hide his coded message.

By 1920 the Baconians' zest for secret messages had cost them much of their credibility, even among those skeptical of Shakespeare's authorship. Most Shakespeare scholars dismissed the Baconians as cranks and crazies and didn't even deign to comment on their work. But as the Baconian era waned, a new and more credible candidate—Edward de Vere, the seventeenth earl of Oxford—moved to the fore.

✌

The case for de Vere, which was set forth in 1920 by an English schoolmaster with the unfortunate name of J. Thomas Looney, appeared to be a strong one. In addition to being the earl of Oxford, de Vere was a cousin of Queen Elizabeth and the ward and later the son-in-law of the lord treasurer, William Burghley. All this gave him more than a passing familiarity with a courtier's life. Best of all, de Vere was an established poet and playwright; in 1598, a contemporary critic named Francis Meres listed de Vere as "the best for Comedy among us."

Unlike Bacon, de Vere would have had good reasons to keep his authorship secret, since the theater was considered a disreputable venue in the circles in which he traveled. Besides, some of those in Elizabeth's court might not like the way they or their ancestors were being portrayed. So, Looney argued, de Vere used a pseudonym. But the earl couldn't resist dropping some hints about his secret identity, so he chose a name derived from one of his crests, which pictured a lion shaking a spear.

Since the earl was a nobleman, his life was much more thoroughly documented than Shakespeare's, and Looney found plenty there to link de Vere and his alleged works. It was known, for example, that de Vere traveled to Italy in 1575, stopping in Padua, Genoa, Venice, and Florence. This could explain the detailed knowledge of these parts evident in Shakespeare's plays.

The most compelling evidence, Looney believed, could be found in Shakespeare's—or rather, de Vere's—most famous play. Like Hamlet's father, de Vere's died young; like Hamlet's mother, de Vere's quickly remarried. De Vere once stabbed a servant of Burghley, which is how Hamlet killed Polonius. And de Vere, again like Hamlet, was captured by pirates, who then spared his life. By the time Looney had finished his analysis, Shakespeare's tragedy seemed to be de Vere's autobiography.

Looney found reflections of de Vere's life in other Shakespeare characters as well. Like Lear, De Vere was a widower with three daughters, of whom the elder two were married. Like Falstaff, he was known for his sharp wit. And like Prospero in *The Tempest*, de Vere had faced stormy weather—albeit metaphorically—in his life.

As for Shakespeare's sonnets, Looney concluded that Henry Wriothesley, the earl of Southampton, fit the role of Shakespeare's "fair youth." Later Oxfordians took this one step farther, speculating that Wriothesley was de Vere's son and that "fair youth" was a punning reference to "Vere youth."

∽

By the mid-twentieth century, the Oxfordians had routed the Baconians to dominate the anti-Stratford position. But, to the academic establishment, the new pretender was no less preposterous than the old.

Indeed, the Oxfordians' efforts to find parallels between de Vere's life and Shakespeare's work suffered from the same obsessive tendencies and loss of perspective as the Baconians' codebreaking. The Oxfordians were determined to force fictional characters into historical figures, but they did so very selectively. For example, as many traditional scholars pointed out, the Oxfordians completely ignored the glaring fact that it was Shakespeare, not de Vere, who named his son Hamnet.

Another major problem with the Oxford-as-Shakespeare theory had to with the dates of Shakespeare's plays. According to most scholars, the King's Men continued to produce new Shakespeare plays until 1614. But de Vere died in 1604. At that point, only twenty-three of Shakespeare's thirty-eight plays had appeared in published editions or been mentioned in printed sources. So there are fifteen plays—including *King Lear, Macbeth, Antony and Cleopatra, The Winter's Tale,* and *The Tempest* (certainly some of the playwright's most accomplished works)—that weren't staged until after de Vere's death.

Some Oxfordians responded to the dating problem by suggesting that de Vere must have started the plays before he died, then someone else finished them. Others went farther, arguing that the dates assigned to the plays were wrong and that almost all of them were written before 1604. The Oxfordians, like all other anti-Stratfordians, had going for them the general dearth of documentation that has plagued all of the traditional biographers. They were correct to assert that some of the plays' dates were based on some speculation and extrapolation, but they were wrong to claim that they were therefore arbitrary.

On the contrary, the traditional dates are based on a variety of contemporary references to Shakespeare and his works. For example, Francis Meres's 1598 work lists twelve of the plays and lauds Shakespeare's works as "most excellent" for comedy and tragedy. This is the same Meres who, you'll recall, the Oxfordians embraced for his praise of de Vere as a writer. But they conveniently disparage his testimony when it's used to support the traditional dating. Moreover, Meres's work raises another embarrassing question for Oxfordians: If their man wrote Shakespeare's plays, why are de Vere and Shakespeare discussed separately in the same work?

Other contemporary references to Shakespeare also bolster the traditionalists' case. Robert Greene mentions Shakespeare in a 1592 pamphlet, and Ben Jonson does so in a number of works. The Oxfordians have argued that Meres and Greene and Jonson all could have been using de Vere's pen name, just as we might refer to Samuel Clemens as Mark Twain, but this seems unlikely. Jonson's 1623 eulogy of Shakespeare refers to him as the "Sweet Swan of Avon," and it's hard to imagine he was thinking of anyone other than the man from Stratford-on-Avon. For most scholars, Jonson's words clinch the case for Shakespeare as Shakespeare.

Still, the Oxfordians and the Baconians—at least those who have not been carried away by their passions—deserve credit for pointing out the gaps in the record and for raising questions that the Shakespeare establishment would have preferred to ignore. In the past decade, the works of the latest Oxfordians, such as Charlton Ogburn and Joseph Sobran, have gained some grudging respect from traditional scholars. Increasingly, academics have taken it on themselves to respond to the anti-Stratfordians, and those responses have themselves been useful and provocative.

That's not to say, however, that the Oxfordians have won over many Shakespeareans to their side. For the vast majority of scholars, the documentary record, though limited, is clear and sufficient. As Shakespearians often joked, the man who wrote Shakespeare's plays was Shakespeare.

The Oxfordians have accused academics of snubbing them because they were amateurs. But the greater snobbery is to assume that only a university-educated aristocrat could turn out to be a literary genius. Shakespeare should not be denied his achievement just because he was the son of a small-town glove-maker.

To investigate further

Delia Bacon, *The Philosophy of Shakspere's Plays Unfolded* (London: Groombridge & Sons, 1857). Nathaniel Hawthorne, who wrote the preface to Bacon's book, was apparently moved by her sincerity but disheartened by her increasingly obsessive need to haunt the graveyards where she was convinced proof of Bacon's authorship would be found. His preface concludes that "it is for the public to say whether my countrywoman has proved her theory." Later Hawthorne came to regret even that tepid support, stating that "this shall be the last of my benevolent follies, and I never will be kind to anybody again."

Ignatius Donnelly, *The Great Cryptogram: Francis Bacon's Cipher in the So-Called Shakespeare Plays* (Chicago: R. S. Peale, 1888). According to Donnelly, Bacon wrote not just Shakespeare's plays but also (in his spare time) Spenser's *The Faerie Queene* and Sidney's *Arcadia*.

Mark Twain, *Is Shakespeare Dead?* (New York: Harper & Brothers, 1909). Twain was actually as concerned with the general question of literary immortality (including his own) as he was with Shakespeare's. But he's always delighted to insult the experts, whom he calls "these Stratfordolators, these Shakesperiods, these tugs, these bangalores, these troglodytes, these herumfordites, these blatherskites, these buccaneers, these bandoleers. . . . "

Edwin Durning-Lawrence, *Bacon Is Shakespeare* (New York: John McBride Company, 1910). Say what you will about Durning-Lawrence, he was a good loser. So confident was he that he'd solved the *honorificabilitudinatibus* problem that he offered a hundred guineas to anyone who came up with another anagram with the same qualities. A Mr. Beevor proposed Abi Inivit F. Bacon Histrio Ludit, which translated as "Be off, F. Bacon, The actor has entered and is playing." Durning-Lawrence paid him the money.

J. Thomas Looney, *"Shakespeare" Identified* (New York: Frederick A. Stokes Company, 1920). The Oxfordian Looney should not be confused with George Battey the Baconian.

Calvin Hoffman, *The Murder of the Man Who Was Shakespeare* (New York: Julian Messner, 1955). The case for Marlowe, which starts off with the great advantage that he was a much more important writer than de Vere. But, like the Oxfordians, the Marlovians have to get around the basic problem of their hero's death, in this instance a much-publicized murder in 1593. Hoffman's answer is that Marlowe faked his own death to avoid being prosecuted for heresy.

Frank Wadsworth, *The Poacher from Stratford* (Berkeley: University of California Press, 1958). A fair and succinct summary of the rival claims up to that time.

James McManaway, *The Authorship of Shakespeare* (Amherst, Mass.: Folger Shakespeare Library, 1962). The establishment position, as issued by the establishment.

S. Schoenbaum, *Shakespeare's Lives* (Oxford: Clarendon Press, 1991). A scholarly yet highly readable survey of Shakespeare's biographers.

Charlton Ogburn, *The Mysterious William Shakespeare* (McLean, Va.: EPM Publications, 1992). Ogburn, the leading Oxfordian, inherited the mantle from his parents, both of whom also wrote books on the subject. Ogburn has been more successful than any of his predecessors in forcing the academic establishment to pay attention, and his book even earned a respectful response in the mainstream journal *Shakespeare Quarterly*.

Irvin Leigh Matus, *Shakespeare, in Fact* (New York: Continuum, 1994). A systematic rebuttal of the anti-Stratfordian arguments.

John Michell, *Who Wrote Shakespeare?* (London: Thames & Hudson, 1996). The most recent and most compelling case that Shakespeare's works were a group effort involving Bacon, de Vere, Marlowe, and Shakespeare himself.

Joseph Sobran, *Alias Shakespeare* (New York: The Free Press, 1997). The latest and one of the best of the pro-Oxford books.

Mark Anderson, "The Countenance Shakes Spears," *Harper's,* April 1999. A description of the work in progress of Roger Stritmatter, an Oxfordian who has found that passages underlined in a Bible that once belonged to de Vere show up in various forms in Shakespeare's plays. Traditionalists have responded that the Oxfordians are, once again, being misleadingly selective.

Chapter 18

Was Captain Kidd a Pirate?

I n December 1698, in an effort to coax pirates out of the seas, England's King William III offered a pardon to anyone who surrendered. There were two exceptions, pirates whose crimes were so heinous that they were beyond redemption. One was "Long Ben" Avery. The other was Captain William Kidd.

Kidd's reputation for ruthlessness and barbarity continued to spread, even after his death on the gallows in 1701. Many a ballad recalled his deeds and misdeeds; one, for example, has Kidd tell how he disposed of a disgruntled crew member: "I murdered William Moore/And left him in his gore/Not many leagues from shore." The pirate stories of Washington Irving, Edgar Allan Poe, and Robert Louis Stevenson were all inspired, at least in part, by Kidd.

The Kidd of legend was ill-tempered, hugely powerful, and insatiably greedy. He was also rich, and he died without revealing where he'd buried his treasure. In the three centuries since then, treasure hunters have searched the shores and dredged the bottoms of rivers and seas from New York to the Indies, East and West. In 2000, the Discovery Channel financed an expedition to the African coast, where divers found what may be the wreckage of Kidd's flagship. But as for the treasure, they came up empty-handed.

Kidd, for his part, always denied that there was a treasure, and—even more vehemently—that he was a pirate. He maintained that his adventures had been entirely in the service of his country and that his voyage had been sponsored by high-ranking officials, including King William himself.

"My lord," Kidd said after a London jury sentenced him to die for piracy and murder, "it is a very hard sentence. . . . I am the innocentest person of them all."

Surprisingly, quite a few historians reached the same conclusion.

૭

The record of Kidd's trial, which started on May 8, 1701, and ended the next day, still exists—and offers a close look at the man and his actions.

Both the prosecution and the defense agreed on some basic facts. Kidd arrived in London in 1695, looking for someone to sponsor a privateering expedition. Like pirates, privateers robbed ships at sea, but with a big difference: they were licensed by one nation, and they were limited to attacks on the ships of hostile nations. By the late sixteenth century, privateering was a fairly common and inexpensive way to undermine an enemy's trade. Kidd was an experienced privateer, having raided various French ships in the Caribbean.

In London, Kidd gained the support of Lord Bellomont, a member of Parliament and a leading figure in the ruling Whig Party. Bellomont persuaded four other Whig peers to put up the cash for a ship, and the Admiralty granted him a privateering license. The king agreed to put up three thousand pounds, then reneged on the money but still lent his support in return for 10 percent of the profits.

Kidd's commission was somewhat unusual in that it authorized him to capture not just enemy ships but also pirate ships. This may have been added to make a venture involving the king sound a bit less mercenary, though it also indicated that the government was becoming increasingly fed up with pirates who interfered with British trade.

Kidd set sail from London in the thirty-four-gun *Adventure Galley*. In January 1697 he arrived at Madagascar, a well-known pirate base off the eastern coast of Africa. Here were nearly two hundred pirates, including the aptly named Captains Hoar and Shivers, but Kidd made no effort to apprehend any of them.

Almost a year later, having wandered about the coasts of Africa and Asia, Kidd had seized nothing but a few small vessels, and both his crew and his backers were getting itchy. The crew members, who'd signed on for a share of the booty and didn't get paid unless they captured something, were by some accounts near mutiny. Back in London, the government worried that Kidd would soon cross the line from privateer to pirate—if he hadn't already done so. The *Adventure Galley* had made no moves against any of the pirates at Madagascar or elsewhere, and she'd fled from some British Navy ships encountered off the coast of Africa.

With the ship leaking and supplies short, the mood on board was increasingly tense. On October 30, 1697, according to the testimony of crew members at Kidd's trial, the captain got into an argument with a gunner, William Moore. Kidd called Moore a "lousy dog." Moore replied, "If I am a lousy dog, you have made me so. You have brought me to ruin and many more." Kidd then picked up a bucket and slammed it down on Moore's head. The gunner died the next day.

Then, on January 30, 1698, hope appeared on the horizon in the form of the four-hundred-ton *Quedah Merchant*. Here, finally, was a prize worth taking. The merchant ship, flying an Armenian flag, was heading north filled with silk, calico, sugar, opium, guns, and gold. Kidd gave chase and ultimately seized the ship and its cargo.

It's at this point that the prosecution and defense stories, as presented at Kidd's trial, diverge. To prosecutors, this was clearly an act of piracy. The *Quedah Merchant* had an English captain, and it was carrying goods belonging to a leading member of the Indian emperor's court, who had powerful connections with the East India Company—an English venture. What's more, Kidd did not take the ship or his goods home to be judged a legal prize, as the contract with his Whig benefactors required. Instead, he dispersed some of the booty among his crew and kept the rest for himself. Kidd's crew members, taking advantage of the king's offer of immunity, testified to all this.

Kidd, for his part, insisted that the *Quedah Merchant* was not an English ship, its captain and connections notwithstanding. Its captain had shown him a "French pass," a document that clearly indicated this was a French ship. The French pass, Kidd maintained, would prove his seizure of the ship was entirely legal.

Kidd cross-examined his ex–crew members, who admitted that they'd heard him speak of the pass, though they hadn't actually seen it. Repeatedly, Kidd asked the court to delay his trial until the jurors could examine the French pass for themselves.

The judges would have none of this, however. The pass was never produced in court, and the trial moved expeditiously forward. The jurors took only an hour to find Kidd guilty of Moore's murder, and another half hour to find him guilty of piracy.

⁓

Many historians were not so sure.

Though Kidd never produced the French pass, there was a great deal of circumstantial evidence indicating that it might have existed. For one thing, Kidd could have hidden out at Madagascar or some other pirate refuge, but he chose to return to America, even though he knew there was a warrant out for his arrest. Why? According to Kidd, it was because he knew the pass would prove his innocence.

Kidd said that before arriving in Boston, he'd sent the pass to Lord Bellomont, his business partner and the newly appointed governor of Massachusetts. Bellomont replied with a reassuring letter, saying that he had no doubts he could get the king to pardon Kidd. Only then did Kidd turn himself in, confident his benefactor would protect him. But Bellomont betrayed him, throwing him in the Boston jail and then shipping him to London in irons.

Bellomont's letter to Kidd, which mentioned the French pass explicitly, convinced many historians that Kidd hadn't made it up. The governor, it seemed, was in a very awkward position. As Kidd's partner, he would have loved to see the *Quedah Merchant* declared a legal prize—for then he'd get his share of the profits. But as governor, he couldn't afford to appear sympathetic to an accused pirate. Ultimately, his political position was more important to him than the profits, so he had Kidd arrested.

Captain Kidd hanging in chains.

*After being hanged, Captain Kidd's body was displayed by the Thames, a warning
to other pirates. Why was so much attention focused on a man who, in the words of
one historian, "never cut a throat or made a victim walk the plank, who was no
more than a third- or fourth-rate pirate"? Library of Congress.*

Kidd's notoriety was a tremendous embarrassment not just to Bellomont but also to his fellow investors—all prominent members of the Whig Party. Their Tory opponents, who saw this as a chance to embroil the Whigs in a scandal, were calling for a vote of censure. For their part, the Whigs were quick to portray Kidd as a privateer turned pirate, to make clear that he'd gone bad *after* they'd made their deal with him. And, to make Kidd's position even worse, the East India Company wanted to make an example of him, to discourage other pirates and to mollify their friends in India.

To many historians, then, Kidd was no fearsome pirate, but a mere pawn in a political game. Many suspected that Bellomont, or perhaps someone else high up in the government, kept the French pass from Kidd to ensure a guilty verdict. And in 1911, while searching through the Public Record Office in London, a writer named Ralph Paine found the proof: there, for all to see, was the French pass that Kidd had seized from the *Quedah Merchant*. Apparently it had sat in the Public Record Office for the two centuries since Kidd's trial.

The pass convinced Paine that Kidd was an innocent man. True, Kidd had not followed the legal steps for declaring the *Quedah Merchant* a legitimate prize, but that was because his crew had mutinied—and absconded with much of the booty. True, too, the *Adventure Galley* had gone on to capture other ships that clearly weren't French, but that was also the work of the mutinous crew and not the captain. And true, Kidd had struck William Moore, but only because he was one of the mutineers. Besides, Paine argued, in an age when captains routinely flogged sailors for trifling misdemeanors, Kidd's blow was downright restrained.

Captain Kidd, in Paine's view, had been "unfairly dealt with by his patrons, misused by his rascally crew, and slandered by credulous posterity."

crxo

More recently, historians have generally taken a more balanced view of Kidd, portraying him as neither the barbarous pirate of legend nor the entirely innocent victim of unscrupulous politicians. There's no doubt that it was grossly unfair to keep from him the French pass, which would have strengthened his defense against the piracy charge pertaining to the *Quedah Merchant*. But, according to the testimony of various crew members, Kidd had hoisted a French flag on the *Adventure Galley* to trick the *Quedah Merchant*'s captain into showing him the French pass. (It was common for merchant ships to carry papers of various nationalities, in the hope that the right one might turn away a privateer or a pirate.) So, these crew members asserted, Kidd knew perfectly well that the ship wasn't French, even if it did have a French pass.

Moreover, there was the matter of the other, albeit smaller, ships seized after the *Quedah Merchant*. Kidd was charged with—and found guilty of—four other counts of piracy. For each, his defense was the same—his crew had mutinied, and acted without his consent. But there was really no more reason to believe Kidd's version than that of the crew members who testified against him.

Kidd was, the majority of historians now agree, a pirate—though not a particularly successful one. His misfortune, according to his latest biographer, Robert C. Ritchie, was that he crossed the line from privateer to pirate at just the time when the latter was least likely to be tolerated. Partly this was because of the struggle between the Whigs and the Tories in Parliament. But, Ritchie demonstrated, Kidd's bad timing went beyond that.

During the late 1690s, both parties—Whig and Tory—were increasingly determined to eliminate the threat pirates presented to the trade of the British Empire. That's why King William offered to pardon pirates. That's why the Whig ministers commissioned Kidd to capture pirates as well as enemy ships. And that's why Kidd's piracy, though nowhere near the worst of his era, brought down on him the wrath of the British government.

The concerted effort of the British government to put an end to piracy didn't succeed immediately, but Kidd was by no means the only pirate to suffer. Throughout the empire, the Royal Navy cracked down, as did local forces. In 1718, for example, Virginians and Carolinians converged on the lair of Edward Teach, also known as Blackbeard, who died in a fierce struggle. By 1730, the era when pirates freely roamed the seas was over.

And what of Kidd's buried treasure?

Alas, there was even less to this than to the rest of his legend. Kidd, perhaps because he didn't fully trust Bellomont, left eleven bags of gold and silver with John Gardiner of Gardiner's Island, off the coast of Long Island. But Gardiner didn't want to tangle with Bellomont, and after Kidd's arrest he turned all of it over to the governor, who sent it on to England.

Most of Kidd's treasure probably ended up in the hands of his crew, many of whom deserted long before he reached Boston. Mutinous or not, these men had signed up in the hope of getting rich, and it's hard to imagine they walked away empty-handed. And once they had the money in their hands, they were far more likely to spend it than to bury it.

To investigate further

Graham Brooks, ed., *The Trial of Captain Kidd* (Edinburgh: William Hodge, 1930). Transcripts of the trial, with a balanced commentary by Brooks.

Daniel Defoe, *A General History of the Pyrates* (Columbia, S.C.: University of South Carolina Press, 1972). Originally published in 1724, this classic history was originally attributed to a "Captain Charles Johnson." Only in the twentieth century did most (but not all) scholars conclude that it was written by Defoe, the author of *Robinson Crusoe* and *Moll Flanders*.

Ralph Paine, *The Book of Buried Treasure* (New York: Macmillan, 1922). As the title indicates, Paine was more interested in searching for treasure than a French pass, but it was the latter that he discovered.

Willard Bonner, *Pirate Laureate* (New Brunswick, N.J.: Rutgers University Press, 1947). Traces the growth of the Kidd legend, from sailors' ballads to the works of Irving, Cooper, Poe, and Stevenson.

Alexander Winston, *No Man Knows My Grave* (Boston: Houghton Mifflin, 1969). The fine line between privateering and piracy, as exhibited in the lives of Henry Morgan, Woodes Rogers, and William Kidd.

Robert C. Ritchie, *Captain Kidd and the War Against the Pirates* (Cambridge, Mass.: Harvard University Press, 1986). How the British Empire brought an end to the golden age of pirates.

David Cordingly, *Under the Black Flag* (New York: Random House, 1995). An informative and entertaining survey of pirates in fact and faction, based on a 1992 exhibit at the London Maritime Museum.

Chapter 19

Was Mozart Poisoned?

Soon after her husband's death, Constanze Mozart told a remarkable story about the *Requiem,* a Mass for the dead that Mozart was working on just before he died in December 1791.

Earlier that year, Constanze recalled, a mysterious messenger had arrived at the Mozarts' apartment in Vienna. He inquired whether Mozart would be willing to write the *Requiem,* in return for a generous payment. The composer—whose most recent opera, *Don Giovanni,* had flopped and who was therefore desperately in need of cash—quickly agreed. The messenger paid the first half of the money, then left, staying only long enough to warn Mozart that he shouldn't try to find out who'd placed the order for the piece.

Mozart worked on the *Requiem* night and day. He became obsessed with it, fainting several times but unable to stop composing. Constanze described her husband's state of mind to Friedrich Rochlitz, who published a collection of anecdotes about Mozart in 1798. "He always sat quietly and lost in his thoughts," Rochlitz wrote. "Finally he no longer denied it—he thought for certain that he was writing this piece for his own funeral."

Another of Mozart's early biographers, a confidant of Constanze, was Franz Niemetschek. He told the story this way, also in a 1798 work: "Mozart began to speak of death, and declared that he was writing the *Requiem* for himself. Tears came to the

Mozart was convinced that he was writing his famous Requiem—*a Mass for the dead—for his own funeral. Library of Congress.*

eyes of this sensitive man. 'I feel definitely,' he continued, 'that I will not last much longer; I am sure I have been poisoned.'"

Mozart never finished the *Requiem,* though even in its incomplete form it's considered a masterpiece. Constanze's story undoubtedly added to the aura surrounding the work and its composer; here was Mozart, driven to the heights of creativity, and ultimately driven to his death, by forces neither he nor others could fully understand. What could be a more appropriate ending to Mozart's brief (he was only thirty-five) but brilliant life?

It's a very satisfying story. And there was never any doubt it originated with Constanze; Rochlitz and Niemetschek both said they heard it from her, as did Vincent and Mary Novello, who published a similar account in 1828. But obvious questions remained: Who was the mysterious stranger who commissioned the *Requiem?* And who, if anyone, poisoned Mozart?

～

Rumors that Mozart had been murdered surfaced soon after his death, even before the 1798 accounts by Rochlitz and Niemetschek. On New Year's Eve of 1791, a Berlin newspaper reported that "because his body swelled up after death, people even thought he had been poisoned." One of the earliest suspects was Franz Hofdemel, the husband of one of Mozart's pupils. Hofdemel attacked his wife and committed suicide on the day of Mozart's funeral, leading some to speculate that his wife was pregnant with the composer's child. But there was no real evidence connecting Hofdemel with Mozart's death.

A more credible suspect emerged in the 1820s in the person of a former Austrian court composer, Antonio Salieri. Salieri's name appears in a number of entries in Beethoven's "conversation books," which his guests used to communicate with the deaf composer. Beethoven's son, Karl, and another visitor, Anton Schindler, both wrote in the notebooks that Salieri had confessed to poisoning Mozart; others recorded that the rumor he'd done so had spread throughout Vienna.

What was Salieri's motive?

Envy. Salieri, or so the rumor mill had it, recognized Mozart's genius—and hated him for it. It was unbearable for Salieri to watch Mozart surpass him as the leading composer at the Viennese court, especially since Mozart was often crude and arrogant, while Salieri was always courtly and correct. This was a highly compelling idea, at least as a literary conceit. The first to mine it theatrically was Alexander Pushkin in an 1830 play. Most recently, Peter Shaffer's 1980 Broadway hit *Amadeus,* which was later turned into a movie, again presented Salieri as a mediocre but eminently serious musician unable to bear the spectacle of the brilliant but boorish Mozart. Shaffer stops short of portraying Salieri as a poisoner; instead, the court composer merely hastens Mozart's demise through various plots that leave his victim impoverished and despondent.

The problem with the case against Salieri, either as murderer or intriguer, is the same as that against Hofdemel: there's no evidence. The alleged confession mentioned in Beethoven's conversation books was repeated nowhere else; in fact, according to the diary of one Beethoven's pupils, the pianist Ignaz Moscheles,

Salieri explicitly denied poisoning Mozart. True, Moscheles then went on to say that Salieri "had damaged him morally through intrigues, and thereby poisoned many an hour for him." But other than a few other similar, gossipy references, there's no real evidence that Salieri disliked Mozart, let alone murdered him.

∽

The next poisoner to be proposed was not an individual but an organization: the Freemasons.

The Masons made for a suitably sinister suspect, since they were a secret society with all sorts of mysterious rituals that seemed, to nonmembers, to verge on the occult. Mozart joined a small Viennese Masonic lodge in 1784. He was an active member, composing a number of pieces with Masonic themes, including *The Magic Flute,* his last completed work.

It was not until the mid-nineteenth century that scholars recognized the Masonic allusions in *The Magic Flute.* For example, the number 18, which is of great significance in Masonic rituals, also plays an important part in Mozart's opera. At the beginning of Act II there are eighteen priests and eighteen chairs, and the first section of the chorus they sing is eighteen bars long. Moreover, the orchestral introduction to this scene contains eighteen groups of notes.

The original printing of the libretto in 1791 provides more explicit evidence that Mozart and his librettist (and fellow Mason) Emanuel Shikaneder meant the opera as, at least partly, a Masonic allegory. The title page of the libretto includes a five-pointed star, a square and a trowel, and an hourglass—all Masonic symbols.

The first to propose that the Masons poisoned Mozart was G. F. Daumer, in 1861. He argued that Mozart had antagonized his fellow Masons by revealing some of their secrets in *The Magic Flute.* So, Daumer argued, the Masons—or rather, an inner circle of Masons—took their revenge. This theory was picked up by many other nineteenth- and twentieth-century writers.

Like the Hofdemel and Salieri theories, however, the Masonic conspiracy theories had no real evidence behind them. True, most (though not all) scholars accepted that there was a Masonic component in *The Magic Flute*, but there was no reason to believe that the Masons weren't perfectly happy to be associated with the opera and its composer. Indeed, after Mozart's death his lodge held a memorial ceremony, and printed copies of the main speech made in his honor. The conspiracy theorists also have never been able to explain why the Masons would murder Mozart but not Shikaneder, who, as librettist, was at least equally responsible for the opera's allegorical elements.

The conspiracy theory is an unfair slur on the Masons who, though undeniably cultish, also included some of the most respected citizens of Vienna. Indeed, the lodges were a meeting place for much of the city's intellectual elite. Similarly, in America, the Masons counted among their members George Washington, Benjamin Franklin, and Thomas Jefferson, and in France many leading republicans joined.

The republicanism of many Masons was hardly reassuring to Austria's Emperor Leopold II, however. Leopold watched the revolutions abroad with a great deal of worry, and responded by cracking down on the Masons at home. He closed many of their lodges and had his police carefully monitor the rest. It was in response to this pressure, some historians have speculated, that Mozart and Shikaneder decided to produce a Masonic opera. Their hope was that *The Magic Flute* would convince the public, and the conservative government, that there was nothing to fear from the Masons.

If so, they hoped in vain; by the mid-1790s Leopold had outlawed the Masons completely, and their membership and influence dwindled. But, to get back to Mozart, he remained a loyal Mason until his death. And there's every reason to believe that his fellow Masons remained equally loyal to him.

∽

If Mozart was poisoned, the most likely culprits were probably his doctors, albeit unintentionally.

Constanze reported at least one incident of doctors "bleeding" him, and there may have been others, since the treatment was still common in the late eighteenth century. In Mozart's weakened state, especially if he was suffering from a kidney disease, as many medical historians believe, the treatment may very well have contributed to his death.

Other than the bleeding, medical historians don't have much to go on. Mozart's death certificate listed the cause of death as "heated military fever," a diagnosis that means nothing to doctors today. Mozart's visitors, including Constanze, described his symptoms so diversely and so vaguely that he could have been suffering from any number of ailments, among them bacterial endocarditis, Henoch Schönlein syndrome, leukemia, staphylococcal bronchopneumonia, and cerebral hemorrhage.

At a medical symposium held in 1991, on the two-hundredth anniversary of Mozart's death, the top two candidates were clearly kidney failure and rheumatic fever, but there was no clear consensus among the experts—except that none of them believed he was poisoned.

As for Mozart's own belief to the contrary, that could easily have been the result of delirium or depression brought on by just about any of the illnesses that led to his death. No doubt, too, the visit of the mysterious messenger who commissioned the *Requiem* would have focused his mind on death, his own in particular. It's easy to imagine the weakened composer turning the mysterious messenger into a messenger of death. Indeed, Shaffer suggested that Salieri, knowing that Mozart was preoccupied with death, disguised himself as the messenger to drive his rival over the edge.

The truth about the messenger, which was finally revealed 173 years after Mozart's death, was less diabolical but no less strange. In 1964, Otto Deutsch published a document, discovered in the archives of Wiener Neustadt, a town about thirty miles south of Vienna. Titled the "True and Detailed History of the Requiem by W. A. Mozart, from its inception in the year 1791 to the present period of 1839," it was written by Anton Herzog, a musician employed by a Count von Walsegg, a major landowner in the region.

The count, Herzog explained, was a passionate music lover who liked to buy the works of promising composers and pass them off as his own. In February 1791 the count's young wife died, and he decided he wanted to commemorate her death with an especially majestic *Requiem*. So he sent a servant to Mozart, with his usual generous offer and his equally standard admonition not to try to find out who'd commissioned the work.

Herzog and his fellow musicians humored their boss. "That the count wanted to mystify us, as he had done with the [other pieces he'd commissioned], was well known to all of us," he recalled. "In our presence he always said it was his composition, but when he said that he smiled."

So Mozart's final masterpiece, it turned out, was written not for some ghostly harbinger of death, but for an eccentric plagiarist. Constanze, no fool, may have circulated the story of the unknown messenger in the hope that it would add to her dead husband's rapidly growing reputation—not to mention the rapidly growing value of his compositions. If so, she succeeded beyond her dreams, for the *Requiem* came to be seen as one of Mozart's masterpieces. And so it remains, regardless of how it came to be written.

To investigate further

Otto E. Deutsch, *Mozart: A Documentary Biography,* trans. from the German by Eric Blom, Peter Branscombe, and Jeremy Noble (Stanford, Calif.: Stanford University Press, 1965). An extensive selection of primary sources.

Paul Nettl, *Mozart and Masonry* (New York: Da Capo Press, 1970). Originally published in 1957, this remains the most comprehensive treatment of the subject.

Wolfgang Hildesheimer, *Mozart,* trans. from the German by Marion Faber (New York: Farrar, Straus, & Giroux, 1982). Originally published in Germany in 1977, this is more an extended essay than a traditional biography. The portrait of Mozart as a frivolous boor, albeit a brilliant one, may have partly inspired Shaffer's *Amadeus.*

Peter Shaffer, *Amadeus* (New York: Harper & Row, 1980). A flop with historians, but a hit with theater- and moviegoers.

H. C. Robbins Landon, *1791: Mozart's Last Year* (New York: Schirmer Books, 1988). A lively chronicle of the year that portrays Mozart, partly in response to the Hildesheimer/Shaffer image, as a responsible husband and citizen.

Gernot Gruber, *Mozart and Posterity,* trans. from the German by R. S. Furness (Boston: Northeastern University Press, 1991). How Mozart has been interpreted, from the eighteenth century through the twentieth.

William Stafford, *The Mozart Myths* (Stanford, Calif.: Stanford University Press, 1991). Debunks the myth of foul play, as well as various other myths about Mozart—such as that he was a social reformer or a nationalist.

Dalhousie Review (Summer 1993). Most of the issue's contents are devoted to papers given at a 1991 symposium titled "Medicine in the Age of Mozart."

Maynard Solomon, *Mozart* (New York: HarperCollins, 1995). A psychoanalytically influenced biography that focuses, quite persuasively, on Mozart's relationship with his father.

Chapter 20

Why Did Freud Abandon His Seduction Theory?

I must mention an error into which I fell for a while," Freud wrote in his 1925 autobiography, "and which might well have had fatal consequences for the whole of my work."

Freud's "slip" was his "seduction theory," in which he passionately believed during the early 1890s. The theory's name was misleading, for it had to do not with seduction but with child abuse. Freud formulated the seduction theory while treating eighteen patients exhibiting a range of nervous disorders. Each of these patients, Freud learned, had been sexually molested as a child.

Freud was tremendously excited, for he thought he'd identified the roots of a great many patients' symptoms. In a paper presented to the Viennese Society for Psychiatry and Neurology in April 1896, Freud compared his findings to the discovery of the source of the Nile. Privately, he wrote to his friend and fellow doctor Wilhelm Fliess that he expected his seduction theory to bring him both fame and fortune.

Yet in September 1897, Freud dramatically reversed himself. "I want to confide in you immediately the great secret that has been slowly dawning on me in the last few months," he wrote, again in a letter to Fliess. "I no longer believe in my [seduction] theory." One problem with the theory, Freud admitted, was that the revelations of child abuse hadn't led to a successful treatment of any of his patients. They continued to suffer from the same symptoms. But the theory's biggest flaw was that these symptoms were so common. If everyone who suffered from them had been abused as a child, that would mean—Freud now realized—that child abuse was rampant throughout Viennese society. In fact, since Freud himself shared many of his patients' symptoms, he must also have been abused as a child, if the seduction theory were correct.

Faced with these implications, Freud abandoned the seduction theory. But he continued to believe that there was something to the stories his patients had told him. In 1905, in his *Three Essays on Sexuality,* Freud announced a new and even more revolutionary theory. His patients had not actually been abused, Freud now asserted. Rather, what they had repressed and were continuing to repress were their childhood fantasies. The patients had not had sex, but they had *desired* sex. More specifically, the patients, as children, had wanted (if they were girls) to sleep with their fathers and (if they were boys) their mothers.

Thus was born the "Oedipus complex." With it came the concepts of infantile sexuality and the unconscious mind, the two pillars of Freud's new science of psychoanalysis. And all this came about, according to Freud, because he had to drop his once-beloved seduction theory.

Freud's disciple and biographer Ernest Jones concurred that this was the crucial turning point in Freud's thinking, and other intellectual historians followed suit. By the 1950s and 1960s Freud was enshrined among the greatest thinkers of all time, and his abandonment of the seduction theory was the prime example of his intellectual courage and honesty.

In the 1970s, however, the consensus view of Freud fell apart. Feminists, offended by some of his misogynistic ideas (e.g., that the driving force in women's behavior was penis envy), led the charge. Other scholars followed with criticism ranging from Freud's use of cocaine to the ineffectiveness of psychoanalysis. But most traumatic of all, for Freud's followers, were a series of works that drastically revised Freud's account of his great breakthrough. The Oedipus complex, according to these revisionists, did not rise from the ruins of the seduction theory. That story was a lie. Even worse, his critics asserted, was Freud's reason for lying. He lied so that no one would ever learn his true—and truly scandalous—reason for abandoning the seduction theory.

To the dismay of orthodox Freudians, one of the most vociferous critics came from within their own ranks. This was Jeffrey Masson, a young American psychoanalyst who, until 1980, was the heir apparent to the director of the Freud Archives at the Library of Congress.

It was at that point that Masson began looking through Freud's letters to his friend Fliess. A selection, edited by Freud's daughter Anna, had been published in 1950, but Masson's inspection of the archives revealed that many of Freud's letters to Fliess had been omitted. On closer examination it was clear that the missing material had to do with Freud's thoughts on the seduction theory. These letters demonstrated, Masson recognized, that Freud hadn't abandoned the theory as quickly or as certainly as he later indicated; on the contrary, he continued for months and perhaps years to hold out some hope that he could prove it correct.

Masson asked Anna Freud why she'd deleted this material, and she said she didn't want to confuse readers by exposing her father's doubts. To Masson these doubts were of historic import. The letters showed not only that Freud continued to believe his patients had told him the truth about being abused, but also that the seduction theory was, indeed, correct. Freud's patients had been abused, Masson believed.

Why, then, had Freud walked away from his own findings? According to Masson, Freud's male colleagues were scandalized by the theory and its implied allegations of widespread abuse. So Freud, desperate for their approval, backed down. "With the greatest reluctance," Masson wrote in his 1984 book, "I gradually came to see Freud's abandonment of the seduction hypothesis as a failure of courage."

Masson found additional evidence for his position in Freud's letters to Fliess about a patient named Emma Eckstein. Eckstein

suffered from painful or irregular menstruation. Freud referred
her to Fliess, who decided she needed an operation on her nose.
In retrospect it's clear that Fliess, who believed that the nose was
the body's dominant organ and that it was the source of Eckstein's menstrual problems, was a quack. To make matters worse,
Fliess bungled the operation by leaving gauze in the wound. Eckstein suffered a massive hemorrhage, and she continued to bleed
long after Fliess was done with her.

Freud's report on Eckstein, in a letter he wrote to Fliess after
the operation, described the continuing bleeding as psychoso-
matic. It was the result, he added, of Eckstein's sexual desire for
Freud. This was a patently absurd diagnosis, almost a parody of
the Freudian concepts of repressed sexuality and transference. To
Masson such a ridiculous diagnosis also demonstrated how far
Freud would go to curry favor with a colleague, and how quick
he was to attribute a patient's symptoms to fantasies rather than
to an actual traumatic event. The analogy to the seduction theory
was clear: Freud was unable to confront Fliess with the uncomfortable truths that his nasal theory was wrong and that he'd
botched the operation, just as he was unable to confront his Viennese colleagues with the equally uncomfortable truths that child
abuse was rampant and the seduction theory was correct.

Masson's book generated a tremendous amount of contro-
versy. The *New York Times* called it "a Watergate of the psyche,"
and it was embraced by many feminists and others who believed
that the abuse of children, especially girls, had been underestimated and ignored for too long. Masson, who was fired from
his job at the Freud Archives, became a hero to the antiabuse
movement.

The scholarly response, however, was generally unfavorable—
and not just from orthodox Freudians. Even many who were disillusioned with Freud or psychoanalysis were generally uncon-
vinced by Masson's arguments. The Eckstein case, they argued,
was an analogy, not proof. Just because Freud had been overly def-
erential, perhaps even cowardly in his relationship with Fliess, that
didn't mean that Freud had acted that way in other situations.

In fact, many scholars pointed out, the abandonment of the
seduction theory was an act of considerable courage, for the idea

Freud (left) with his close friend and onetime mentor Wilhelm Fliess, a quack who believed he could solve most of a patient's problems by nose operations. A. W. Freud et al., Sigmund Freud Copyrights.

that replaced seduction—that children fantasized about having sex with their parents—was hardly one likely to ingratiate Freud with the medical establishment. The Oedipus complex was at least as radical an idea as widespread child abuse. Indeed it was more radical, since many physicians recognized that at least some child abuse took place, while no one had thought of Oedipus as anything other than an ancient Greek myth.

On only one point did Masson prevail. The newly released letters to Fliess persuaded most scholars that Freud continued to hope he could salvage the seduction theory well after he renounced it in his September 1897 letter to Fliess. After Masson, it became difficult to argue that the Oedipus complex was a direct consequence of the abandonment of the seduction theory; instead, it was clear that he only gradually dropped one and embraced the other. But as to his reason for dropping the seduction theory, the traditional account, in which Freud came to suspect that his patients had not actually been abused, withstood the challenge from Masson.

☞

If loyal Freudians thought that they could relax, having fended off Masson, they were very much mistaken. A new and more sustained attack was still to come, this time from an assortment of scientists, philosophers, and literary critics. Of these, the literary critic Frederick Crews probably sparked the most debate, partly because his work first appeared in the *New York Review of Books,* long considered a Freudian bastion.

In essays published in 1993 and 1994, Crews agreed with Masson that Freud lied about why he abandoned the seduction theory. Yet unlike Masson, who believed Freud backed away from his patients' stories of abuse because of cowardice, Crews accused Freud of essentially making up those stories in the first place. So eager was Freud to prove his seduction theory, according to Crews, that he encouraged his patients to recall having been abused as children. And the patients, who were none too stable to start with and eager to please their doctor, obliged with descriptions of abuse that, in fact, had never taken place.

To prove his case, Crews delved into Freud's papers from the 1890s. He found repeated admissions that, prior to their analysis, Freud's patients had no idea that they'd supposedly been molested as children. "Only the strongest compulsion of the treatment," Freud wrote in 1896, "can induce them to embark on a reproduction of [the molestation scenes]." It was not that Freud intentionally invented the stories, Crews said, but that he grossly underestimated the extent to which his patients were susceptible to his suggestions.

Gradually, however, Freud realized that the stories of childhood abuse he was hearing weren't true. Perhaps he also realized that was why his therapy wasn't working, or perhaps some of the patients retracted the stories. But by then it was too late: Freud had already presented the seduction theory to his colleagues, and he was too embarrassed to admit that his findings were the result of a fatally flawed form of therapy. Freud was trapped. If he continued to maintain that the abuse stories were true, some of his disillusioned patients might start contradicting him in public. But if he admitted that he'd planted the abuse stories in his patients' minds, he'd be disgraced as a therapist.

And then the wily Freud found the way out of his predicament. He invented a theory that conceded the abuse never took place but that still attributed the stories to the patients, not the therapist. The stories, Freud explained, were the products of the patients' unconscious and repressed desires. And so was conceived, according to Crews, the Oedipus complex.

Crews's version of the origins of psychoanalysis was even more disturbing than Masson's. Masson's coward was replaced by an outright charlatan. Freud, in short, was a fraud. And, Crews stressed, patients and others continued to suffer as a result.

A particular concern of Crews was the rise, during the 1980s and 1990s, of what became known as "recovered memory" therapies. Many psychologists, seizing on the Freudian concept of repressed sexual memories, encouraged adults to recall childhood abuse, and this led to the prosecution of many alleged abusers. Critics of the therapies, Crews among them, believed that much of this abuse had not occurred and that the recovered memories were, like the stories of Freud's patients, the products of a therapist's suggestion.

To Freud's defenders, this attack seemed ironic as well as unfair. On the one hand, they'd finally disposed of Masson, who accused Freud of deserting the victims of childhood abuse. Then along came Crews, who blamed Freud's ideas for encouraging patients to "recall" abuse that didn't take place. How could Freud be responsible both for letting abusers get away with it and for accusing innocent people of abuse? Some exasperated Freudians suggested that the two attacks ought to cancel each other out.

Alas, for Freudians the critics were not so easily dismissed. The various attacks on Freud damaged both the prestige and the business of psychoanalysis. True, the decline in the number of pyschoanalytic patients had a lot to do with new drug therapies; Prozac was quicker and cheaper than analysis. But the attacks on the intellectual underpinnings of psychoanalysis also took their toll. If Freud couldn't be trusted to tell the truth about the origins of psychoanalysis, how could patients be expected to trust their emotional well-being to his successors?

Still, though his most ardent critics would deny this, Freud's status as one of the most important thinkers of all time remains secure. The critics have succeeded in proving that Freud's version of his major breakthrough was inaccurate; his abandonment of the seduction theory was neither as immediate nor as complete as he claimed. But most intellectual historians have been reluctant to attribute to Freud motives as base as those presumed by Masson or Crews. Equally possible, in the view of some scholars, is that Freud oversimplified—and yes, misrepresented the truth—for the sake of a dramatic narrative.

Moreover, regardless of the origins of Freud's ideas, regardless even of what good or bad they've wrought, their continued influence on science, philosophy, art, and literature—and on the way we think about ourselves—is undeniable. Like it or not, after Freud, no one had to read Sophocles to know something about Oedipus.

To investigate further

Sigmund Freud, *The Standard Edition of the Complete Psychological Works of Sigmund Freud,* trans. under the general editorship of James Strachey in collaboration with Anna Freud (London: Hogarth Press, 1953–1974). Of these twenty-four volumes, the most relevant are volume 7 (*Three Essays on the Theory of Sexuality,* published in 1905 and including the first public retraction of the seduction theory) and volume 20 (*An Autobiographical Study,* published in 1925 and with a subtly different recollection).

Jeffrey Masson, ed., *The Complete Letters of Sigmund Freud to Wilhelm Fliess,* trans. from the German by Masson (Cambridge, Mass.: Belknap Press, 1985). The unexpurgated version and, regardless of whether you find Masson's interpretation persuasive, a revealing look at Freud's thoughts in the making.

Ernest Jones, *The Life and Work of Sigmund Freud* (New York: Basic Books, 1953–1957), three volumes. Jones, himself an important figure in the history of psychoanalysis, wrote what remains the most comprehensive biography.

Jeffrey Masson, *The Assault on Truth* (New York: Farrar, Straus, & Giroux, 1984). Some sense of the Freudians' reception to Masson can be gauged from Janet Malcolm's description of him as "a veritable Iago, papered over with charm yet filled with motiveless malignity."

Peter Gay, *Freud* (New York: W. W. Norton, 1988). An authoritative biography that, though it fails to directly address most of the recent Freud critics, reaffirms its subject's intellectual importance and integrity.

Paul Robinson, *Freud and His Critics* (Berkeley, Calif.: University of California Press, 1993). A vigorous defense of Freud.

Frederick Crews, *The Memory Wars* (New York: A *New York Review* Book, 1995). Includes not just Crews's lively essays but also many of the equally interesting responses that also appeared in the *New York Review of Books*.

Frederick Crews, ed., *Unauthorized Freud* (New York: Viking, 1998). A collection of essays by many of the leading anti-Freudians, including the literary critics Mikkel Borch-Jacobsen and Stanley Fish, the philosophers Frank Cioffi and Adolf Grunbaum, the psychoanalyst Rosemarie Sand, the biologist Frank Sulloway, the psychologist Malcolm Macmillan, and the mathematician Allen Esterson. The range of contributors shows from how many different sides Freud is under attack.

Chapter 21

Could the *Titanic* Have Been Saved?

The small ocean liner *Carpathia*, with Captain Arthur Rostron at the helm, steamed into New York Harbor on the night of April 18, 1912. It was greeted by the mayor's tugboat and a fleet of other boats, all sounding their bells and whistles and sirens. More than forty thousand people waited on the dock, including a swarm of reporters who immediately surrounded the passengers as they walked down the gangway.

These passengers were the survivors of the *Titanic*, the unsinkable ship that a few days before had, unthinkably, sunk.

The *Carpathia* had first heard the *Titanic*'s SOS just after midnight of April 14. Rostron instantly changed course to rescue the giant ship. Though he had to plot his way through the same ice field that had ripped apart the *Titanic*, Rostron pushed the *Carpathia* up to seventeen knots, faster than his ship had ever gone before.

Four hours later, the *Carpathia* reached the site of the *Titanic*'s last radioed position. They were about about an hour and a half too late: the *Titanic*, with 1,502 passengers and crew members still on board, had sunk. Rostron spent the next four hours searching for survivors. By 8:00 A.M. he'd picked up the 705 people who'd made it into the *Titanic*'s lifeboats.

It was at that point that Captain Stanley Lord's ship, the *Californian,* arrived on the scene. Rostron, understandably eager to get the survivors to New York, left it to Lord to make a final search and headed off. Lord found no other survivors, and reset his original course. Nine hours after the Carpathia docked in New York, the *Californian* quietly slipped into Boston.

Lord wouldn't avoid the limelight for long. In a few days, the world's attention would shift from the *Carpathia* to the *Californian.* A number of Boston newspapers reported, after talking to members of the *Californian's* crew, that the ship had been much closer to the sinking *Titanic* than the *Carpathia* had been; indeed, at about 11:00 P.M. on the night of April 14, Lord and his crew had actually seen a ship just a few miles to the southeast. Not long after, some of those aboard the *Titanic* had spotted a ship to the northwest.

Then, soon after midnight (and also soon after the *Titanic* had hit the fatal iceberg), officers of the *Californian* had seen what appeared to be a rocket go off over the other ship. Over the next couple of hours, as the *Titanic* fired its distress signals, the *Californian's* officers and crew members watched seven more rockets burst in the sky.

And yet Lord did nothing. The *Californian* would go down in history—in the words of historian Leslie Reade—as "the ship that stood still." Not until sometime after 5:00 A.M. did Lord set a course toward the *Titanic's* final position.

Ever since, historians have wondered: Could the *Californian* have saved those aboard the *Titanic?* And if so, why did Lord do nothing?

స్రా

Among those who greeted the *Carpathia* in New York was Senator William Alden Smith of Michigan, who wasted no time in forming a subcommittee to investigate the disaster. On April 19, the day after the *Carpathia* docked, Smith was already interviewing survivors at the Waldorf-Astoria. Once the reports surfaced in Boston that the *Californian* had seen the sinking ship's distress signals, Smith subpoenaed Lord and his crew.

The Titanic *on its first (and last) voyage. Library of Congress.*

The *Californian,* according to the testimony of its captain and crew, was en route from London to Boston when, on the night of April 14, it found itself in the same ice-laden section of the North Atlantic as the *Titanic.* Unlike the *Titanic*'s Captain Edward Smith, who doomed his ship by speeding ahead in spite of the ice, the *Californian*'s captain was a very cautious man. Lord ordered the ship stopped for the night.

At about 11:00 P.M., the *Californian*'s wireless operator, Cyril Evans, tapped out a rather informal message to the *Titanic,* which he knew was somewhere in the area: "Say, old man, we are surrounded by ice and stopped."

The *Titanic*'s operator, Jack Phillips, was annoyed by the interruption. He'd been busy all day sending messages for the ship's wealthy passengers, and had no time to chat. "Shut up! Shut up! You are jamming me!" he responded.

Evans, who'd been up all day and who was perhaps a bit put off by the unfriendly response, turned off his set and went to bed. Since the *Californian* had only one wireless operator, it was at this point essentially out of radio contact. When the *Titanic* started sending out its SOS, at about 12:15 A.M., there was no one who could have heard it awake on the *Californian*.

But what of the rockets? Why hadn't the *Californian* responded to the *Titanic's* distress signals?

Lord testified that he'd seen only one rocket go off, then went to bed himself. When his officers later informed him that they had seen other rockets, he was half asleep, so he didn't realize they could be distress signals. And since his officers didn't press the point, he slept on.

Besides, Lord told the senators, he still wasn't so sure they were distress signals. Ships routinely used various sorts of flares to greet passing ships. Distress signals were usually bigger and noisier, and no one on the *Californian* had heard anything during the night. Lord had no idea why some ship was sending up rockets that night, but he had no reason to believe, at least back then, that the ship was in trouble.

In fact, Lord continued, he was certain that the ship he and his officers saw was *not* the *Titanic*. They knew the *Titanic* was in the area, of course, since Evans had been in touch with it by radio. But the ship Lord spotted was far too small, and his officers had seen it steam off—in perfectly good shape—at about 2:00 A.M. That's why it hadn't even occurred to anyone on the *Californian* to wake up Evans and check for an SOS. It was only at about 4:00 A.M. that Lord's officers, perhaps feeling somewhat uneasy about the rockets, woke Evans, who then learned from other ships that the *Titanic* had hit an iceberg. Once Lord was informed, he immediately ordered the *Californian* into action.

Lord's explanation didn't satisfy Senator Smith. He asked the U.S. Navy to check if there was another ship in the vicinity of the *Californian* and the *Titanic* that night, and the navy said it didn't know of any. Smith checked the *Californian's* log from that night and found there was no reference to any rockets—in spite of the testimony of Lord and his officers. Even more suspicious, the April 15 entry in the scrap log, sort of a rough draft of the official log, was missing. To Smith it looked like Lord, anticipating an inquiry into the *Californian*'s actions, had attempted to cover up its inexcusable inaction.

Smith concluded that the mystery ship described by Lord and his officers never existed. "That ice floe held but two ships—the *Titanic* and the *Californian*," he announced.

The Senate subcommittee report harshly condemned Lord: "The committee is forced to the inevitable conclusion that the *Californian* . . . was nearer the *Titanic* than the nineteen miles reported by her captain, and that her officers and crew saw the distress signals of the *Titanic* and failed to respond to them in accordance with the dictates of humanity, international usage, and the requirements of law."

A British Board of Trade hearing that followed later in the month was equally damning. "When she first saw the rockets, the *Californian* could have pushed through the ice to the open water without any serious risk and so have come to the assistance of the *Titanic*," concluded Lord Charles Mersey. "Had she done so she might have saved many if not all of the lives that were lost."

⁂

Lord did not take any of this sitting down, and he found plenty of supporters. Many other seamen, especially, were convinced that the shipping establishment had decided to make Lord a scapegoat, in the hope that it would distract attention from the gross negligence of the White Star Line, which owned the *Titanic,* and the British Board of Trade, which was responsible for safety on the seas.

There was no denying that both organizations had plenty to answer for.

For starters, there was the fact that Captain Smith had ordered the *Titanic* to maintain its speed of twenty-two knots, the fastest it had ever gone, in spite of having received eight messages from other ships (including the *Californian*) about the ice in the vicinity. It may have seemed somewhat ungracious to criticize Smith— who did, after all, heroically go down with his ship—but to many it seemed that Captain Lord was taking a lot of the blame for Captain Smith's mistake.

Worst, there was the lingering suspicion that Smith's reckless speed had been a result of pressure, if not a direct order, from Bruce Ismay, the White Star Line's managing director and a passenger on the *Titanic's* first (and last) voyage. It was not only Lord's defenders who wondered whether Ismay, in his eagerness to prove that the *Titanic* was not only the largest and most luxurious liner but also the fastest, had urged Smith to speed ahead. There were even reports that Ismay had pocketed one of the warnings about ice, so that Smith wouldn't slow down.

That Ismay survived the wreck was itself an embarrassment, for this was an age that still took very seriously the idea of "women and children first." Since more than 150 women and children died on the *Titanic* (along with more than 1,300 men), many felt that Ismay, like Smith, should have gone down with the ship, or at least shouldn't have gotten on a lifeboat until he made sure there were no more women or children on the *Titanic.* But at least Ismay had a chance to deny the charges that he'd in any way influenced Smith's decisions, and neither the Senate nor the Board of Trade hearing found him guilty of anything other than being one of the lucky survivors.

If the company got off easy, in the view of Lord's supporters, the Board of Trade was even more fortunate. The Board of Trade determined how many lifeboats a ship needed by a formula based on a ship's weight; the *Titanic's* owners had exceeded the board's requirements by putting on board 14 regular lifeboats and 4 collapsible ones. Those 18 boats could fit a total of 1,178 people. Yet the *Titanic* itself could hold more than 3,500, and there were more than 2,100 aboard on its maiden voyage.

Whatever else or whoever else was to blame, then, it was clear that the board's grossly outdated regulations also were responsible. Moreover, the agency's mandate was to further the interests of British shipping, and the White Star Line was among its most powerful constituents. So it was no wonder that Lord's supporters were outraged that this was the agency empowered to pass judgment over the captain of the *Californian.*

But in fairness to both the the Board of Trade and to Senator Smith's subcommittee, neither the British nor the American hearings were the whitewash that Lord's supporters claimed they

were. Both hearings examined the failings of Smith, the White
Star Line, and the regulations, and though these were not high-
lighted quite so boldly as Captain Lord's, neither were they covered up. Indeed, both the U.S. and British governments quickly
passed new legislation requiring ships to carry enough lifeboats
to hold all their passengers and crew members. Similarly, the
Titanic tragedy—in particular, the image of Cyril Evans asleep in
his bunk while the *Titanic* sank nearby—also convinced both governments to require twenty-four-hour radio watches.

These changes were undoubtedly good for shipping safety,
but they did nothing for Stanley Lord. Fired by the *Californian*'s
owners, he continued to maintain that the ship seen from the *Californian* was not the *Titanic* and that the ship seen from the *Titanic*
was not the *Californian*.

∽

Lord died in 1962, the same year that his most loyal defender,
Leslie Harrison, identified what he believed was the mystery ship
that had been seen from both the *Titanic* and the *Californian* that
night.

Harrison was the general secretary of the Mercantile Marine
Service Association, which represented ship captains and champi-
oned Lord's cause. The mystery ship, according to Harrison, was
an Icelandic fishing vessel called the *Samson*. As proof, Harrison
presented what was allegedly an old journal in which one of the
Samson's crew members admitted that the *Samson* had been
between the *Titanic* and the *Californian*. The *Samson*, which had
been illegally hunting seals, feared that either the *Titanic* or the
Californian might catch it with the goods, so it sped away from
both as quickly as possible.

Harrison's case fell apart, however, when other investigators
placed the *Samson* in Iceland on both April 6 and April 20. For
such a small boat to have made a three-thousand-mile journey
almost across the Atlantic and back in just fourteen days was
impossible.

Lord's defenders thought they'd finally gotten a break in 1985,
when a joint American and French effort, led by oceanographer
Robert Ballard, located the wreck of the *Titanic*. The ship, it

turned out, was farther east than its final SOS coordinates. That put the *Titanic* about twenty-one miles away from the *Californian's* logged position that night—apparently too far away for Lord or any of his officers to have seen it. But, Ballard pointed out, if the *Titanic* had drifted east of where its officers thought it was, the *Californian* probably did the same, putting the two back in each other's view.

The discovery of the *Titanic*, along with Harrison's determined lobbying, finally prompted the British Department of Transport to reopen the case. The department's report, released in 1992, offered Lord a partial vindication. It concluded that the *Californian* was probably seventeen to twenty miles from the *Titanic*, too far to have seen the sinking ship and probably too far to have reached it in time, even if Lord had started up immediately after the first rocket was spotted.

It took Lord more than two hours to reach the *Carpathia* on the morning of April 15, and there's every reason to assume it would have taken even longer to maneuver through the ice in the darkness. And two hours after the first rocket had gone off, the *Titanic* had already sunk. So, the report said, Lord could not have saved anyone aboard.

Still, the report also made clear that Lord's inaction was inexcusable. Even if he couldn't have saved the *Titanic*, he certainly ought to have tried. And even if he hadn't seen the *Titanic*, he had seen one rocket, and his officers had seen seven others. An experienced seaman could not have mistaken these for anything other than distress signals, yet neither Lord nor his officers bothered to wake up their wireless operator to check out what was wrong.

Most recent historians of the *Titanic* have agreed with the 1992 report. The rockets seen from the *Californian* most probably came from the *Titanic;* there's no evidence that any other ship was nearby. But even if they didn't come from the *Titanic*, they came from some ship that was in need of help—and Lord's response was to go to bed. There were many reasons why Lord may have stayed in bed. Perhaps he was a coward. Or perhaps he was such a martinet that his officers were afraid to bother him when they sighted additional rockets. Or perhaps he didn't feel he should have to put his ship at risk just because someone else was more foolhardy than he about speeding through the ice.

Whatever Lord's reason, it wasn't good enough.

To investigate further

Tom Kuntz, ed., *The Titanic Disaster Hearings* (New York: Pocket Books, 1998). Transcripts of the 1912 Senate hearings.

Walter Lord, *A Night to Remember* (New York: Holt, Rinehart, & Winston, 1955). A real page-turner about the disaster by a popular historian who was no relation and in fact one of the harshest critics of Captain Lord.

Leslie Harrison, *A Titanic Myth* (London: William Kimber, 1986). The case for Captain Lord.

Walter Lord, *The Night Lives On* (New York: William Morrow, 1986). Lord revisits the sinking, in the light of new evidence and theories that emerged after *A Night to Remember*.

Robert Ballard, *The Discovery of the Titanic* (New York: Warner Books, 1987). A firsthand account of the twelve-year search for the sunken liner, with stunning and eerie photos by the divers.

Michael Davie, *Titanic: The Death and Life of a Legend* (New York: Alfred A. Knopf, 1987). A journalist's thorough investigation into the many things that went wrong, from the shortage of lifeboats to the lack of binoculars for the lookouts.

Don Lynch, *Titanic* (New York: Hyperion, 1992). Illustrated with haunting paintings by Ken Marshall as well as hundreds of photographs that evoke the ship's Edwardian splendor.

Leslie Reade, *The Ship That Stood Still* (New York: W. W. Norton, 1993). The case against Captain Lord.

Robin Gardiner and Dan van der Vat, *The Riddle of the Titanic* (London: Weidenfeld & Nicolson, 1995). The central mystery of the *Titanic* saga, according to Gardiner and van der Vat, is why Captain Smith, who knew there was ice ahead, continued at high speed. The book pursues a conspiracy theory that the White Star Line hoped to sink the ship (which was actually not the *Titanic* but her sister and near twin, the *Olympic*) as part of an insurance scam. After tantalizing readers with the evidence supporting the theory, Gardiner and van der Vat ultimately (and reasonably) reject it as highly improbable.

Daniel Butler, *"Unsinkable"* (Mechanicsburg, Pa.: Stackpole Books, 1998). A straightforward retelling of the *Titanic*'s story that strips away many myths, not just about the *Californian* but also about how and why the ship sank, and how various individuals and classes behaved that night.

Chapter 22

Did Any of the Romanovs Survive?

The three-hundred-year-old Romanov dynasty came to a bloody end in July 1918.

Conditions had steadily deteriorated for the family since March 1917, when Czar Nicholas II reluctantly abdicated, leaving the government in the hands of Alexander Kerensky's moderate "Whites." Many of the Whites—in contrast to the Bolshevik "Reds"—favored a constitutional monarchy, and their treatment of the former czar and his family was accordingly polite, albeit wary. The Romanovs were confined to their palace near St. Petersburg, but other than that, life went on much as before the Revolution; the family engaged in a thoroughly royal round of lessons, walks, tennis, and teas. Outside the palace, however, the world had changed. By August, the danger of an angry mob breaking into the palace forced Kerensky to evacuate the family to the Siberian town of Tobolsk.

In November 1917, with the Bolsheviks now in control, the Romanovs' lives took a sharp turn for the worse. Gone were the royal routines and the sympathetic White guards; now the family ate black bread and soup, while hostile Bolshevik guards painted over the windows, helped themselves to the family's possessions, and scrawled obscenities on the walls. In May 1918 the family was moved to the town of Ekaterinburg, and it was there, in the early morning hours of July 18, that they apparently died.

One of the guards, Pavel Medvedev, later described the scene to White investigators. The family was awakened and ordered into the basement of the house. First came Nicholas, carrying his ailing son, the thirteen-year-old Alexei. Next came the ex-czarina, Alexandra, followed by their four daughters, twenty-two-year-old Olga, twenty-one-year-old Tatiana, nineteen-year-old Maria, and seventeen-year-old Anastasia. Also present were the family doctor, cook, maid, and valet. The Bolshevik officer in charge, Yakov Yurovsky, arranged the eleven prisoners against the wall, as if for a family portrait. Then he called in the death squad and informed them that the Ural Executive Committee had decided to execute them. At that point Yurovsky shot the ex-czar, who died instantly.

Each member of the firing squad had been assigned a victim, but the room was so small that they were unable to get into position, and their first shots failed to kill the former czarina or her daughters. Their agony was further prolonged by the rows of diamonds they'd hidden in their corsets; bullets ricocheted off them and around the room. Finally, using their bayonets and rifle butts, the guards finished them off.

The burial of the family was equally chaotic, partly because the guards were more interested in getting hold of the diamonds than in getting rid of the bodies. They dumped them in some nearby mine shafts, then returned the next day to look for a more concealed spot. When their truck got stuck in the mud, they decided to bury the corpses right there.

The official announcement of the ex-czar's death mentioned none of the gory details. On July 20 *Pravda* reported that Nicholas had been executed on the orders of the local Ekaterinburg Soviets. It added, equally tersely, that the rest of the family had been "sent to a safer place."

That last phrase left the world to wonder about the family's fate. There was, after all, only the single eyewitness—and Medvedev's testimony was given to Whites, who had a vested interest in portraying the Bolsheviks as thugs and murderers. Almost instantly, stories spread about one or another family member having escaped, usually with the help of a compassionate guard.

Czar Nicholas and his daughters in their Siberian prison, sometime in early 1918. Beinecke Rare Book and Manuscript Library, Yale University.

Most of the claimants were easily dismissed as impostors, but not all; some even garnered the support of surviving relatives and acquaintances of the imperial family.

Without any bodies to prove they were dead, it seemed impossible to lay the Romanovs to rest.

Amid the many Romanov claimants, one stood out. Known by various names at different points in her life, to her supporters she was always "Anastasia."

She first drew the attention of the world in February 1920, a couple of weeks after attempting to commit suicide by jumping into Berlin's Landwehre Canal. After her rescue, she told a fantastic tale about a Polish soldier carrying her out of the cellar in Ekaterinburg, unconscious but alive. With his help, she managed to cross Russia in a wagon. She reached Romania, then decided to go to Berlin to seek help from her aunt, Princess Irene of Prussia. But she despaired of convincing Irene of her identity and decided to throw herself in the river instead.

An impressive number of Russian exiles accepted her, noting the remarkable resemblance between the woman pulled from the canal and the supposedly dead Anastasia. Among the believers were Nicholas II's first cousin, Grand Duke Andrei, and Anastasia's own cousin, Princess Xenia. In New York, where she took the name Anna Anderson, the claimant was the toast of the town; she was wined and dined by various wealthy socialites eager to be seen with the alleged grand duchess.

But most of the living Romanovs quickly lined up against Anderson. In October 1928 twelve Romanovs and three of Alexandra's relatives signed a joint declaration stating that "the woman now living in the United States . . . is not Grand Duchess Anastasia." Contrary to popular legend, the dowager empress, Anastasia's grandmother, refused to meet her, or even to hear her name mentioned.

In 1938 Anderson took her case to court, in an effort to get her share of what remained of the Romanov estate. The evidence against her was substantial: not only did most of her relatives reject her, but in 1927 a woman named Doris Wingender had identified her as Franziska Schanzkowska, a Polish factory worker who had lived with her until 1920.

For someone claiming a life worthy of a fairy tale, Anderson was a difficult heroine. She was often imperious, antagonizing even her strongest supporters. She refused to speak Russian, further fueling suspicions that she was a fraud. Her supporters offered reasonable explanations: Why shouldn't she be imperious? She was brought up in the imperial family. Why should she speak Russian? This was the language she associated with the traumatic murders of her parents and siblings.

Still, it all made for a weak case. After numerous delays, in 1970 the West German Supreme Court rejected her appeal.

✑

For most historians, the Anna Anderson case was a sideshow; the main events were the investigations within the Soviet Union itself. The first of these was undertaken by the Whites, who re-captured Ekaterinburg just eight days after the executions sup-posedly took place. The White government assigned Nicholas Sokolov, a professional investigator, to find out what happened to the Romanovs.

Sokolov took six years to finish his investigation. By then, of course, the Bolsheviks had recaptured not just Ekaterinburg but also all of Russia, and Sokolov's report had to be published in Paris. The 1924 book proclaimed that the Reds' initial announce-ment was a lie; it was not just the former czar, Sokolov claimed, but also the entire family who were killed on July 18. For starters, there was the testimony of the guard Pavel Medvedev, who claimed not to have participated in the shootings but to have heard the shots and seen the bodies in the basement. Sokolov also pointed to a large collection of jewelry and other Romanov belongings found at the scene of the shooting and the nearby mine shaft. And there was a captured telegram, dated July 17, in which the Ekaterinburg Reds informed Moscow that the "family suffered the same fate as its head."

Two years after Sokolov's report, the Soviets issued their own, written by Pavel Bykov. Remarkably, Bykov agreed with Sokolov; the only significant difference in their accounts was that Sokolov said the bodies had been burned, while Bykov said they were buried. Bykov's report reversed eight years of Soviet denials; the government now conceded that the entire family had died in Ekaterinburg, though Bykov continued to maintain that the decision had come from the local Ekaterinburg Soviet, not Moscow. Bykov himself had been a member of the Ekaterinburg Soviet.

The Sokolov and Bykov reports convinced most of the world that no member of the imperial household survived. If the Whites and the Reds could agree on a common story, most his-torians decided, that alone was a very good reason to believe it. But some remained skeptical, noting that neither Sokolov nor Bykov had found any remains of the bodies themselves.

Among the skeptics were two British journalists, Anthony Summers and Tom Mangold, who tracked down the files on which Sokolov had based his report. They found that Sokolov

had "meticulously included all evidence that supported his premise that the entire family had been massacred . . . but omitted evidence that hinted or stated categorically that something else had
happened." The latter included testimony from local citizens that
the former czarina and her daughters had been spotted in and
around Ekaterinburg *after* July 18.

Summers and Mangold concluded that the original Soviet
announcement—that only the ex-czar had been shot—was in fact
true. In his effort to make the Reds appear brutal and bloodthirsty, Sokolov had dismissed the evidence that some family
members survived. But why would Bykov, writing on behalf of
Lenin and the Soviet leadership, want to cover up the fact that
the Bolsheviks had *not* killed the rest of the family?

The answer, according to Summers and Mangold, had to do
with secret negotiations between the Soviets and the Germans
that took place early in 1918. The Germans wanted to save
Alexandra, who was a cousin of Kaiser Wilhelm. And Lenin was
perfectly willing to use the family as a bargaining chip to extract
concessions from the Germans. He ordered the family removed
from Ekaterinburg, but then the German deal fell apart, and the
family was no longer of any use. At that point the Romanovs
either escaped or were killed; Summers and Mangold weren't
sure which. Either way, the whole thing was an embarrassment
to Lenin, so it was easier for Bykov just to go along with the
Sokolov story of an Ekaterinburg execution. Better that than to
admit that Lenin had used the family members as pawns, then
either killed or lost them.

Most historians rejected the Summers and Mangold thesis.
The evidence of the German negotiations was circumstantial at
best—and some of it indicated that the talks, if they took place
at all, fell through before July. That would have left Lenin plenty
of time to switch gears and allow the executions to proceed at
Ekaterinburg. As for the newly found Sokolov files, many historians pointed out that the investigator may have left out of his
report the reported sightings of family members simply because
he hadn't believed them. A close look at the testimony indicated
that the witnesses *thought* they'd seen some family members, but
they weren't absolutely certain.

Still, Summers and Mangold had given new hope to the romantics who hoped that an heir to the Romanov throne had somehow survived. The only way to extinguish that hope would be to find the victims' bodies, and in the 1970s a well-known Russian filmmaker named Geli Ryabov set out to do just that.

⁓

Ryabov's first big break came in 1978, when he tracked down the eldest son of Yakov Yurovsky, the man who'd been in charge of guarding the Romanovs in Ekaterinburg. To Ryabov's delight, the younger Yurovsky handed him a copy of his father's report on the execution. The report confirmed the Bykov version—in which the bodies were buried, not burned. Better yet, it included a precise description of the burial place: about twelve miles northwest of Ekaterinburg.

Ryabov's second break was teaming up with a local man, Alexander Avdonin, who knew his way around Ekaterinburg and was equally interested in finding the bodies. On May 30, 1979, again to his delight but also to his horror, Ryabov uncovered three skulls and assorted other human bones just where the Yurovsky report said they'd be. But now Ryabov and Avdonin got nervous; this was still pre-*glasnost,* and they were none too sure how the authorities would react to the discovery of the Romanov bones, if indeed that's what these were. Ryabov and Avdonin decided to return the bones to their burial place, and they swore not to tell anyone what they'd found until times had changed.

It was not until ten years later that Ryabov decided the time was right. On April 10, 1989, the weekly *Moscow News* broke the story that the Romanov bones had been found in a swamp near Ekaterinburg. Two years later, Russian troops arrived at the site, dug up the reburied bones, and also found some additional skulls, ribs, vertebrae, leg bones, and arm bones.

Were these the Romanovs? To know for sure, scientists had to compare DNA extracted from the bones to DNA taken from the blood of a living relative of the Romanovs. British scientists turned to, among others, Queen Elizabeth's husband, Prince Philip, who in the intertwined worlds of European royalty also happened to be Alexandra's grandnephew. The prince agreed, and donated his blood. In July 1993, after ten months of work, Peter Gill and Pavel Ivanov announced that the DNA evidence made them 98.5 percent sure that these were the Romanovs' bones. Later tests indicated an even higher degree of certainty.

DNA tests also revealed, once and for all, the identity of Anna Anderson. Anderson had died in 1984, after marrying a wealthy doctor in Charlottesville, Virginia. But Gill was able to obtain a tissue sample that a Charlottesville hospital had routinely preserved, after Anderson was operated on there. Gill compared DNA from the tissue with DNA from the Ekaterinburg bones and found they were unrelated. He then compared Anderson's DNA with a sample from a German farmer named Karl Maucher, who was a grandnephew of the Polish peasant Franziska Schanzkowska. It was a 100 percent match.

Only one mystery remained. The Ekaterinburg graves held parts of nine skeletons, even though the imperial household had consisted of eleven people—the seven family members, the doctor, and the servants. That left two members of the imperial party unaccounted for. One of the missing bodies was clearly Alexei's, since none of the skeletons was that of a thirteen-year-old boy. Scientists disagreed about the other: a Russian team team concluded it was Maria, while a visiting American team insisted it was Anastasia. Either way, it left open the possibility that an heir to the Russian throne survived the massacre at Ekaterinburg.

But even romantics and monarchists (of which there are still plenty in Russia) had to concede that it was a very faint possibility. Yurovsky's report, like Medvedev's, described a scene so bloody that it's highly unlikely that Alexei—or Maria or Anastasia—could have survived. The Yurovsky report also offered an explanation for the missing bodies: in the confusion, the chief jailer recalled, two of the bodies were buried separately from the rest. If they're uncovered, as remains possible, that could remove any lingering doubts.

Meanwhile, in July 1998, the bones of Nicholas, Alexandra, and three of their children were reburied, this time in St. Petersburg, and in a dignified though hardly imperial ceremony. For many historians, the Romanovs' deaths signaled the coming of state terrorism, and the millions of other deaths that would mark Soviet rule. The meaning of the Romanovs' return to St. Petersburg was much less clear.

To investigate further

Mark Steinberg and Vladimir Khrustalev, *The Fall of the Romanovs* (New Haven, Conn.: Yale University Press, 1995). A useful collection of documents including letters between Nicholas and Alexandra, parts of their diaries, minutes of government meetings, and other official papers.

John F. O'Conor, *The Sokolov Investigation* (New York: Robert Speller & Sons, 1971). Includes translations of sections of Sokolov's report, along with a harshly critical commentary.

Anthony Summers and Tom Mangold, *The File on the Tsar* (New York: Harper & Row, 1976). An impressive investigation of the investigator, even though the discovery of the Romanov bones ultimately disproved the Summers-Mangold theory.

Peter Kurth, *Anastasia* (Boston: Little, Brown, 1983). An entertaining albeit overly credulous investigation of Anna Anderson.

Edvard Radzinsky, *The Last Tsar,* trans. from the Russian by Marian Schwartz (New York: Doubleday, 1992). Radzinsky is a prominent Russian playwright, and that's both the book's strength and its weakness. As literature, it's engrossing and evocative; as history, it's frustratingly vague and undocumented.

Marc Ferro, *Nicholas II,* trans. from the French by Brian Pearce (New York: Oxford University Press, 1993). A solid though uninspired biography that's undermined by Ferro's belief that some family members survived.

Robert K. Massie, *The Romanovs* (New York: Random House, 1995). A thrilling historic and scientific detective story that's especially good at describing the DNA evidence and the rivalries among the Russian, British, and American scientists.

Peter Kurth, *Tsar* (Boston: Little, Brown, 1995). A magnificently illustrated portrait of the lost world of Nicholas and Alexandra; even a Marxist historian couldn't help but be moved by the snapshots of the family before and during their imprisonment.

Orlando Figes, *A People's Tragedy* (New York: Viking, 1996). A comprehensive history of the Russian Revolution, from the end of the nineteenth century to the death of Lenin. Figes is scholarly and fair, yet he captures the passions of the period.

Chapter 23

Did Hitler Murder
His Niece?

On the morning of September 19, 1931, a twenty-three-year-old woman, Geli Raubal, was found dead in Adolf Hitler's Munich apartment. Raubal, who was the daughter of Hitler's half-sister, had been shot with his pistol. The gun was found next to the body.

For Hitler, the timing couldn't have been worse. The previous year's elections had increased the number of Nazis in the Reichstag from 12 to 107, bringing the party to the brink of power. A scandal now—especially one, as this shaped up to be, involving sex and murder charges—could quickly push Hitler and the Nazis back to the fringes of German politics.

And, indeed, anti-Nazi newspapers jumped all over the story. Stories soon circulated about how the twenty-three-year-old woman had been Hitler's lover as well as niece. The Munich *Post* reported that Raubal had a broken nose, implying that Hitler had killed her in a fit of rage—possibly because he'd found out she was sleeping with someone other than he, possibly because she'd threatened to tell the public about some of her uncle's unusual sexual practices. Others suggested that Raubal had been driven to suicide, either by Hitler's violent jealousy or his sexual demands.

Questioned by detectives, an apparently shaken Hitler reported that he'd last seen her the day before the body was found.

They'd argued about her plan to take singing lessons in Vienna, and she was angry that he forbade her to go on her own, but then she'd calmed down. So, Hitler continued, he left for a campaign rally in Nuremberg. It was there that he learned of her death. He immediately rushed back to Munich, stopping only for a speeding ticket that he got near the halfway point.

The staff at Hitler's apartment had little to add to Hitler's story. They recalled Raubal rushing out of Hitler's bedroom, visibly upset, but they had no idea what had upset her or what had happened next.

The police found no signs of a broken nose, or any other evidence that Raubal had been assaulted. They ruled the death a suicide. But since there were many Nazi sympathizers high up in the Bavarian Ministry of Justice, many suspected the police had been pressured to cut short their investigation. The household staff, too, could have been pressured by Nazi officials, especially since Party officials were already on the scene when the detectives arrived.

So, at least for historians, the investigation remained open. And their search for evidence that he murdered Raubal has led them into the very dark recesses of Adolf Hitler's mind.

Among those who suspected Hitler of murdering Raubal were some ex-members of his inner circle. The most prominent was Otto Strasser, who published an influential Nazi newspaper and whose brother, Gregor, was the party's deputy führer. Gregor, who later challenged Hitler for the party leadership, was killed in 1934; Otto fled to Switzerland.

In his 1940 book *Hitler and I,* Otto Strasser cited three pieces of evidence for murder: first, a conversation he'd had with a priest who told him that he'd buried Raubal as a Catholic, something he would not have been allowed to do if he believed she committed suicide; second, a conversation with his brother, in which Gregor said that he'd heard directly from Hitler that he'd shot Raubal; and finally, a story (the source of which Strasser didn't give) that Fritz Gerlich, a well known anti-Nazi editor, had been planning to publish a major exposé on the murder in the

Hitler and Eva Braun, who became his mistress after the death of his niece (and according to many reports, his previous lover) Geli Raubal. Copyright Baldwin H. Ward and Kathryn C. Ward/CORBIS.

March 12, 1933, issue of his newspaper. But on March 9, Nazi storm troopers broke into the newspaper's offices, destroyed all the files, and arrested Gerlich. Gerlich, like Gregor Strasser, was killed in 1934. Otto Strasser didn't spell out a motive for the murder, but he implied that it was a result of Hitler's anger about Geli seeing other men.

Ernst Hanfstaengl, once Hitler's foreign press secretary, provided more specifics: Raubal was not only seeing other men, he said, she also was pregnant by one. The prospective father was an art teacher and, worst of all from Hitler's perspective, a Jew. Raubal had met the teacher in 1928, and now she wanted to marry him. For a Jew to take away his niece—his lover—was the ultimate dishonor, personally and politically. So, Hanfstaengl reported, Hitler forced Raubal to commit suicide. How he did so wasn't clear from Hanfstaengl's account, though he implied it had something do with threats about her mother. In any case, Hanfstaengl added, Hitler's family all took this story to be true; he himself had learned it from Brigid Hitler, the wife of Hitler's brother, Alois.

In his 1944 book *Der Führer,* the German historian Karl Heiden argued that it was SS chief Heinrich Himmler, not Hitler, who was responsible for Raubal's death. In fact, Heiden argued, Hitler was in love with Raubal, and wanted to marry her. But Himmler wanted to avoid a scandal, either because he suspected Raubal was sleeping with another man, or because she'd threatened to go public about her uncle's sexual practices. Heiden wasn't sure whether she was murdered or pushed to suicide, but he was confident the Nazis were to blame. His source, he said, was a friend of Raubal's mother.

The problem with all these accounts was that they were based on unsubstantiated rumors, mostly circulated by relatives and former associates of Hitler, who were often less concerned about the truth than with settling grudges and exonerating themselves. These were people whose testimony later historians, quite reasonably, considered suspect. (It should be quickly added, in fairness to Heiden, that unlike either Strasser or Hanfstaengl, he'd always been an enemy of Hitler. But his story, too, came from an unhappy relative.)

Moreover, Hitler's speeding ticket provided him with an alibi. It was not, to be sure, an airtight alibi, given that the police and other witnesses to the ticket may have sympathized with the Nazis or been intimidated by them, but there was no evidence to contradict it either. As for Heiden's accusation that Himmler was responsible, that seemed illogical; if his motive had been to avoid a scandal, he certainly would not have left the body in Hitler's apartment, or left Hitler's gun beside it.

So, though murder couldn't be ruled out, the police's verdict of suicide seemed more likely. But some crucial (and titillating) questions remained: Did Hitler drive his niece to suicide? And what was the nature of their relationship?

∽

There was no doubt, in Heiden's mind, that Hitler's intentions toward Raubal were more than avuncular.

One story Heiden told, without naming his source, concerned a letter Hitler wrote to Raubal; in it he "expressed feelings which could be expected from a man with masochistic-coprophil inclinations, bordering on . . . unidinism." More bluntly, what Heiden meant was that Hitler became sexually excited by having a woman urinate on him. The letter never reached Raubal, instead falling into the hands of a blackmailer. In 1929, according to Heiden, Nazi Party treasurer Franz Schwarz paid off the blackmailer and recovered the letter.

Hanfstaengl told the story of a different blackmail attempt, this one a year later. He recalled running into Schwarz in 1930, just after the treasurer had bought from a blackmailer a folio of pornographic sketches that Hitler had made of Raubal. Hanfstaengl glanced at the drawings, horrified, and suggested Schwarz tear them up. But Schwarz said he couldn't—since Hitler wanted them back.

Heiden wasn't sure that Hitler moved beyond fantasizing about his niece, but Hanfstaengl thought he did. He quoted a conversation—admittedly one he'd only heard thirdhand—in which Raubal told a friend that her uncle was a "monster" and that "you would never believe the things he makes me do." And, as Hanfstaengl pointed out, there was a precedent for incest in the family: Hitler's parents were second cousins, and Hitler's mother, who was twenty-two years younger than his father, called him "Uncle."

Otto Strasser, like Hanfstaengl, had no doubt that the relationship between Hitler and Raubal had been consummated and that it was by no means a normal sexual relationship. In a 1943 interview with agents of the OSS (the wartime predecessor of the CIA), Strasser was explicit about the unidinism. He claimed he'd heard about it directly from Raubal and that she'd found the whole thing "disgusting."

As with the murder allegations, these stories about Hitler's sex life had to be approached with some skepticism. Neither Hanfstaengl nor Strasser was a particularly reliable source, and *their* sources were often unnamed or even less reliable. Nor did Strasser bother to explain why Raubal had supposedly chosen him—at that time a close colleague of the man she supposedly wanted to get away from—as a confidant. So it wasn't surprising that Hitler's most respected biographers of the past two generations—Alan Bullock in 1952 and Ian Kershaw in 1998—both expressed serious doubts about whether Hitler and Raubal ever consummated their relationship, let alone engaged in any sort of unusual sex. The evidence just wasn't sufficient.

Still, unlike the murder accusation, the rumors of an unusual sexual relationship had a certain logic to them. Psychobiographers, especially Freudians, tended to see sexual secrets lurking everywhere, so they were especially inclined to find them in a psychopath such as Hitler. William Langer, a psychiatrist who prepared the 1943 OSS report on Hitler, believed Raubal (and Strasser) were telling the truth about the unidinism. Langer also cited interviews with another woman, the film actress Renate Muller, who reported similarly unpleasant sexual encounters with Hitler in 1932. "From a consideration of all the evidence," Langer wrote, "it would seem that Hitler's perversion is as Geli has described it."

And one could hardly fault the Freudians for considering it significant that, of the seven women who were at various times reported to have had sex with Hitler, six either committed or attempted suicide. (The six include Raubal, on the assumption that she wasn't murdered, as well as Eva Braun, who died with Hitler in 1945.) Whatever Hitler was doing to the women he slept with, it seemed, was making them deeply unhappy.

But, as the less Freudian of Hitler's biographers pointed out, none of that proved that sexual issues were the root of the problem for Hitler, or the women he slept with. One did not have to believe Hitler was a sexual pervert to explain why these women would have committed suicide; he clearly had plenty of other disagreeable traits, to put it very mildly. Indeed, one might very well assume that any woman who chose to get into a relationship with Hitler already had some serious problems.

Raubal, of course, did not choose Hitler. She moved in with her uncle because she and her mother had no place else to go, and that remained the case for as long as she lived. She was trapped in the household of a man who was intensely attracted to her and who was ruthless in his efforts to keep her from seeing anyone else. His refusal to let her go to Vienna was just one of a series of escalating restrictions he'd placed on his niece ever since she first moved in with him in 1929.

One did not have to assume that he was forcing her to have some sort of perverted sex to imagine him treating her cruelly. One did not even have to assume they had any sex at all to believe he drove her to suicide.

This was the conclusion Bullock and Kershaw reached, and a majority of historians have followed their leads. Hitler, in the majority view, probably did not murder Raubal. And (though the consensus on this point is much weaker) he probably didn't have sex with her, or if he did, it probably wasn't the nature of the sex that was the direct cause of her death. But he was a tyrant—a domestic tyrant in 1931, even before he became a national tyrant two years later.

For Geli Raubal, death must have seemed the only escape.

For many, including the ex-Nazi memoirists, Raubal's death was a crucial turning point for Hitler. Hanfstaengl, for example, wrote that "with her death the way was clear for his final development into a demon." Hitler's official photographer, Heinrich Hoffmann, echoed those sentiments. "At this time," he recalled, "the seed of inhumanity began to sprout in Hitler. His appetite for carnage grew monstrously only after Geli's death." This kind of analysis was clearly self-serving; if Hitler became a monster only after her death, then they could be forgiven for having allied themselves with him in his earlier, presumably more reasonable, period.

But it wasn't only the ex-Nazis who believed Raubal's death transformed Hitler. Many of the Freudian biographers, whose motivation was certainly purer than the ex-Nazis, tended to see Raubal's death as a crucial stepping-stone in his development as a murderer. Even if he didn't kill her, they've argued, the loss of the woman with whom he was obsessed somehow unleashed the monster in him. The Freudian influence has been considerable; even Bullock, though he found the evidence for an affair insufficient, believed that Raubal's death changed Hitler and that there was "probably something sexual" to Hitler's anti-Semitism.

For most historians, however, Raubal's death doesn't suffice to explain Hitler's genocidal ambitions. Nor have the various other sexually based explanations—which include a supposedly missing testicle and an encounter Hitler allegedly had with a syphilitic Jewish prostitute—satisfied most historians, especially historians of the Holocaust. Indeed, to trace the death of millions back to a single cause presents moral as well as practical problems that historians and philosophers continue to struggle with.

One thing is clear: Raubal's death, however deeply it affected Hitler, did not turn him into a killer. He already had blood on his hands; in spite of the conveniently selective memories of the ex-Nazi memoirists, Nazi thugs had already murdered and beaten hundreds if not thousands of people prior to September 1931, undoubtedly with Hitler's knowledge and approval. By no means was Geli Raubal's suicide the first death for which Hitler was responsible.

To investigate further

Otto Strasser, *Hitler and I*, trans. from the German by Gwenda David and Eric Mosbacher (Boston: Houghton Mifflin, 1940). Part history, part self-justification— a combination that's undeniably titillating but by no means trustworthy.

Konrad Heiden, *Der Führer*, trans. from the German by Ralph Manheim (New York: Lexington Press, 1944). Full of details that made it an important source for later historians.

Ernst Hanfstaengl, *Hitler* (London: Eyre & Spottiswoode, 1957). Like Strasser's book, an ex-Nazi's apologia/memoir.

Walter Langer, *The Mind of Adolf Hitler* (New York: Basic Books, 1972). The OSS report from 1943—making this, in a way, the official U.S. government position on Adolf Hitler.

Joachim Fest, *Hitler*, trans. from the German by Richard and Clara Winston (New York: Harcourt Brace Jovanovich, 1973). The best German biography of Hitler.

John Toland, *Adolf Hitler* (Garden City, N.Y.: Doubleday, 1976). An anecdotal and very readable biography. As for Raubal, Toland's theory was that it was her jealousy, not Hitler's, that led to her suicide. He came to this conclusion after interviewing a couple of the surviving household staff members. They told him that just prior to her death, Raubal had been very upset because she'd found a letter from Eva Braun to Hitler.

Alan Bullock, *Hitler and Stalin* (New York: HarperCollins, 1991). Bullock's 1952 biography of Hitler remains a classic, even though this more recent dual biography incorporates new research.

Ronald Hayman, *Hitler and Geli* (London: Bloomsbury, 1997). Hayman is the latest to argue that Hitler shot Raubal.

Ian Kershaw, *Hitler* (London: Allen Lane, 1998). The latest and arguably the best biography of Hitler to date.

Ron Rosenbaum, *Explaining Hitler* (New York: Random House, 1998). An entirely fascinating and often brilliant mix of intellectual history and piercing interviews. Rosenbaum reveals the underlying motivations of historians, and in doing so makes an important contribution to our understanding of Hitler. This chapter is heavily indebted to Rosenbaum.

Chapter 24

Why Did Hess Fly to Scotland?

The Battle of Britain is still recalled as the nation's "finest hour," a time of hardship and heroism. On May 10, 1941, Luftwaffe bombs caused massive damage in the heart of London. That same night, a lone German pilot slipped through Britain's coastal defenses and parachuted to the ground, not far from the duke of Hamilton's estate in Lanarkshire, Scotland.

A Scottish farmer found the pilot nursing a wrenched ankle and, armed with a pitchfork, took him into custody. The pilot would say only that he was on a "special mission" and had to see the duke.

The duke arrived at ten the next morning. Speaking in English, the pilot told Hamilton that Hitler wanted to stop the fighting, and that he had flown to England for peace talks with Hamilton and other sympathetic Englishmen. The pilot also identified himself to Hamilton: he was Rudolf Hess, deputy führer of the German Reich.

Predictably, Hess's flight created sensational headlines around the world. Hess was the Nazi Party chief, the virtual coauthor of *Mein Kampf*, a member of Hitler's inner circle. Surprisingly, the official reactions that quickly followed from Berlin and London were pretty much the same: Hess was a madman, though perhaps an idealistic one. He'd acted entirely on his own, without the knowledge or encouragement of Hitler or Churchill or any responsible person in either government.

From the start, there were many who doubted the official line that Hess acted alone. Some believed Hitler sent his old friend and associate to make peace with England, perhaps so he could could turn his armies against Russia instead. Others suspected an even darker secret: that Hess, far from arriving out of the blue, had good reason to believe he'd be met by friends, including some high up in the British government.

಄

If Hitler knew anything about Hess's mission in advance, he didn't show it. Eyewitness accounts from his mountain retreat, where he called top aides to deal with the crisis, described their führer as grief-stricken and the scene as utter confusion. Chief of Staff General Franz Halder wrote in his diary that Hitler "was taken completely by surprise."

Once it was clear Hess was in British hands, Berlin quickly issued a series of press statements regretting Hess's "hallucinations" and assuring the world that they would have no effect on the war.

Hitler ordered the arrest of various Hess associates, including the deputy führer's valet, Karlheinz Pintsch, and his friend and unofficial adviser, Albrecht Haushofer. Haushofer admitted to the Gestapo that he'd discussed with Hess their mutual interest in peace with Britain, and most historians believe he was the one who planted the idea of a peace mission in Hess's head. Haushofer also admitted that he'd talked to Hess about his many British friends—including the duke of Hamilton.

Also arrested were astrologers and fortune-tellers throughout Germany. According to Nazi press reports, Hess's mental disorder may have left him vulnerable to their influence.

It's tough to say how much of this activity was real and how much was a show. Certainly the Nazis were masters of propaganda, and the Hess affair required all their skills. For the Germans to send a peace emissary in the midst of the Battle of Britain, let alone one as high-ranking as Hess, would inevitably be construed as a sign of weakness. So it was clearly crucial that Hitler distance himself from Hess.

Some witnesses, including Pintsch, thought Hitler was acting, and that he knew far more about this mission than he let on. Both Haushofer and Hess's wife, Ilse, said they were under the impression that Hess had discussed the general idea of a peace mission with Hitler, though neither claimed Hitler knew any specifics. Others later recalled a May 5 meeting between Hitler and Hess during which voices were raised, perhaps because Hess was telling Hitler about his plan.

Among those who never bought the official story was Stalin. In spite of his 1939 nonaggression pact with Germany, he didn't trust Hitler. When German forces invaded Russia in June, just a month after Hess's flight, he saw it as proof that he'd been right. Hess, he believed, must have been part of some German-British conspiracy to call off the Battle of Britain and instead jointly destroy the Bolsheviks.

Stalin never relinquished his suspicions. As Churchill recalled in his 1950 history of the war, Stalin confronted him about Hess in 1944, during their meeting in Moscow. Churchill repeated the official version: Hess was a "medical case" whose escapade had nothing to do with the march of events. Annoyed by Stalin's skepticism, Churchill insisted that he'd stated the facts as he knew them and that he expected them to be accepted. Stalin replied, "There are lots of things that happen even here in Russia which our Secret Service do not necessarily tell me about."

The implication was clear: it was not just Germans but also British spies who were involved in the Hess plot.

∽

With the demise of the Soviet Union and the opening of many KGB archives, Western historians could for the first time get a glimpse of the type of intelligence that fueled Stalin's suspicions. In 1991 British historian John Costello published the results of his study of the KGB Hess files. Costello concluded that Stalin had been right all along.

The files included a report from a Soviet agent who described the Hess flight as "not the act of a madman . . . but the realization of a secret conspiracy by the Nazi leadership to strike a peace with Britain before opening the war with the Soviet Union." Another agent began by explicitly saying that "the disseminated story that Hess arrived in England unexpectedly is not correct."

According to the Soviet spies, Hess had long been in correspondence with the duke of Hamilton—though Hamilton didn't know it. Apparently British spies had intercepted Hess's letters to Hamilton. They'd then sent back answers in Hamilton's name, encouraging Hess to come. The whole thing had been a British trick played on the unsuspecting deputy führer.

Costello found similar theories in a U.S. Army Intelligence file from 1941 that was declassified in 1989. The Soviet and American reports were so similar, in fact, that Costello concluded they must both have had the same source. Both, for example, recount the same line from a doctor who examined the German pilot soon after his capture. When the pilot announced he was Rudolf Hess, the doctor wisecracked that the hospital also had a patient who thought he was Solomon.

For Costello, the new evidence exploded the myth of the heroic England bravely holding out against the Nazi onslaught. Instead, the British government was portrayed as deeply ambivalent about the war, with a significant "peace party" actively working to replace Churchill with a prime minister more likely to appease Hitler. Churchill's opponents held out little hope that they could defeat Hitler; with Pearl Harbor still months away and American isolationists strongly opposed to war, the only certainty was that continuing the fight alone would mean the continuing loss of lives and property. To Costello it made no sense that Hess, however fanatical or naive or crazy he may have been, would drop out of the sky without some reason to believe that the duke of Hamilton would be waiting to meet with him.

Others, most notably the British historian Peter Padfield, found convincing the evidence that the British lured Hess to England, but concluded that it was probably a Secret Service operation, not an anti-Churchill plot. Like Stalin, Padfield suspected that the Hess mission was part of a British campaign designed to persuade Hitler to abandon the Battle of Britain and focus his forces on Russia instead. And, Padfield speculated, Hitler, too, had reasons to send his deputy to England. If the peace mission

Stalin, for one, believed that Rudolf Hess's trip to Scotland was not the act of a madman but part of a secret Nazi-British plot to join forces against the Soviet Union. Here is Hess in prison, in 1945. Library of Congress.

failed, Hitler may have reasoned, Stalin would assume that that ensured the Battle of Britain would continue. That would give Hitler the chance to catch the Soviets off guard.

By this theory, Hess was a pawn of both Churchill and Hitler. Churchill hoped to persuade Hitler to go east, while Hitler hoped to persuade Stalin he was going west.

જી

Provocative as their books were, neither Costello nor Padfield succeeded in changing the consensus view of the Hess mission. For one thing, just because Soviet and American spies agreed on something didn't mean it was right. More likely, according to most historians, both drew on the same sources, and those sources were wrong. The full story may emerge in 2017, when all the British government files on Hess will be unsealed.

From the British secret service files already open, though, it's clear that Hess's friend Albrecht Haushofer (though not Hess himself) had been in touch with the duke of Hamilton. Some of Haushofer's letters indicate a close relationship between Haushofer and Hamilton—so close that Costello saw homosexual undertones.

In September 1940 Haushofer wrote to Hamilton, inviting the duke's "friends in high places" to "find significance in the fact that I am able to ask whether you could find time to have a talk." Haushofer, probably with Hess's knowledge, was clearly feeling out the possibility of peace talks.

Yet Haushofer's letter never reached Hamilton. It was intercepted by British intelligence, which held on to it for five months. Why they did so is unclear. Perhaps it was because Churchill had made clear peace talks were out of the question. Or perhaps the Secret Service responded in Hamilton's name, intending to bait Haushofer and instead snaring Hess.

Whatever the bait, it's clear the deputy führer was eager to bite. Hess knew of Hitler's grudging admiration for Britain and of his unmitigated hatred of the Russian Bolsheviks. Regardless of whether he'd ever explicitly discussed it with Hitler, Hess knew that a successful peace mission would certainly please the führer. Moreover, this was an opportunity for Hess to regain some of the power he felt slipping away. Hess had been Hitler's number-two man in the early days of Nazism, but by 1941 his influence was declining as a result of rivals such as Martin Bormann and of Hitler's concentration on military matters.

The best explanation of Hess's motives may still be the one Churchill wrote in 1950. After describing Hess's jealousy of the generals who'd overshadowed him, he imagined Hess's thoughts: "They have their parts to play. But I, Rudolf, by a deed of superb devotion will surpass them all and bring to my Fuehrer a greater treasure and easement than all of them put together. I will go and make peace with Britain."

Hess's peace plan was doomed to fail. Driven by loyalty and ambition, and perhaps deceived by the British Secret Service, he failed to see that by 1941 the time for peace had passed. It was not just Churchill, but also the British public who were now firmly committed to the war.

Churchill recognized that the Hess mission was completely irrelevant to the course of the war. That was clear from the moment he first learned that Hess had landed in Britain. After the duke of Hamilton met with Hess, the duke hurried to give his report to the prime minister. Churchill, who had planned to see a movie that evening, listened impatiently, then responded: "Well, Hess or no Hess, I am going to see the Marx Brothers."

To investigate further

Winston Churchill, *The Grand Alliance* (Boston: Houghton Mifflin, 1950). Volume 3 of Churchill's magnificent history of World War II, full of not just the author's recollections but also his directives, telegrams, and other documents that illuminate the British government's pursuit of the war.

Ilse Hess, *Prisoner of Peace* (London: Britons Publishing Co., 1954). Hess's letters to his wife and son from England, Nuremberg, and Spandau Prison.

James Douglas-Hamilton, *Motive for a Mission* (London: Macmillan, 1971). As the son of the Duke of Hamilton, Douglas-Hamilton grew up immersed in the Hess mystery. Surprisingly, though, his book is more about Haushofer than either Hamilton or Hess. Haushofer emerges as a fascinating and tragic figure: with ties to both the Nazis and the resistance, he ended up despising himself and welcoming his death at the hands of the Gestapo.

W. Hugh Thomas, *Hess: A Tale of Two Murders* (London: Hodder & Stoughton, 1988). Thomas, a British surgeon who examined Spandau's inmate, discovered to his amazement that he had none of the scars that should have remained from Hess's World War I injuries. Thomas concluded that the man who died in prison in 1987 couldn't have been Hess. His theory was that Himmler shot down the real Hess over the North Sea, then sent his carefully schooled double to England. Thomas's 1979 book *The Murder of Rudolf Hess* makes many of the same arguments. A 1989 Scotland Yard report reasonably concluded otherwise.

John Costello, *Ten Days to Destiny* (New York: William Morrow, 1991). Though Costello didn't succeed in overturning the traditional view of the Hess mission, his book makes a convincing case that at least some British leaders were not averse to a deal with Hitler.

Peter Padfield, *Hess* (London: Weidenfeld & Nicolson, 1991). Hess as the pawn of *both* Hitler and Churchill.

Louis Kilzer, *Churchill's Deception* (New York: Simon & Schuster, 1994). Goes even farther than Costello in arguing that some inside the British government were behind the German invasion of Russia. Though provocative, Kilzer (like Stalin) is too eager to explain everything by conspiracies. Sometimes (though, of course, not always) the official story also turns out to be the real story.

Chapter 25

Was Gorbachev Part of the August Coup?

The Russian equivalent of America's legendary smoke-filled rooms—the place where politicians make their secret deals—is the steam bath. So it did not seem extraordinary, on August 17, 1991, that some of the most powerful figures in the Soviet Union gathered to take a bath at the luxurious Moscow facilities of the KGB.

Present were Prime Minister Valentin Pavlov, Defense Minister Dmitri Yazov, Central Committee Secretary for Defense Oleg Baklanov, Central Committee Secretary for Personnel Oleg Shenin, and the president's chief of staff, Valery Boldin. Their host, according to the later testimony of all six, was KGB chairman Vladimir Kryuchkov.

Nowhere to be seen amid the steam was their boss, Soviet president Mikhail Gorbachev. Gorbachev was vacationing with his family in the Crimea. He would first hear about the meeting the day after, when Baklanov and Boldin arrived at the vacation dacha known as Foros. They were accompanied by General Valentin Varennikov, the commander of Soviet ground forces, and General Yury Plekhanov of the KGB.

As Gorbachev later told the story, he was working on the final draft of a speech when his security chief told him he had visitors. That was already a matter of concern, since people didn't just drop in on the Soviet president. Gorbachev's first reaction was to call Kryuchkov to find out what was going on. He discovered the line was dead. So were his four other lines.

At that point the delegation from the steam bath entered the room. Baklanov informed Gorbachev that they represented the "State Committee for the State of Emergency." Gorbachev responded that he'd never authorized such a committee. Baklanov said Gorbachev should sign a decree declaring a state of emergency or turn over his powers to the vice president, Gennady Yanayev. Gorbachev refused.

As he later put it, "using the strongest language that the Russians always use in such circumstances, I told them where to go."

For the next three days Gorbachev was cut off from the outside world, unable to make or receive any calls and surrounded by a double ring of guards. He was able to watch on television the next day's press conference in Moscow, during which members of the emergency committee announced that, since the president was ill, Vice President Yanayev had assumed his duties.

By tuning in to the BBC and the Voice of America on a transistor radio, Gorbachev was able to follow some of the momentous events that followed. Russian president Boris Yeltsin denounced the takeover as an illegal coup and called for popular resistance. The committee declared martial law and ordered large numbers of tanks and armored personnel carriers into Moscow.

By midmorning of August 19, the Russian government building known as the White House was surrounded both by Soviet troops and by tens of thousands of Russian citizens. Some formed human chains to prevent the tanks from moving forward. At noon Yeltsin dramatically mounted a tank near the White House and appealed to the troops to give their allegiance to the elected Russian government, not the emergency committee.

As the day wore on, it became clear that the soldiers were not willing to fire on Russian citizens. Two days later the troops withdrew, Gorbachev returned to Moscow, and the leaders of the coup were arrested. Democrats were euphoric: by the end of the year, the Soviet Union had been disbanded, Gorbachev had reluctantly retired, and Yeltsin—the first democratically elected presi-

Two Soviet tank drivers, surrounded by protesters in Moscow's Menazh Square on August 19, 1991. Copyright Reuters/CORBIS.

dent of Russia—had replaced him as the most powerful figure in the country.

This fairly straightforward account of the August 1991 coup, featuring Gorbachev as the heroic victim and Yeltsin as the democratic hero, has been accepted by most Western leaders, journalists, and historians. Gorbachev himself recounted the story, in numerous interviews and in two books. Yet the Russian people, even as they celebrated the coup's demise, were much more skeptical. They had lots of questions about the roles played by each of the story's heroes, and these questions continue to plague both Gorbachev and Yeltsin.

∽

Among the first to challenge Gorbachev's view of the coup were, not surprisingly, the members of the emergency committee.

Not all of them were in a position to do so. Two—Minister of Internal Affairs Boris Pugo and Gorbachev's military adviser Marshal Akhromeev—committed suicide before they could be arrested. Two others—Pavlov and Yanayev—were too drunk to say anything coherent at first.

Once they sobered up, Pavlov and Yanayev joined their coconspirators in insisting that they'd gotten the go-ahead for the state of emergency from Gorbachev himself. According to the committee members, they'd gone down to the Crimea to tell Gorbachev everything was set. Then, to their surprise, he'd backed off, pretending to be sick.

As Pavlov told the Russian prosecutors: "Gorbachev decided to play a game that he could not lose. If he stayed there [at Foros] and the state of emergency worked, he would come to Moscow later, having recovered from his illness and taken charge. If it didn't work, he could come and arrest everyone, and once again as president he would take charge."

The committee members' case depended on proving that, contrary to the president's claim, he was not held incommunicado at Foros. They were helped by some confusion about the timing: one source said phone lines were cut at 4:32 P.M. on August 18, another said it was 5:50 P.M. And a close ally of Gorbachev later recalled speaking to the president at 6:00 P.M. that day—after the lines were supposedly cut.

Of course, all of the conspirators had good reason to blame Gorbachev for the coup: if they could convince people they were just following the president's orders, they could hardly be accused of usurping his power. Still, many Russians found their version of the story as credible as Gorbachev's.

For one thing, the conspirators were all close associates of the president. Indeed, Gorbachev had appointed and promoted them, in spite of the fact that they were all clearly hostile toward his policies of *perestroika* and *glasnost*. Publicly, Kryuchkov usually toed the line; he spoke of creating a more open organization (and he even promoted a beauty contest whose winner was crowned "Miss KGB"). But in private he made no secret of his belief that Gorbachev's reforms had gone way too far.

Gorbachev had plenty of warning that his ministers couldn't be trusted. In December 1990 Foreign Minister Eduard Shevardnadze, the leading liberal in Gorbachev's government, dramatically resigned because of the growing power of reactionary forces in the government. "Let this be my contribution, if you like, my protest, against the onset of dictatorship," he said.

In June the U.S. ambassador, Jack Matlock, received an even more specific warning from the mayor of Moscow, Gavriil Popov, a leading democrat. Popov signaled to Matlock that the room was bugged by the KGB and that they couldn't talk freely. Then the mayor handed the ambassador a note that read: "A coup is being organized to remove Gorbachev."

On the same sheet, Matlock asked who was behind it. Popov wrote the names of Pavlov, Kryuchkov, Yazov, and Anatoly Lukyanov, Speaker of the Supreme Soviet—all of whom were involved in the coup two months later. Matlock then passed on the warning to Gorbachev. Since Matlock had only Popov's word to go on, he didn't name any of the plotters, which may have lessened the impact of his warning. Still, Gorbachev's response was disturbingly (and in some minds, suspiciously) nonchalant: the president merely thanked the ambassador for his concern and told him not to worry about it.

Even in public, the hard-liners didn't always try to conceal their strong opposition to Gorbachev's reforms. Pavlov was especially outspoken in his criticism of a new treaty that Gorbachev was negotiating with the leaders of the Soviet republics, and that would have severely curtailed the power of the central government. Many of the conspirators later said they acted to forestall the signing of the treaty, which had been scheduled for August 20.

How could a politician as astute as Gorbachev ignore such clear warning signs? To those who sympathized with the hard-liners on the committee, Pavlov's answer made sense: Gorbachev himself must have been behind the coup. Perhaps he chickened out at the last minute, or perhaps he wanted to let the committee members do his dirty work. But whether he actively participated in the planning or just encouraged the plotters, he was not their innocent victim.

The revisionist interpretation of the coup was unkind to Yeltsin as well. In an open letter to the Russian president, Kryuchkov accused him of staging the heroic defense of the White House to bolster his own reputation. Kryuchkov denied that he ever ordered an attack on the White House. Moreover, he wrote, Yeltsin was fully aware of that, since the KGB chief had called him personally to tell him.

Like the attacks on Gorbachev, the criticism of Yeltsin was to a considerable extent self-serving. The committee members may have been embarrassed to portray themselves as dupes, victims of Gorbachev's manipulations and Yeltsin's histrionics. But, legally and politically, that was a lot better image than the orthodox view of them as power-hungry, bloodthirsty, neo-Stalinist reactionaries.

∽

The criminal trial against the alleged conspirators brought additional frustration for the supporters of Gorbachev and Yeltsin.

At first, prosecutors charged the leaders of the coup with treason against the USSR. By the end of 1991, however, the USSR had broken up into independent countries. Defense lawyers argued that there was no legal basis for charging their clients with treason against a country that no longer existed.

Prosecutors eventually settled on conspiracy charges, but the trial was delayed again and again because of additional legal arguments and the illnesses of various defendants. Finally, in December 1993, the new Russian parliament—now dominated by an anti-Yeltsin coalition of nationalists and ex-Communists—granted amnesty to all the defendants.

Of the fifteen defendants, only one refused the amnesty. Unwilling to concede that he had committed any crime for which he could be amnestied, General Varennikov demanded a trial. Varennikov was also undoubtedly aware that the Military Collegium of the Russian Supreme Court, like the newly elected parliament, was stacked with enemies of both Gorbachev and Yeltsin.

The trial took place in August 1994. An angry Gorbachev took the stand, denying he had anything to do with the coup. The court ignored his testimony and acquitted Varennikov.

Gorbachev and his supporters denounced the verdict, comparing it to Stalin's show trials of the 1930s. The charge had a great deal of merit: both the new parliament and the court reflected how drastically Russian politics had changed since the postcoup euphoria. A disastrous economy and political disarray among the democrats had swept into power a collection of ultra-nationalists and pro-Communists who had much more in common with the emergency committee members than with either Yeltsin or Gorbachev.

By the mid-1990s, those who took part in the coup were celebrated as heroes in conservative circles. In fact, two members of the committee were among the new parliamentary delegates. The White House, once the symbol of Yeltsin's resistance to the coup, was now in the control of his enemies. Yeltsin remained president until the end of the decade, but with his power and his reputation much diminished.

As for Gorbachev, he continued to argue his case, though it seemed that no one in Russia was listening. His only consolation was that he remained a hero abroad, especially to Western leaders such as George Bush and Margaret Thatcher, who considered him their partner in ending the Cold War.

Western journalists and historians, with a bit more distance from and a bit more objectivity about Soviet politics, also continued to admire Gorbachev. They emphasized that, whatever

Gorbachev's flaws, he implemented a complete reversal of Soviet foreign policy, and he introduced an unprecedented degree of freedom to the Soviet Union, including semidemocratic elections and a multiparty system.

Undeniably, he made all sorts of compromises with and promises to the hard-liners in his government, but that didn't make him one of them. Perhaps some of his conservative ministers genuinely did think they could convince Gorbachev to go along with their coup, or at least held out some hope that he would. Certainly Gorbachev grossly miscalculated how far they'd go to stop his reforms. But that's a far cry from proving he wanted anything to do with the coup.

Gorbachev's memoirs, though often self-serving and sanctimonious, present a convincing defense against the charge that he colluded with the conspirators. "The transformation of the country into a viable democratic federation as well as the general plan of perestroika, the sweeping reforms and the new thinking in the sphere of international politics—these had become my life's work," he wrote.

"Why then would I want to lift my hand against it?"

To investigate further

Mikhail Gorbachev, *The August Coup* (New York: HarperCollins, 1991). Inevitably, since it appeared just months after the coup, much of the book consists of reworked previous statements and speeches, but these still make for a useful document.

David Remnick, *Lenin's Tomb* (New York: Random House, 1993). Intimate and revealing vignettes from the last days of the Soviet Empire.

John Dunlop, *The Rise of Russia and the Fall of the Soviet Empire* (Princeton, N.J.: Princeton University Press, 1993). Dunlop makes a strong case that the plotters had reason to believe Gorbachev could be convinced to side with them. Somewhat academic in its style but still compelling.

Victoria Bonnell, Ann Cooper, and Gregory Freidin, eds., *Russia at the Barricades* (Armonk, N.Y.: M. E. Sharpe, 1994). A collection of documents, interviews, and eyewitness accounts of the coup.

Valery Boldin, *Ten Years That Shook the World* (New York: Basic Books, 1994). A venomous and vindictive portrait of Gorbachev, written by his chief of staff while he awaited trial for his part in the coup.

Boris Yeltsin, *The Struggle for Russia* (New York: Times Books, 1994). Disorganized and sometimes disingenuous, but entertaining and informative. Yeltsin has little good to say about his archrival, though he stops short of accusing Gorbachev of planning or approving the coup. Instead Yeltsin concludes, somewhat ambiguously, that Gorbachev was its "chief catalyst." As for the revisionist attacks on Yeltsin's own role in the coup, he admits he had a telephone conversation with Kryuchkov during which the KGB chief told him the emergency committee would not use military force. But Yeltsin adds that there were good reasons not to believe him.

Jack Matlock, *Autopsy on an Empire* (New York: Random House, 1995). Matlock, who was the U.S. ambassador to Moscow under Reagan and Bush, provides a firsthand account of the Soviet collapse. Unlike the works of most diplomats, Matlock's is not just a valuable historical document but also a valuable work of history.

David Pryce-Jones, *The Strange Death of the Soviet Empire* (New York: Henry Holt, 1995). An unusual and often interesting mix of interviews with former leaders, dissidents, and other Soviet observers.

Mikhail Gorbachev, *Memoirs* (New York: Doubleday, 1995). Like its author, the book goes on too long but remains important.

Archie Brown, *The Gorbachev Factor* (Oxford: Oxford University Press, 1996). The best overall defense of Gorbachev's record as a genuine reformer—a better defense, in fact, than Gorbachev's own memoirs.

Amy Knight, *Spies without Cloaks* (Princeton, N.J.: Princeton University Press, 1996). The first chapter is the most recent and most thorough case against Gorbachev. The rest of the book argues that the postcoup KGB continues to be a dangerous and independent force in Russia.

David Remnick, *Resurrection* (New York: Random House, 1997). A surprisingly hopeful view of postcoup Russia, especially since most of the book chronicles the country's descent into chaos, corruption, and crime.

Index

Abdullah Al Mamun, 19–20

Achilles, 34, 35, 40

Adventure Galley (ship), 144–45, 148, 149

Aegus, 26, 27

Africa

  Egyptology, 18–25

  human origination in, 5–8

afterlife, 18, 24

Agamemnon, 34, 38, 40

Ailly, Pierre d', 111

Akhromeev, Marshal, 206

Alcock, Leslie, 64–65

Alexander the Great, 35

Alexandra, czarina of Russia, 178, 180, 182, 184

Alexei (Russian Prince), 178, 184

alphabet, Linear A and B, 29, 30–31

Amadeus (Shaffer play and film), 153, 156

Amazons, 26

Ambrosius, Aurelius, 10–11

Amenemhet III, pharaoh of Egypt, 19

Anastasia (Russian princess), 178, 179–80, 182, 184

Anatomical Society, 105

ancestor worship, 81

Anderson, Anna, 180, 184

Andrei (Russian grand duke), 180

Andrews, E. Wyllys, 73

Androgeos, 26

angels, 84, 85, 90

Anglo-Saxons, 10–11, 60, 61

anthropology, 56

anti-Semitism, 193

Antony and Cleopatra (Shakespeare), 139

archeological findings

  Arthurian legend, 64–65

  Easter Islander origins, 78, 81

  Egyptian pyramids, 18–22

  human origins, 1–8

  Mayan civilization, 67–73

  Minoan and Mycenaen cultures, 27–32

  Nazca lines, 52–58

  Stonehenge, 11–15

  Troy site, 34–41

architecture, 23

Arc, Jacque d', 187

Argolic Peninsula, 38

Argonauts, 26

Ariadne, 26, 27

Aristotle, 111

Arthur, King, 10, 11, 59–66

Ashmolean Museum (Oxford), 27

Asia

  paper and print inventions, 98

  search for route to, 108–12

astronomical theories

  Egyptian pyramids, 18, 22

  Mayan civilization, 67

  Nazca lines, 53–55, 57

  Stonehenge, 14–16, 55

Athenians, 26, 27, 30

Atkinson, Richard, 11–12, 14–15, 16

Aubrey Holes (Stonehenge), 14, 15

Austria

Freudian psychoanalysis, 159–66

Mozart's death-cause theories,
151–57

Avalon, 59, 62–63

Avdonin, Alexander, 183

Aveni, Anthony, 52, 56, 57, 58

Avery, "Long Ben," 143

Avignon (France), 93, 94

Aztecs, 68

Bacon, Delia, 136

Bacon, Francis, 136–37

Baconians, 136–38, 139, 140

Bahamas, 109

Bahn, Paul, 79

Bahrdt, Karl Friedrich, 45

Baklanov, Oleg, 203, 204

Ballard, Robert, 174–75

Battle of Britain, 195, 196–98, 199

Becan (Mayan city), 71

Beethoven, Karl, 153

Beethoven, Ludwig van, 153

Begley, Walter, 137

Belize, 72

Bellomont, Lord, 144, 146, 148, 150

Belzoni, Giovanni, 20

Bible

Gutenberg, 96, 97, 98

scholarship, 45–49

Bibliothèque Nationale, 96

bird designs, Inca, 56

Blackbeard (Edward Teach), 149

Blegen, Carl, 30, 39–40

bluestones, 13, 14

Boldin, Valery, 203

Boleyn, Anne, 102

Bolivia, 78

Bolsheviks

Hitler's hatred of, 197, 200

Romanov executions by, 177–78,
181, 183–85

See also Soviet Union

Bonampak (Mayan city), 71

Bormann, Martin, 200

Bosworth Field, battle of, 102

botany, 78

Bothwell, earl of (James Hepburn),
127–28, 129–31, 132

Boule, Marcellin, 2, 3, 4, 5

Brace, C. Loring, 4

Brackenbury, Sir Robert, 102

Bradley, Marion Zimmer, 60

Brauer, Gunter, 7–8

Braun, Eva, 191

Britain. See England

British Board of Trade, 172, 173

British Secret Service, 200, 201

Bronze Age

Minoan remains, 27, 31

Stonehenge theory, 10, 11

Trojan remains, 39

Buchanan, George, 127, 131, 132

Buck, Sir George, 105

bull-leaping, 28–29

Bullock, Alan, 191, 192–93

bulls, as important Cretan symbol,
26, 28–29

Burghley, William, 138

Burgundians, 83, 84

Burton, Richard, 60

Bush, George, 209

Butler, Eleanor, 102

Bykov, Pavel, 181, 182, 183

Cadbury Castle, 64–65

calcium sulfate, 72

calendar, Mayan, 67, 68

Californian (ship), 169–76

Calvert, Frank, 34–35

Camelot, 60, 61, 64, 65

Camelot (musical), 60

Canary Islands, 108–19

Cann, Rebecca, 5, 6

Capitulations (contract), 112–13

Caracol (Mayan city), 68, 71

Carnarvon, earl of, 20

Carpathia (ship), 168–69, 175

Carriere, Jean-Claude, 121

Carter, Howard, 20

Casket Letters, 130, 131

Catherine, St., 90

Catherine of Aragon, 102

Catholicism. See Roman Catholicism

Cave, A. J. E., 4

Caze, Pierre, 87

Celsus, 44–45

cenotaphs, 23

Central America, Mayan civilization
    in, 67–74

Chariots of the Gods? (von Däniken),
    53

Charles II, king of England, 105

Charles VI, king of France, 86

Charles VII, king of France, 83–84,
    85–86, 87, 88, 90

Chase, Arlen and Diane, 71–72

child abuse, 159–60, 162, 163
    faulty memories of, 164–65

Chinon (France), 84, 85, 87, 88, 90

Christianity, 43–48. See also Protes-
    tantism; Roman Catholicism

Christian Right, 48

Churchill, Winston, 196, 197, 198,
    199, 200, 201

Clarkson, Persis, 55–56, 57

clay tablets
    Hittite, 40
    Minoan, 29, 30

Coleridge, Samuel Taylor, 136

Columbus, Christopher, 108–16

Columbus, Ferdinand, 111, 112, 115

Cook, Captain James, 75–76, 79

Copan ruins, 67, 68

Coptic Museum (Cairo), 46

Coras, Jean de, 118, 119, 121, 122,
    123, 124

Costello, John, 197–98, 199, 200

Coster, Laurens, 93, 98

Crete, 26–33

Crews, Frederick, 164, 165, 166

Crossan, John Dominic, 48–49

crucifixion, 43–44, 45, 48, 49

cryptology
    authorship of Shakespeare's plays,
        136–37
    Mayan documents, 71–72
    Minoan/Mycean alphabet, 30–31

crypts, 23

"curse of the pharaohs," 20

Cuzco (Peru), 56, 57

Daedalus, 26

Dalgleish, George, 130

Däniken, Erich von, 53, 57

Dardanelles, 34, 35

Darnley, earl of (Henry Stuart),
    126–27, 129, 130, 131–32

Darwin, Charles, 2

dating methods
    Mayan calendar, 68
    mitochondrial DNA, 5, 6–7
    pottery shards, 55–56, 69, 70
    radiocarbon, 11, 12, 46, 78

Daughter of Time, The (Tey), xi–xii,
    100

Daumer, G. F., 154

dauphin of France. See Charles VII,
    king of France

Davis, Natalie Zemon, 121–24

Dawson, Charles, 3

Demarest, Arthur, 72
dental evidence, 105
Deutsch, Otto, 156
de Vere, Edward, 138–41
Discovery Channel, 143
DNA
  human origins dating by, 5, 6–7
  Romanov identification by,
    183–84
Don Giovanni (Mozart), 151
Donnelly, Ignatius, 136–37
Dorpfeld, Wilhelm, 39, 40
Dritzehn, Andreas, 94–95, 98
drought, Mayan, 72
drug therapies, 166
Druids, 11, 23
Durning-Lawrence, Edwin, 137

earthquakes
  Hisarlik site, 39–40
  Minoan civilization destruction
    theory, 31–32
Easter Island, 75–82
East India Company, 145, 148
Eckstein, Emma, 161–62
ecstatic revelation, 47
Edward II, king of England, 106
Edward III, king of England, 106
Edward IV, king of England, 101,
    102, 106
Edward V, king of England, 101,
    102, 104–5
Egypt
  Nag Hammadi documents, 46
  purpose of pyramids, 18–25
Ekaterinburg, Russia, 178–79, 181,
    182, 183, 184
Elizabeth I, queen of England, 126,
    129, 130–31, 132, 136, 138
El Spar (Arab sheik), 136
Emmaus, 44

England
  Arthurian legend, 59–65
  authorship of Shakespeare's plays,
    134–41
  Hitler's speculated peace over-
    tures to, 195–96, 197, 198,
    200–201
  Hundred Years War, 83–84, 88,
    90
  Kidd piracy legend, 143–50
  Mary of Scotland, 125–31
  Piltdown man bones, 3
  Richard III's reputation, xi–xii,
    100–107
  sinking of *Titanic,* 168–76
  Stonehenge, 10–16
"Enterprise of the Indies," 108–9,
    111, 112
Eschenbach, Wolfram von, 60
Evans, Arthur, 27–31, 32
Evans, Cyril, 170–71, 174
Eve (hypothetical human ancestor),
    5, 6–7
evolution theory, 2

Falstaff (Shakespearean character),
    139
Falwell, Jerry, 48
Ferdinand, king of Spain, 108–9, 110,
    112–13, 114, 115
fertility ritual, 56
Fichet, Guillaume, 92
Finlay, Robert, 124
First Flower People, The (Solecki), 5
First Folio (1623), 137
Fliess, Wilhelm, 159–64
fossils, human origins, 1–8
France
  Arthurian legend, 60
  Joan of Arc, 83–91
  Neandertal man fossil, 4

printing introduced into, 93
return of Martin Guerre, 117–24
France, Anatole, 88
Franklin, Benjamin, 155
Freemasons, 154–55
Freud, Anna, 161
Freud, Sigmund, 159–67
  revisionist views of, 160–66
Freudian theory
  Hitler biography, 191, 192–93
  seduction theory abandonment,
    159–66
  See also psychoanalysis
Fuhlrott, Johann, 1, 2, 6
Führer, Der (Heiden), 189–90
Funk, Robert, 48, 49
Fust, Johann, 95–98

Galapagos Islands, 78
Gama, Vasco de, 108
Garden of Eden, 114–15
Gardiner, John, 150
Gardiner's Island (N.Y.), 150
genetics. *See* DNA
Geoffrey of Monmouth, 10–11, 13,
  59–61, 64
geography, 108–16
geology, 13–14
Gerald of Wales, 62
Gerlich, Fritz, 187–88
Germany
  Arthurian legend, 60
  Hess's flight to Scotland, 195–201
  murder/suicide of Hitler's niece,
    186–93
  Neandertal fossil find, 1–2
  printing press invention, 92, 94–98
  rationalism, 45
  Romanovs and, 179–80, 182
Gildas (Welsh monk), 61–62
Gill, Peter, 184

Gillieron, Émile, 29
glaciers, 13–14
glasnost, 207
Glastonbury Abbey, 62–64
Gnosticism, 46–47
gold, 36–38, 150
Golden Fleece, 26
Goneim, Zacharia, 22
Gorbachev, Mihail, 203–11
Gorlois, duke of Cornwall, 59
gospels, 44–49
Great Britain. *See* England
Great Pyramid of Khufu, 19–20,
  21–22
Great Trilithon, 11–12
Greece, 23
  Minoan and Mycenaean cultures,
    26–32
  Trojan War, 34–41
Greene, Richard, 140
Guatemala, 72
Guerre, Martin, 117–25
Guerre, Pierre, 117–19, 122, 124
Guinevere, Queen, 59, 60, 62
Gutenberg, Johann, 92–98
Gutenberg Bible, 96, 97, 98

Halder, Franz, 196
Hamilton, duke of, 195, 196, 198,
  200, 201
Hamlet (Shakespeare), 138
Hanfstaengl, Ernst, 188–92
Harawa pyramid, 19
Harrison, Leslie, 174, 175
Haushofer, Albrecht, 196, 197, 200
Hawkins, Gerald, 14, 15, 55, 57
Hector, 34, 40
Heiden, Karl, 189–90
Helen of Troy, 34, 36, 40
Helmasperger, Ulrich, 95
Helmasperger Instrument, 95

Hengist (Saxon), 59

Henry IV, king of England, 106

Henry VI, king of England, 100, 106

Henry VII, king of England,
    100–101, 102, 104–5

Henry VIII, king of England, 102

Hepburn, James. *See* Bothwell, earl of

heresy, 84, 85

Herodotus, 18, 34, 35

Herzog, Anton, 156–57

Hess, Ilse, 197

Hess Rudolf, 195–202

Hetepheres (Egyptian queen), 21–22

Heyerdahl, Thor, 76–80

hierographic inscriptions, 19

Himmler, Heinrich, 189

Hisarlik, Turkey, 34–36, 38, 39–41

Historia Rerum (Pius II), 111

History of King Richard III, The
    (More), 101–2, 104

History of the Briton (Nennius), 62

History of the Kings of Britain
    (Geoffrey of Monmouth),
    10–11, 59, 60–61, 64

Hitler, Adolf
    Hess flight to Scotland, 195–96,
        197, 198–99
    niece's suicide, 186–94

Hitler, Alois, 189

Hitler, Brigid, 189

Hitler and I (Strasser), 187–88

Hittite civilization, 40

Hodell, David, 72

Hofdemel, Franz, 153

Hoffmann, Heinrich, 192

Holocaust, 193

Homer, 29, 34, 35, 36, 38–39, 40, 41

Horsa (Saxon), 59

Hotu Matua, 79

human origins, 1–8

Hundred Years War, 83–84, 88, 90

Iliad (Homer), 34, 35, 39, 40

Imago Mundi (d'Ailly), 111, 114–15

Incas, 56, 68, 76, 79

Indian Ocean, 108

Indies (Asia), 108–15

infantile sexuality, 160, 163, 165

Inquisition, 84–85, 88

Institute for Antiquity and
    Christianity, 48

Iran, 4–5

Iraq, 4–5

Ireland
    Arthurian legend and, 59
    Stonehenge and, 10–11, 13

Irene (Prussian Princess), 180

Irish Sea, 13

irrigation system, 56

Irving, Washington, 143

Isabeau, queen of France, 83, 87

Isabella, queen of Spain, 108–9, 110,
    112–13, 114, 115

Ismay, Bruce, 173

Italy, 93

Ivanov, Pavel, 184

James I, king of England (James VI
    of Scotland), 11, 128, 131, 136

Jason, 26

Jefferson, Thomas, 45, 155

"Jefferson Bibles," 45

Jesus of Nazareth, 43–50
    quest for historical, 45–49

Jesus Seminar (1985), 48–49

Joan of Arc, 83–91
    trial of rehabilitation, 85–86

John, gospel of, 44, 46

Jones, Ernest, 160

Jones, Inigo, 11

Jonson, Ben, 140

Joseph, 18

Josephus, 43–44

Judaism, 43–44, 193
Judas Iscariot, 44
Junius, Hadrian, 93

Kairatos Valley (Crete), 27–28
Kellaway, G. A., 13–14
Kennedy administration, 60
Kerensky, Alexander, 177
Kershaw, Ian, 191, 192
KGB
    coup against Gorbachev, 203, 204,
        207
    Hess's flight to Scotland, 197–98,
        199–200
Khafre, pharaoh of Egypt, 20
Khufu, pharaoh of Egypt, 18, 19–23
Kidd, Captain William, 143–50
Killarus, Ireland, 11
King Lear (Shakespeare), 139
King's Men theater, 134, 139
King Tut's tomb, 20
Kirk o' Field (Scotland), 127, 132
Knights of the Round Table, 60
Knosorov, Yuri, 70–71
Knossos (Crete), 27–32
Knox, John, 127, 131, 132
Kon-Tiki (Inca chief god), 76, 79
Kon-Tiki expedition, 77–78, 79
Korfmann, Manfred, 40
Kosok, Paul, 53–55, 57
Krapina (Yugoslavia), 4
Krings, Matthias, 6–7
Kroeber, Alfred, 52
Kryuchkov, Vladimir, 203, 204, 207,
    208

labyrinth (Knossos, Crete), 26–27
La Chapelle-aux Saints fossil, 4
Ladurie, Emmanuel Le Roy, 123
Lake Chichancanub, 72
Lancelot, 60

Landa, Diego de, 70, 71
Langer, William, 191
Las Casas, Bartolomé de, 109, 111,
    112, 114, 115
last supper, 44, 48–49
legend. See mythology
Lenin, V. I., 182
Leopold II, emperor of Austria, 155
Le Pen, Jean-Marie, 88
Leslie, Bishop John, 127
Le Sueur, Guillaume, 121
Library of Congress, Freud Archives,
    161
Linear A and Linear B alphabets, 29,
    30–31
linguistic analysis
    Cretan alphabet, 29, 30–31
    Easter Islanders script, 78–79
    Mayan manuscripts, 70–71
Looney, J. Thomas, 138–39
Lord, Captain Stanley, 169–76
Louvre (Paris), 20
Love's Labour's Lost (Shakespeare),
    137
Luke, gospel of, 44, 46, 47–48
Lukyanov, Anatoly, 207
lunar eclipses, 14, 15
Luther, Martin, 47, 49

Macbeth (Shakespeare), 139
Mack, Burton, 48
Madagascar, 144–46
Madeiras, 111
Magic Flute, The (Mozart), 154–55
Mainz (Germany), 92, 94, 95, 97, 98
Mainz Psalter (1457), 96
Malory, Thomas, 60
Mancini, Dominic, 105
Mandeville, John, 111, 114
Mangold, Tom, 181–83
Margaret, St., 90

Maria (Russian princess), 162, 178, 184

Marinatos, Spyridon, 31–32

Mark, gospel of, 44, 46

Marlowe, Christopher, 136

Marquesa islands, 79, 80

Mary, queen of Scots, 126–33

Masonic order, 154–55

Masson, Jeffrey, 161–64, 165, 166

mastabas (Egyptian tombs), 23

Matlock, Jack, 207

Matthew, gospel of, 44, 46

Maucher, Karl, 184

Mayan civilization, 67–74

McLuhan, Marshall, 92

Medvedev, Pavel, 178, 181, 184

Meidum pyramids, 23

Mein Kampf (Hitler), 195

Mejia, Toribio, 52

Memorable Decision, A (Coras), 121, 122

Mendelssohn, Kurt, 23

Mentelin, Johann, 92

Mercantile Marine Service Association, 174

Meres, Francis, 138, 140

Merlin, 10, 11, 13, 59

Mersey, Lord Charles, 172

Metropolitan Museum of Art, 20

Mexico, 67–74

Middle East
    Egyptology, 18–25
    Neandertal remains, 4–5, 6, 8

Minoan culture, 29–32

Minos, king of Crete, 26, 27, 29

minotaur, slaying of, 26–27, 28, 32

mitochondrial DNA, 5, 6–7

moai (Easter Island statues), 75–76, 77, 78, 80, 81

molecular biology, 5, 6–8

Montaigne, Michel de, 121

"Moonshine on Stonehenge" (Atkinson), 15

Moore, William, 143, 145, 146, 148

Moray, earl of (James Stewart), 128–30, 131

Mordred, 59

More, Thomas, St, xi–xii, 101–2, 104, 105, 106

Morison, Samuel Eliot, 113, 115

Morley, Sylvanus, 67–68, 70, 71

Morte d'Arthur (Malory), 60

Mortillet, Gabriel, 2

Morton, John Cardinal, xi, 104

Moscheles, Ignaz, 153–54

Mount Badon, battle of, 61, 62, 65

Mount Carnmenyn, 13

Mount Foel Trigarn, 13

Mozart, Constanze, 151–52, 155–56, 157

Mozart, Wolfgang Amadeus, 151–58

mtDNA. *See* mitochondrial DNA

Muhammad Ali al-Samman, 46

Muller, Renate, 191

Municipal Library of Lille, 105

murder theories
    English "princes in the tower," xi–xii, 100–107
    Hitler's niece, 186–93
    Mary of Scotland's husband, 126–31
    poisoning of Mozart, 151–57
    survival of Romanovs, 177–85

Mycenaean culture
    Stonehenge carvings linked with, 12, 14–15
    Theseus legend linked with, 30–31, 38, 41
    Troy excavations and, 38

mythology
    British Isles, 10, 11, 59–65

Greece, 26–32
    Trojan War, 34–41

Nag Hammadi documents, 46
Napoleon Bonaparte, 20
Naranjo (Mayan city), 68
National Library of Berlin, 70
natural disaster theories
    destruction of Crete, 31–32
    Easter Island moai, 81
    Mayan civilization collapse, 72
Nazca lines, 52–58
Nazi Party
    alleged peace bid to Britain, 198
    Hess's position in, 195, 200
    and Hitler's niece suicide, 186–87,
        189, 192–93
Neandertals, 1–9
Nennius (Welsh monk), 62
Netherlands, 93–94
New Testament, 44, 46, 47–48, 49
New World
    Columbus's voyages, 109, 111,
        112–13
    Spanish conquests, 68, 73
New York Review of Books, 164
Nicholas II, czar of Russia, 177, 178,
        180, 184
Niemetschek, Franz, 151–52, 153
Nile River, 18–19
Nonaggression pact (1939), 197
Novello, Vincent and Mary, 152

Odyssey (Homer), 34, 35, 41
Oedipus complex, 160, 161, 163,
        164, 165, 166
Ogburn, Charlton, 140
Olga (Russian princess), 178, 182
Origin of Species, The (Darwin), 2
Orinoco River, 114
Orléans, battle of, 84, 88

OSS, 190, 191
out-of-Africa theory, 5–8
Oviedo, Gonzalo Fernandez de, 111,
        112
Oxford, earl of (Edward de Vere),
        138–41
Oxfordians, 138–41
Oxford University, 27, 56

Pacariqtambo (Peru), 57
Pacific Ocean, 77–78, 81
Padfield, Peter, 198–99
Pagels, Elaine, 47
Paine, Ralph, 148
paleoclimatology, 72
Pansette. See Tilh, Arnaud du
paper, 98
Paradise, 114–15
Paria Peninsula (Venezuela), 114
Paris (Trojan warrior), 34, 40
Parthenon, 29
Parzival, 60
Pasiphae, 26
Pavlov, Valentin, 203, 206, 207, 208
penis envy, 160
pentecostalists, 47
perestroika, 207
Peru, 73
    Easter Islander theorized origins
        in, 75–79
    Nazca lines, 52–58
pharaohs of Egypt, 18–25
Philip (British prince consort), 183–84
Phillips, Jack, 170
Piazzi Smyth, Charles, 22
Piccolomini, Aeneas Silvius (later
        Pope Pius II), 96
Picts, 59, 61
Piggott, Stuart, 13
Pilate, Pontius, 43–44
Piltdown man, 3

Pintsch, Karlheinz, 196
piracy, 143–50
Pius II, Pope, 96, 111
Plato, 29
Plekhanov, Yury, 203
Plutarch, 26–27, 32, 34
Poe, Edgar Allan, 143
Polo, Marco, 111, 114
Polynesia, 76, 78, 79, 80
Popov, Gavriil, 207
Portugal
    and Columbus's voyage, 111, 113
    human origin fossils, 5, 7
pottery
    Galapagos, 78
    Mayan, 69, 70
    Nazca lines and, 55–56
pre-Inca Indians, 79
Preseli Mountains, 13, 14
Priam, king of Troy, 34, 36–40
"princes in the tower," xi–xii,
    100–107
printing press invention, 92–99
privateering, 144–45, 149
Prospero (Shakespearean character),
    139
Protestantism, 123, 127, 128, 129,
    131, 132
Prozac, 166
psychoanalysis
    Freudian origins of, 159–65
    reasons for decline, 165–66
Pugo, Boris, 206
Pushkin, Alexander, 153
pyramids of Egypt, 18–25

Quedah Merchant (ship), 145–46, 148,
    149

Radford, C. A. Ralegh, 64, 65
radiocarbon dating, 11, 12, 46, 78
Raleigh, Walter, 136

rationalism, 45
Raubal, Geli, 186–93
Reade, Leslie, 169
recovered memory therapies, 165
Reds. See Bolsheviks
regional continuity theory, 5, 7, 8
Reiche, Maria, 54–55, 57
Reiche, Renate, 57
Reims (France), 84
Reinhard, Johan, 56
Reisner, George Andrew, 21–22
repressed sexuality, 162, 165
republicanism, 155
Requiem (Mozart), 151–52, 156–57
resurrection, 43–45, 46, 47–48
Return of Martin Guerre, The (Davis),
    121–24
Return of Martin Guerre, The (film),
    121, 123
Richard (English prince), 101, 105
Richard II, king of England, 106
Richard III, king of England, xi–xii,
    100–107
Richard III (Shakespeare), xi, 100
Richard III Society, 100, 105–6
Richard of Gloucester. See Richard III
Riffe, Walter, 94
Ritchie, Robert C., 149
Rizzio, David, 126–27, 132
Robertson, Pat, 48
Rochlitz, Friedrich, 151, 152, 153
Roggeveen, Jacob, 75, 80
Rols, Bertrande de, 117, 118, 119,
    121–24
Roman Catholicism
    Joan of Arc heresy, 84–85
    of Mary, queen of Scots, 127, 130,
    131
Roman Empire
    Britain and, 11, 59, 61
    crucifixion of Jesus and, 43–44
Romanov dynasty, 177–85

Romanticism, 136
"Rongorongo" script, 78–79
Rostron, Arthur, 168–69
Ruggles, Clive, 57
Ruin of Britain, The (Gildas), 61–62
Russia. *See* Soviet Union
Ryabov, Geli, 183–84

St. Petersburg, Russia, 184–85
Sala, Pierre, 86
Salieri, Antonio, 153, 156
Salisbury Plain (England), 10–16
Samson (fishing ship), 174
Saqqara pyramid (Egypt), 23
sarcophagi, 19, 22, 23
Saxons, 59, 62
Schaaflhausen, Hermann, 1–2
Schanzkowska, Franziska, 180, 184
Schiller, Friedrich, 86
Schindler, Anton, 153
Schliemann, Heinrich, 35–39, 40, 41
Schliemann, Sophia, 36, 37
Schöffer, Peter, 96
Scotland
    Hess's flight to, 195–201
    Mary, queen of Scots, 126–31
Scots, 59
Scott, Sir Walter, 126
seduction theory, Freud's
    abandonment of, 159–67
Sekhemkhet, pharaoh of Egypt, 22
Seneca, 111
sexuality
    Freudian theory, 160–66
    Hitler's psychopathologies, 190,
        191–92
Shaffer, Peter, 153, 156
Shakespeare, Hamnet, 139
Shakespeare, William, 86
    authenticity of plays, 134–42
    characterization of Richard III by,
        xi, 100, 101, 105, 106, 107

Shanidar caves (Iraq), 4–5
Shaw, George Bernard, 86
Shenin, Oleg, 203
Shevardnadze, Eduard, 207
Shikaneder, Emanuel, 154, 155
"sign" of Joan of Arc, 84–90
Silverman, Helaine, 56, 58
Simnel, Lambert, 105
sinking of *Titanic,* 168–76
Smith, Captain Edward, 170, 172–73,
    174
Smith, Fred, 8
Smith, William Alden, 169, 171–72,
    173–74
Snefru, pharaoh of Egypt, 23
Sobran, Joseph, 140
Sokolov, Nicholas, 181–82
solar alignment
    Nazra lines and, 53–55
    Stonehenge lines and, 16
Solecki, Ralph, 4–5
solstices, 54, 55
Sophocles, 166
South America. *See* Peru; Venezuela
Southampton, earl of (Henry
    Wriothesley), 139
Soviet Union (former)
    coup against Gorbachev, 203–10
    dismantling of, 204, 206, 208
    Hitler's invasion of, 197, 198–99,
        200
    possible Romanov survivors,
        177–85
    suspicions about Hitler peace
        moves with Britain, 197–200
Spain
    Columbus's voyages, 108–11,
        112–15
    conquests in Mexico and Peru, 68,
        73
    human origin fossils, 5, 7
Stalin, Joseph, 197, 198, 199, 209

statues, Easter Island, 75–81
Stephens, John Lloyd, 67, 73
step pyramids, 23
Stevenson, Robert Louis, 143
Stewart, James. *See* Moray, earl of
Stewart, Mary. *See* Mary, queen of Scots
Stillington, Robert, 102
Stone Age, 10, 11, 36
Stonehenge, 10–17, 55
Stonehenge Decoded (Hawkins), 14
Stoneking, Mark, 5, 6
Strassburg (Germany), 92, 94, 95, 98
Strasser, Gregor, 187–88
Strasser, Otto, 187, 188, 190–91
Stratford-on-Avon (England), 134–35, 136, 140
Straus, William, 4
Strauss, David Friedrich, 45
Stuart, Henry. *See* Darnley, earl of
Stukely, William, 14
sub-Saharan Africa, human origination in, 5–8
Summers, Anthony, 181–83
sun. *See* solar alignment
sun god cult, Egyptian, 23–24
Sussex (England), 3
sweet potatoes, 78

Tacitus, 43
Tahiti, 75, 78
Tanner, Lawrence, 105
Tatiana (Russian princess), 178, 182
Teach, Edward (Blackbeard), 149
Tempest, The (Shakespeare), 139
Temple of the Sun (Inca), 56
Terrestrial Paradise, 114–15
Tey, Josephine, xi–xii, 100
Thatcher, Margaret, 209
Thera volcanic eruption, 31–32
Theseus, 26–32

Thomas, H. H., 13
Thomas, gospel of, 46
Thompson, J. Eric, 67–68, 70, 71
Three Essays on Sexuality (Freud), 160
Tiahuanaco culture, 78
Tikal (Mayan city), 68, 71
Tiki (Easter Islander chief-god), 76, 79
Tilh, Arnaud du (Pansette), 118, 119, 121–23, 124
Tintagel Castle, 64
Titanic (ship), 168–76
tomb robbers, in Egypt, 19, 23
Tory Party, 149
Toscanelli, Paolo del Pozzo, 108, 111, 112
totora reed, 78
Toulouse (France), 118–24
Tower of London, 101, 102, 104, 106
transference, psychoanalytic, 162
treasure
    of Captain Kidd, 143–50
    in Egyptian pyramid tombs, 19–22
    of Priam, 36, 37, 38
Trojan War, 34–35, 38, 39, 40
Troy, 34–42
Troyes, Chrétien de, 60
"True and Detailed History of the Requiem by W. A. Mozart . . ." (Herzog), 156–57
tsunamis, 32
Tudor dynasty
    and Mary, queen of Scots, 126, 129, 130–31, 132, 136, 138
    and Richard III, 100–101, 102, 104–5, 106
Turkey, and Hisarlik evacuations, 36, 38, 40
Tutankhamen, pharaoh of Egypt, 20
Twain, Mark, 86, 134, 136, 140
Tyrell, James, 102

unconscious mind, 160, 165
unidinism, 190, 191
United States
  and Captain Kidd's treasure, 146, 150
  famous eighteenth-century Masons, 155
  intelligence on Hess flight to Scotland, 198, 199–200
  and sinking of Titanic, 168–76
University of Munich, 6–7
Urton, Gary, 57, 58
U.S. Army Intelligence, 198, 199–200
Uther, King, 59, 64

Valley of the Kings (Egypt), 20
Varennikov, Valentin, 203, 209
Venezuela, 114
Ventris, Michael, 30–31
Viennese Society for Psychiatry and Neurology, 159
Vignaud, Henry, 112–13
Vigne, Daniel, 121
Virchow, Rudolf, 2
volcanic eruption, Cretan civilization and, 31–32
Voltaire, 87–88

Wace, Alan, 30
Wace, Robert, 60
Waldvogel, Procopius, 93, 94, 98
Wales
  chronicles of Britons' history, 61, 62, 65
  as source of Stonehenge stones, 13
Walpole, Sir Horace, 104
Walsegg, Count von, 156–57
Warbeck, Perkin, 105

War of the Roses, 102
Washington, George, 155
Westminster Abbey, 105
Whig Party, 144, 145, 148, 149
White, Thomas H., 60
White House (Moscow), 204, 208, 209
Whites (Russian revolutionary faction), 177–78, 181
White Star Line, 172, 173, 174
Wiener Neustadt (Austria), 156
Wilhelm, kaiser of Germany, 182
William III, king of England, 143, 144, 146, 149
William of Newburgh, 60–61
Wilson, Allan, 5, 6
Wingender, Doris, 180
Winter's Tale, The (Shakespeare), 139
woodcut technique, 93
Woodville, Anthony, 101
Woodville, Elizabeth, 101–2
World War II, 195–201
Wright, William, 105
Wriothesley, Henry, 139

Xenia (Russian princess), 180
Xenophon, 34
Xerxes, king of Persia, 35

Yanayev, Gennady, 204, 206
Yazov, Dmitri, 203, 207
Yeltsin, Boris, 204, 206, 208, 209
Ygerna (mother of King Arthur), 59, 64
Yucatán Peninsula, 69, 72–73
Yugoslavia, 4
Yurovsky, Yakov, 178, 183–84

Zuidema, Tom, 56, 58